To Elizabeth
Christmas 1984

THE RIDER'S HANDBOOK

A QUARTO BOOK

THE RIDER'S HANDBOOK

SALLY GORDON

NEW BURLINGTON BOOKS

A QUARTO BOOK

No part of this publication
may be reproduced, stored
in a retrieval system or
transmitted in any form or
by any means electronic,
mechanical, photocopying,
recording or otherwise,
without prior permission of
the publisher.

This book was designed
and produced by Quarto
Publishing Limited
32 Kingly Court, London
W1

Editorial Director Jeremy
Harwood
Art Director Robert Morley
Art Editor Moira Clinch
Editor Victoria Funk
Illustrators Chris Forsey
and Marilyn Bruce
Special Photographs Simon
de Courcy Wheeler

ISBN 0 906286 468

Filmset in Britain by
Brown Knight & Truscott
Ltd.
Colour origination by Sakai
Lithocolour Company Ltd.,
Hong Kong
Printed in Hong Kong by
Lee Fung Asco Ltd.

Special thanks to Jenny
and Steve at the
Hildenborough Riding
Stables; Heather Jackson
for all her advice; Georgina
and Mrs Christine Dodwell
for their advice on Western
riding; Miss Hawley at
Moss Bros and Moss Bros;
Roger Daniels, Peter
Roberts for their assistance.

Published by New Burlington Books
13 New Burlington Street, London W1

Riding in the Carmargue, Southern France.

Contents

Introduction

IT IS NOT DIFFICULT TO UNDERSTAND why riding for recreation and pleasure has achieved its current level of popularity. Unlike many sports, it does not demand natural athletic aptitude or single-minded dedication; nor is it necessary to learn how to ride when a child in order to be a good horseman or woman in later life. For many people, it scores over such sports as tennis, squash, or hockey because it is bound up with a living animal, subject to moods and feeling, with which a close and satisfying relationship can be achieved. Where it was once a pastime mainly for the wealthy, it is now within reach of almost anybody's pocket; it can be enjoyed in urban, suburban or rural locations throughout the world. Anyone can learn to ride – regardless of age, height, weight or sex – as long as they are able to get up into the saddle and possess sufficient determination to work at the rudiments of the learning process.

Having said that anybody can learn to ride, not everyone, of course, wants to. No one should ever be pushed into riding against their will. Even for those who are keen to begin, there are points worth serious consideration. The very reasons that make riding attractive also have their dangers and pitfalls. Like people, horses are individuals and are therefore sometimes unpredictable. Feeling off-colour, displays of bad temper, high spirits or sheer devilment are part and parcel of every living being, but, should they come from your mount when you are riding along a busy road, for example, you have a potentially dangerous situation on your hands. Equally, horses that have been badly trained or treated unkindly, so that they tend to mistrust the human race in general, can be very dangerous in the hands of a novice rider.

Riding will always have its dangerous aspects, but these can be greatly reduced by ensuring that you have the best possible instruction and guidance while you are learning. The selection of a riding school, therefore, is of paramount importance and it pays to inspect all those in your area before making a final choice. Enlist expert advice to help you if you can, but, if none is available, let your common sense guide you. The stables and yard should be clean and well maintained; the grooms or staff should be pleasant, and look clean and neat in appearance; the horses should look in good, sleek condition – well fed and well cared for – and the stable management should be interested in your enquiry and ready to help.

Right: Riding is a leisure activity and sport for riders of all ages. Whether you choose to enter the world of competition or simply enjoy a day in the country, it will give you a lifetime of pleasure.

The Language of Riding

RIDING IS AN ACTIVITY in which the learning process never stops. From the day you first sit on a horse to the day you hang up your riding clothes for good, you will find that you are perpetually discovering new things – new terms connected with the horse or its tack, new aspects of riding technique, or new facets of stable management. As always, however, there is most to learn and remember at the beginning – so much, in fact, that you will inevitably feel that you will never manage to absorb even half of the information. Here, you can help yourself by some prior preparation. It pays to learn the names of some of the elementary items connected with horses and riding, such as what riding clothes are called, the basic points of the horse and the parts of the animal's saddlery, or 'tack', even before you have your first lesson.

Your riding kit

There is no need to buy all the correct riding kit for the first lessons. Riding clothes are expensive and it is best to make sure that you are going to pursue the sport before making such an investment. It is perfectly acceptable for beginners to dress informally, as shown here.

Hard Hat A hard hat is one essential item of riding equipment, and it should always be worn right from the first time you sit on the back of a horse. The chin strap should always be secured, while, if you ever do fall on your head, the hat should be checked by a saddler to make sure the protective crown has not been damaged.

Raincoat Any well-fitting, shower-proof jacket is suitable for riding. Make sure that it is not too tight around the arms, as otherwise your movements will be restricted, but do not select one that is too baggy or voluminous. If you do, your instructor will not always be able to see if you are sitting correctly.

Polo neck sweater or shirt Either of these items of clothing are perfectly acceptable. Choose the one which suits the weather best.

Jeans These should be tough and well-fitting. If they are too baggy round the legs, they will wrinkle against the saddle and lead to considerable discomfort. Stretch slacks can also be worn, provided that they have a strip of elastic under foot to stop them wrinkling your legs.

Shoes These should lace up and be made of tough leather. They should never be fitted with any buckles or other adornment that could catch on the stirrup irons. The heels should be low and the sole should run through the entire length of the shoe — both the sole and the heel.

As soon as you are sure that you are going to

Formal occasions require formal riding outfits, however, these may be subject to variation according to the occasion. **Above:** The outfit illustrated would be suitable and correct for hunting and some types of showing classes.
Right: As riding progresses, it is wise to invest in proper clothing which should be both comfortable and smarten the rider's appearance.

Left: A complete riding outfit is not necessary for the novice's first few lessons. However, a hard hat is always an essential item. **Right:** This shows inappropriate attire for a ride. Loose-fitting or flapping clothes are uncomfortable for the rider and may also be distracting for the horse who may see them from the corner of his eye. Rainboots, shoes, or boots with high heels or decorative buckles may be attractive but are potentially dangerous as they may slip or get caught in the stirrups. Similarly, wet woollen gloves may slip on the reins. The rider should never be without a hard hat.

TYING A CRAVAT

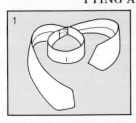
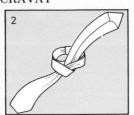
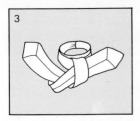
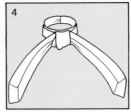
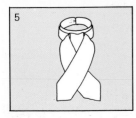

Above: The stock is a specially shaped cravat, usually made of white material and worn with a collarless shirt for formal occasions. It has to be tied in a special way which may seem complicated at first but will soon become second nature.

learn to ride seriously, it is worth buying at least some of the correct equipment. You will not only look more professional but also feel more comfortable.

Hacking jacket This type of jacket is specially tailored for riding. The cut ensures you have sufficient room for free arm and shoulder movement; it also lets the coat fall smartly and properly down over the back of the saddle.

Shirt and tie Any shirt and tie is suitable, although it is conventional to avoid anything too loud, brightly coloured or patterned. Usually, it is acceptable to wear a polo neck sweater under your jacket.

Jodhpurs There are trousers specially designed for riding. They are tight-fitting right down the legs to the ankles, which ensures your legs are not pinched by the stirrup leathers.

Jodhpur boots Jodhpur boots are ankle length boots, which either have elastic sides or fasten with a strap. They are designed to be worn with jodhpurs (or with jeans), but not with breeches.

Gloves Experts disagree on whether riders should or should not always wear gloves. When it is cold, they certainly make for greater comfort. Remember, however, that they must be made of a non-slip material, such as string. Woolen ones are deadly, as they will slip on the reins in the rain or if the reins are even slightly sweaty. Gloves should be well fitting, and not too thick, as this reduces contact with the reins.

For formal occasions, such as hunting or a competition, a suitably formal outfit should be worn. There are a number of variations on this basic pattern, depending on the activity involved.

Bowler hat A bowler is slightly more formal

It is important that the right size horse be chosen for your size. **Top left:** A good example of a rider on an undersized horse. The rider is said to be 'underhorsed'. **Top right:** here the rider is what is known as 'overhorsed'.

Above: The riders here are riding horses of the correct size. **Right:** A horse of 17 hands stands beside a pony of 12.2 hands. Differences, besides body size, are apparent such as the size of the head, ears and muzzle.

than a hard hat, but it is designed to fulfill exactly the same purpose. It is worn by both men and women.

Black jacket This is designed and cut in a similar fashion to the tweed hacking jacket, but, again, it is somewhat smarter.

Stock This is a specially shaped 'cravat', which is usually made of white material and is worn with a collarless shirt. It has to be tied in a special way and is normally secured with a plain gold stock pin (like a tie pin).

Gloves On formal occasions, clean, string gloves should always be worn.

Breeches Like jodhpurs, breeches are designed specifically for riding. They are always worn

with long boots, so they do not necessarily extend to the ankle.

Riding boots Riding boots, unlike jodhpur boots, come up to the knee. At one time they were always made of leather, but, today, special 'rubber' riding boots are available. These are perfectly adequate for most occasions and have the advantages of being considerably cheaper than their leather counterparts.

Stick and spurs A rider formally dressed almost always carries a riding cane and may wear spurs. Canes and whips are available in various designs; they should be rigid and not too long or 'whippy'. Spurs should always be blunted; the best are of stainless steel.

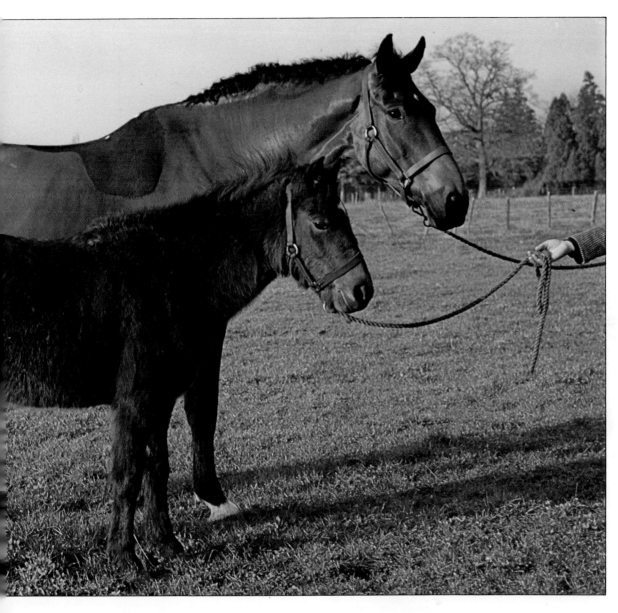

A horse or a pony

One of the first questions asked by most beginners starting to ride is when is a horse a horse, when is it a pony and how do they know which they are riding. The answer is a simple one. The principle factor that differentiates a pony from a horse is height. Horses and ponies are both measured in 'hands', one hand equaling 10cm (4in). The measurement is taken from the ground to the animal's withers, making sure it is standing on level ground, using a special measuring stick. If the measurement is 14.2 hands high (147cm–4ft 10in) or under, the animal is classed as a pony. If it measures 14.3 hands high (149.8cm–4ft 11in) it is a horse.

Although height is the determining factor in establishing whether the animal you are about to ride is a horse or pony, there are also some differences in general appearance between the two. These are most apparent in the head – ponies generally have smaller heads than horses (even in relation to their size), with neat, compact ears, small muzzles and often something of an impish expression. Such 'pony' characteristics, however, become recognizable only with experience, and are not clear-cut points that are capable of rigid definition.

Most pre-teenagers and those in their early teens will learn to ride on a pony. It is not easy to say definitively what size of pony is the right

This illustration shows the various points of the horse. It is generally agreed that the most important points are the limbs and feet as the horse depends on these for locomotion, if not for survival. For this reason, both legs and feet should be as correctly conformed as possible. In fact, this is probably the most valuable asset a horse can possess.

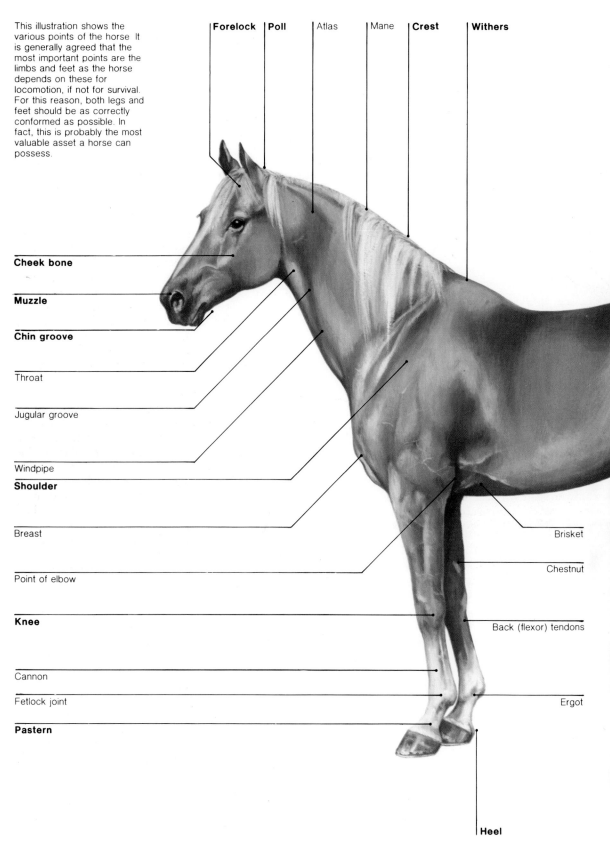

Forelock | **Poll** | Atlas | Mane | **Crest** | **Withers**

Cheek bone

Muzzle

Chin groove

Throat

Jugular groove

Windpipe

Shoulder

Breast

Point of elbow

Knee

Cannon

Fetlock joint

Pastern

Brisket

Chestnut

Back (flexor) tendons

Ergot

Heel

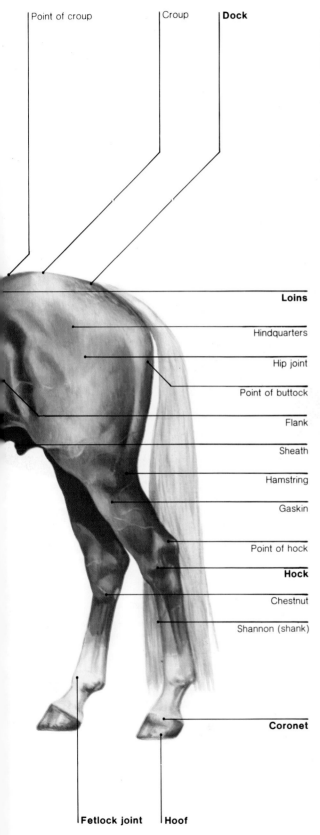

Point of croup

Croup

Dock

Loins

Hindquarters

Hip joint

Point of buttock

Flank

Sheath

Hamstring

Gaskin

Point of hock

Hock

Chestnut

Shannon (shank)

Coronet

Fetlock joint

Hoof

one for any particular height of person; other factors – weight, whether the pony is broad or narrow, and so on – all play a part. As a rough guide, though, it is worth noting that the animal is approximately the right size if you are standing by the animal's side and your eyes are level with its withers.

It is also far better to learn to ride on a pony or horse that is a little too big (within reason) than one that is too small. In general, the larger the animal, the longer its paces and therefore the smoother its ride. Small ponies tend to have a short, somewhat springy action, which is extremely uncomfortable for a novice rider. Also, small ponies seem to possess more low animal cunning than their taller relatives and they can be somewhat unpredictable when being ridden by a beginner. Lastly, it is very difficult to establish a good, correct seat on a pony if it is so small that your legs are practically touching the ground. The obvious corollary, however, is that it is equally difficult if the horse or pony you are riding is so broad that you can scarcely get your legs across its back.

Points of the horse

The names given to the various parts of a horse's body are technically known as the points of the horse. These vary in importance, but there are certain basic ones that should be memorized at the outset, for the instructor will refer to some of them in your first lesson.

One good reason for having a sound knowledge of a horse's points is that this information can, to a large extent, determine the rider's attitude toward the horse. For example, a knowledge of the basic musculature will allow the rider to be almost immediately aware of any injury or weakness in the horse, which, if overlooked by a less knowledgeable rider, might take weeks or even months for the horse to recover from. Also, a basic knowledge of the horse's points will allow the prospective owner to appraise and determine a horse's capabilities.

The horse's tack

Besides the main points of the horse, you should also know the names of the component parts that make up the basic equipment the horse wears when he is to be ridden. There are two major items – the bridle and the saddle. The former fits on the animal's head and is the rider's main means of control. The saddle is buckled on to the animal's back and gives the rider a more comfortable and secure seat than if he or she were to ride bareback.

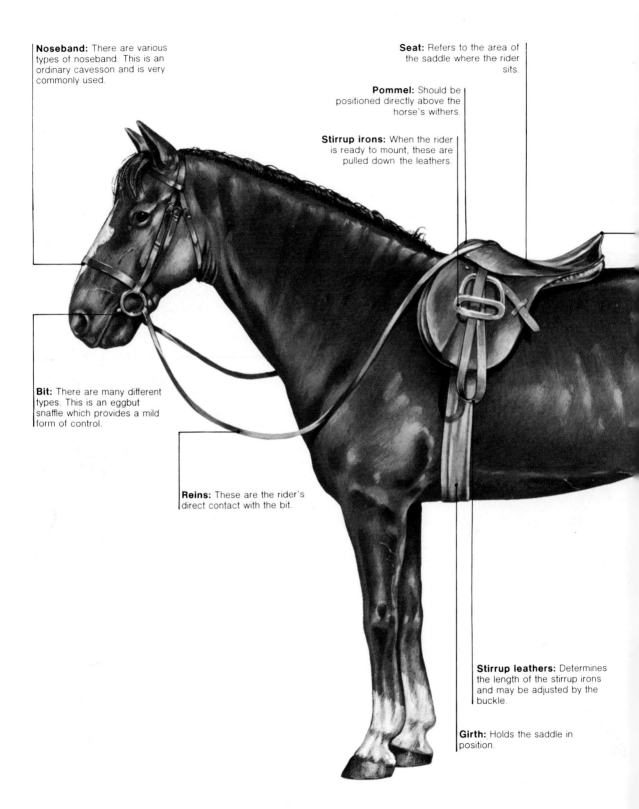

Noseband: There are various types of noseband. This is an ordinary cavesson and is very commonly used.

Seat: Refers to the area of the saddle where the rider sits.

Pommel: Should be positioned directly above the horse's withers.

Stirrup irons: When the rider is ready to mount, these are pulled down the leathers.

Bit: There are many different types. This is an eggbut snaffle which provides a mild form of control.

Reins: These are the rider's direct contact with the bit.

Stirrup leathers: Determines the length of the stirrup irons and may be adjusted by the buckle.

Girth: Holds the saddle in position.

A horse wearing a correctly fitted saddle and bridle. The points annotated are those the novice rider should know.

Right: The saddle fits on the horse's back so that the deepest point corresponds to the lowest part of the horse's spine. The weight of the saddle should lie evenly across the fleshy areas on either side of the backbone.

Cantle: The high ridge at the back of the saddle. The rider should sit well in front of this point.

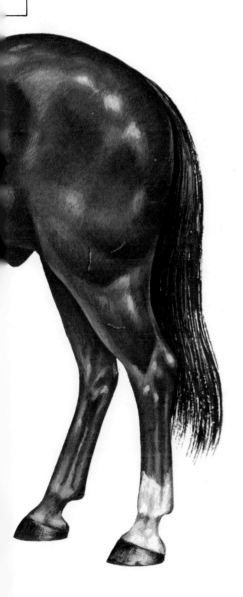

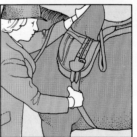

The girth should fit snugly with one finger's width gap between it and the horse.

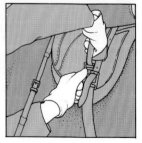

Buckle guards prevent the buckles from marking or injuring the saddle.

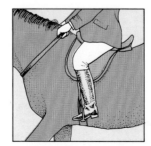

A neckstrap is a good idea for the novice rider to prevent undue pulling on the reins.

A lunging cavesson should be used when a horse is being lunged during your first lesson.

Your First Lesson

Below: Getting to know the horse on which you are going to learn to ride is extremely important. Establishing a friendly relationship right from the start will help to increase your confidence in one another. Take time at the beginning and end of each lesson to pat and talk to the horse.

IN THE EARLY STAGES of your riding career, try to establish and maintain a regular pattern of lessons. If you can only manage to ride once a week, book a course of six half-hour lessons. This is usually sufficient to give you the initial feel of riding and thereafter you can move on to one-hour spells.

The more frequently you have lessons, the more quickly your riding will progress; it is far better to have a half-hour lesson each week than a one-hour lesson once a fortnight. Moreover, you will find it far too tiring to try to ride

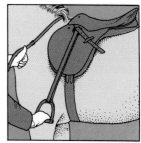

To acquire the proper length, the stirrup iron is pulled down the leather.

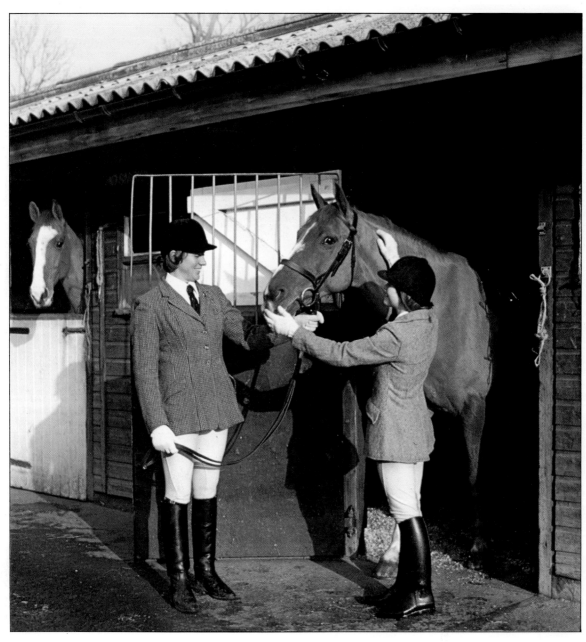

for a full hour at a time at first. If you have been working properly for the first few weeks, your muscles will be aching and your legs will feel as if they are ready to drop off after considerably less than half-an-hour. Much of the technique of riding depends on developing the correct muscles and, until you have done so, you cannot hope to begin to realize your potential as a rider.

At the start of your first lesson you will meet the horse that, providing you suit one another, is likely to be your mount for the next weeks. Try, therefore, to establish a friendly relationship right from the beginning by introducing yourself to him now, even before you get on his back. When he has been led from his stable, walk up to him calmly and directly, approaching him from the front, so that he can see you clearly. Find out his name and talk to him quietly, patting him on his neck. If you do feel any slight nervousness, try to conquer it, or at least do not let it show. Horses are sensitive animals and quickly sense fear or discomfort in a person, which makes them nervous, too. By

and large, they are kind animals and would far rather be friends than at odds with their human masters. Always remember that horses are living animals, with the same sort of feelings and likes and dislikes that we have, and treat them accordingly.

Watch how the horse's handler leads the horse to the school or paddock where your lesson is to take place, for you will soon be doing this yourself. As the horse will have a leading rein attached to his bit – you will be led by the instructor or an assistant for your first few lessons – the reins should be looped evenly around the animal's neck. If one side is almost hanging on the ground, it is inviting the horse to trip. The leader will walk quietly by the horse's shoulder – not in front so the animal is being tugged along – holding the leading rein in his right hand quite close to the bit. Any excess should be coiled in the left hand, so that, again, there is no danger of the horse tripping over it. If the horse does show any reluctance to move, he should be tapped lightly on his side, behind the saddle. Normally, the flat of the

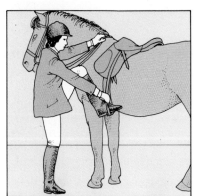

Mounting: With your body turned to face the horse's tail, put your left foot in the stirrup.

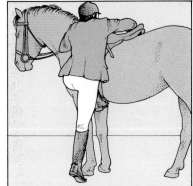

Put right hand and arm across the saddle and turn your body to face the horse's side.

Mistakes - Mounting

Putting the wrong foot in the stirrup iron is a common mistake.

Jumping off your right foot, turn the top of your body to the front.

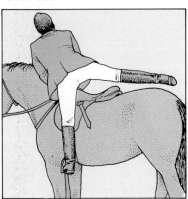

Lift yourself up and swing your right leg over the saddle and put foot in stirrup.

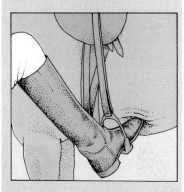

Avoid digging your horse's side with your toe when mounting.

hand is quite sufficient. It is counter-productive to stand in front of the horse and start hauling on the bit – he will probably move backwards in an effort to escape the unpleasant feeling of the bit banging on his teeth.

Mounting the horse

Once in the school, your nervousness or apprehension may well heighten with the thought of actually getting on the horse. There is no need whatsoever to worry about this, provided you think logically about what you are doing, as the picture sequence (see p.17) shows.

The first step is to take up the reins. Even though the assistant will be holding the horse's head, you should get into the habit of holding the reins sufficiently tightly yourself to discourage the horse from moving forward. Take them up in your left hand – together with a good lump of mane if you feel you need the security – and stand by the horse's shoulder facing towards his tail. Take hold of the stirrup iron with your right hand, turn it towards you and put your left foot into it. Hop forward and turn to face the saddle. Then, with your right hand across the seat of the saddle, spring up off your right foot. Swing your right leg across the saddle, trying to avoid hitting the horse's back as you do so, and sit down lightly in the saddle. Put your right foot in the stirrup iron.

The stirrup leathers should lie flat against your legs; if they are twisted one edge will dig into your legs and this will soon be very painful. You must adjust the stirrup leathers too, so they are the right length. It is impossible to give exact instructions as to how to judge the correct length, as this will alter as you settle deeper into the saddle and become more confident. As a guide – always providing that this length does, in fact, feel comfortable – hang your legs straight down and adjust the leathers so the bottom of the iron is level with your ankle bone. The leathers must be of equal length; if your legs are lopsided, you will have no hope of sitting straight and being equally balanced in the saddle.

Position in the saddle

There are two things to be said straightaway about adopting the correct position in the saddle. The first is that it is of paramount importance, for it is only by sitting correctly at all times that you can become an effective and good rider, and the second is that you should not expect it to feel comfortable until you have got used to it. It is not a 'natural' position in

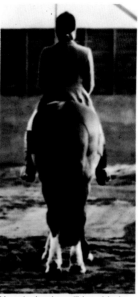

Your instructor will be able to tell you if you are sitting evenly across the horse's back as he/she stands behind you.

Your position in the saddle is probably the most difficult yet most important aspect of learning to ride. Initially, you should make a conscious effort to always be aware of the points mentioned below; eventually these will become automatic and you will be able to concentrate on other areas of your riding.

Shoulders: These must be pulled back so they are square to the horse's shoulders and in line with your hips.

Back: This should be perfectly straight, but not hollow.

Seat: Rest lightly but deeply in the saddle so that you are sitting on your seat bones and not on the fleshy part of your buttocks.

The bottom of the stirrup iron should be level with your ankle bone.

Use the buckle close to the saddle to adjust the length of the leathers.

Head: This is held high and straight. Mentally press your neck back against your collar and look ahead between the horse's ears at all times.

In the early stages of riding hold on to the pommel rather than the rein to avoid a tendency to overpull the reins.

Hands: Rest them on the pommel at first, as this is a purely positional exercise.

Legs: Hang your legs down naturally, so that the inside of the calf rests against the saddle. Your knees should be relaxed and supple, not pressed hard into the saddle.

Mistakes - Position

Above left: This shows the rider sitting incorrectly with humped back, rounded shoulders, looking towards the ground. **Above right:** The rider is wrongly positioned at the back of the saddle with lower legs pushed forward. **Right:** The rider incorrectly points her toes outward while gripping with the back of her legs.

Feet: The ball of each foot rests squarely in the irons. Your feet should point directly forwards, with toes up.

that it is not similar, for instance, to the way you sit in a chair. Instead, it has to be learnt and worked at over many lessons, for the tendency will always be to shift slightly so that you are more comfortable.

Having positioned yourself correctly, the resulting discomfort may make it hard to believe that this position has been devised to give you and your mount the maximum ease of movement, efficiency and control.

If you are sitting up sufficiently straight with your head held high, it will feel as if you are sitting as straight as a ramrod, with your head and shoulders forced back. If you could see yourself, you would see that this was not actually so; in any event, the importance of keeping your head up cannot be sufficiently stressed. Your head is the heaviest single part of your body and its position determines much of the positioning of the rest of it. If you look down, your weight automatically shifts forward. A horse already carries two-thirds of his weight on his forehand, so the last thing he wants is your extra weight on this area.

Your body weight should be on your seat bones, evenly distributed on either side of the saddle, so that you and the horse can balance freely. Your seat is maintained at all times by balance, not by grip. If you grip with your thighs and knees, you are automatically impeding the horse's freedom of movement and pushing your seat upwards in the saddle. Try to relax your knees and hips which will demand some conscious thought and effort.

Your legs should hang straight underneath you, making a straight line from the shoulder and hip to the heel. This should not be done by bending more acutely at the knee, so the lower part of your leg is forced back, but by bringing that part of the leg directly underneath you. Finally the weight of your legs should fall into the heels. In doing this, the temptation is often to stick your toes out, which results in gripping the horse's sides with the back of your leg. Instead of thinking of pressing your heel down, think of bringing your toe up, pointing directly forward.

The first movements

Even before you learn to hold the reins, your instructor will probably ask the assistant to lead the horse forward, so that you can get the feel of the walk. With your hands on the pommel, close the insides of your legs against the horse's side and by so doing you will encourage the horse to move forwards.

At a walk, a horse moves his legs one after the other in a rhythmic sequence. There is no point of suspension and four hoofbeats are heard.

A horse walks by picking up and putting down each foot separately, so that four distinct hoof beats may be heard. This results in a pace that has a gently swinging or swaying movement and, as your aim at all times is to move with the horse, you should let your body sway gently in time with the movement. This is not a conscious movement. If you think about it, you are likely to sway too much, so concentrate instead on maintaining the correct position in the saddle. Keep sitting on your seat bones, with your back straight and your head held up so you look between the horse's ears, and your legs hanging easily beneath you.

Even though you are now in the saddle, you will either be led by an assistant or lunged by your instructor. This means he or she will stand at a given spot – the center of a circle – and control the horse from the end of a long rein attached to his bit, guiding him round and

In your first lessons, your instructor will either control your horse on a lunge rein **(Above)** or ask an assistant to lead you **(Right)** In either case, this will leave you free to concentrate on maintaining the correct position without having to worry about controlling your mount. Your movements will not require a conscious effort on your part. Instead, concentrate on keeping your weight on your seat bones, back straight, legs relaxed beneath you, and head held high with eyes looking between your horse's ears.

round. In either case, you do not yet have to worry about controlling the horse; you can concentrate completely on sitting correctly. Until this becomes second nature, you will find it takes all your concentration.

Holding the reins

Although you need not concern yourself with controlling the horse for a few lessons yet, you must know how to hold the reins. Pick up a rein in either hand, so that they run through your little and third fingers, cross the palms of your hands and emerge between your thumb and first finger. Your thumbs – pointing straight forward – are on the tops of the reins holding them down onto your first finger.

Hold your hands in front of you about 10cm (4in) above the withers with elbows bent and supple by your side. There should be a straight line from the bit, through the reins, hands and arms up to your elbow. You will find this necessitates holding your hands quite forward and the width of the bit apart. Think of holding a book in front of you, your thumbs on top of the pages. In fact, riding a horse is somewhat like reading a book – ideally, you should always be looking four words ahead.

Always remember that the reins are for guiding the horse and not to be clutched for security, maintain your position or correct your balance. Think of them as delicate threads; if you pull on them too hard, they will break.

As soon as the horse moves forward – remember you make him do so at this stage by closing the inside of your leg against his sides – you

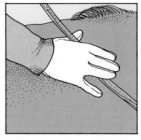

Close fingers around the reins pressing down on to your first fingers with the thumbs.

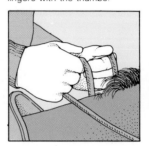

Pass reins inside your hand from third finger to the crook of first finger and thumb.

Right: Reins correctly held.
Below: The end of the reins fall over the horse's neck.

Even if the horse's head moves, maintain a straight line through elbows and hands to the bit.

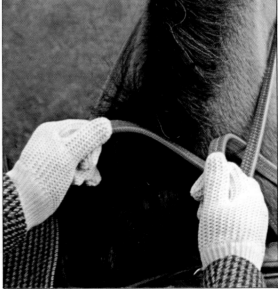

must make sure to follow the movement of his head with your hands. If you keep your hands rigid, you will naturally impede his head movement, thus making it difficult, if not impossible, for him to balance properly. To do this, he needs to be able to move his head freely. You will find that, at a walk, his head moves quite considerably, so let your hands move as well. Again, do not try to move them consciously; just let them follow the movement, so it is the horse's head that moves your hands rather than the other way around.

When you want the horse to slow down or stop, you must pass on your intention to him. Clearly you have to discourage or restrict his forward movement; you do this by pushing him forward with your legs and then squeezing the reins gently so that he meets resistance. In other words, your legs push him up to meet your hands. Do not haul on the reins, leaning

Mistakes - Holding Reins

Holding the reins 'upside down', over top of hands.

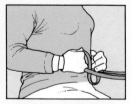

Hands positioned too far back into stomach.

Positioning one hand higher than the other.

Holding reins too low and forcing elbows outwards.

backwards as you do so; instead, brace your back muscles, so you are no longer following the horse's movement, and close your hands on the reins, so that they, too, are no longer following the movement. This should be done gently, as though you were squeezing a sponge.

From walk to trot

If you feel reasonably confident and comfortable at a walk in your first lesson, your instructor may suggest that you try a few strides at the trot. This is a very different pace from the walk. It is a two-time pace – that is, the horse moves opposite diagonal legs together and springs from one pair of diagonals to the other. This makes it a much bouncier, springier gait, so, until you get used to it, prepare to be bounced around in the saddle.

As you progress, you will learn to ride at this pace both by sitting down in the saddle to the movement and rising up and down with it. For this first time, however, take hold of the pommel firmly with both hands, ask the horse to move into a trot by closing the inside of your legs against his sides and then try to maintain your balance as he moves forward. When you want him to return to a walk, try to sit very tall in the saddle – this helps you to maintain your balance as the horse slows down – and ask him to walk by closing your legs against his side and bracing your back muscles.

Dismounting

The last stage of any lesson is dismounting. To do this, take both feet out of the stirrup irons and collect the reins in your left hand. Put your right hand on the pommel, or the side of the horse's neck, and swing your right leg up behind you and over the back of the saddle. As gently as you can, let yourself slide down to the ground, letting your knees bend to take the jar as you land. Be warned – after even half-an-hour on a horse, it takes a second or two to regain your usual muscles and you may well find your first few steps are somewhat staggery. It is not unknown for people to find themselves sitting down on the ground.

Thank your horse for the ride by patting him. Then, with the reins looped round your arm so that he cannot walk off on his own, run the stirrup irons up the side of the leather closest to the saddle so they rest against the top sides of the saddle. This will stop them from banging against the horse's sides as he walks. Take the reins over the horse's head and, holding them together with the leading rein, lead him away.

If you feel insecure at the trot, hold on to the pommel.

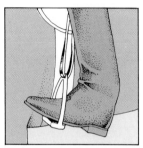
To trot, close your legs firmly against the horse's sides.

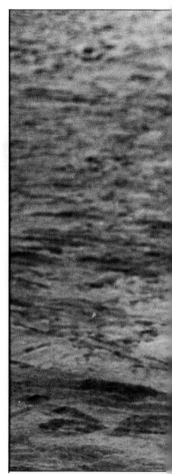

Right: At a trot, the rider hears only two hoof beats as the horse moves opposite diagonal legs together. At one point, all four legs will leave the ground as one diagonal is raised before the other has returned to the ground. This is a much livelier gait and the rider can either sit in the saddle and follow the natural rhythm, or rise slightly out of it for one beat. Much like humans, horses tend to favour one side, making it easier, for example, to stay on the left diagonal for prolonged periods. This, however, is bad for both horse and rider.

Mistakes - Trotting/Dismounting

Trotting: Leaning towards the back of the saddle, lower legs forward.

Conversely, as the horse slows from a trot to a walk, the rider may fall forward.

Dismounting: Right leg in front of the saddle rather than swinging it behind.

Not swinging your right leg high enough so that it catches on the cantle.

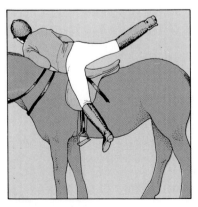

Dismounting: Leaning forward slightly, take both of your feet out of the irons.

Leaning forward with left shoulder, swing right leg up and behind.

Still holding onto the saddle, bend your knees as you land to prevent jarring.

Second Time Around

Check List

(1) Think over all points learned at your first lesson before beginning the second.

(2) Pat and talk to your horse before mounting.

(3) Check your girths before mounting to ensure they are tight enough to keep the saddle in place.

(4) Once in the saddle, think over all aspects of your position to ensure you are sitting correctly.

(5) Sit with head held high, body weight resting on your seat bones, knees and hips relaxed.

(6) Your legs should hang in a straight line with the weight falling into the heels.

RIDING IS LIKE MANY SPORTS; the second time you come to it, it may seem as if you are going backwards rather than making any progress. This may not be your experience, but if it is, do not be discouraged – competent horsemen and women are never made in a single lesson.

Before embarking on your second lesson, try to go over all the points from your first lesson in your mind again. The main thing is the position. If this sounds like endless repetition it is because you simply cannot make progress unless you establish a correct and secure, yet balanced and supple, position in the saddle.

It is likely that you will still be on a leading rein, so take full advantage of this to really work on your position again. Sitting tall is the first aspect to consider. Imagine somebody in the roof of the riding school is pulling on a piece of string attached to the middle of your head and really stretch your neck and back. Alternatively, think of pulling your head and neck right out of your shoulders. Do not worry if you feel you are exaggerating; unless you feel you are doing so, you will probably not be sitting correctly.

Make sure, too, that you are holding the reins correctly – that is, sufficiently short to ensure you have a light even contact with the horse's mouth, but not tight enough to make him try to evade the pressure in his mouth. Practice shortening and lengthening them while the horse is walking.

In addition, concentrate when you want to move forward or go faster on giving the correct signals with your legs and then work on relaxing in the saddle with the movement, not getting left behind and jerked backwards as the horse moves. When you want to slow down, remember the action is a gentle squeeze on the reins, not a fierce tug backwards. In other words, the position of your hands does not alter.

Positional exercises

Earlier, it was briefly mentioned that the position in the saddle should be maintained by balance at all times. This is very important; if you grip with your thighs and knees, you will automatically make the horse tense his back and shoulder muscles. This, in turn, restricts the freedom of his movements. It also pushes you upwards in the saddle so you come off your seat bones. To help you achieve an even balance across the horse's back, let your arms hang down by your sides. Then, without rounding your shoulders, imagine you are carrying two

POSITIONAL EXERCISES

Exercises are invaluable for helping achieve and maintain correct position in the saddle. Later on they can be done at a walk and trot as well as a halt.

Cross arms and bend forward from the waist keeping your lower body still. Slowly straighten up and lean backward the same way, making sure your legs do not shoot forwards. This will help supple your waist.

Put one hand on the pommel and circle other arm from shoulder. Think of trying to pull your hips out of their sockets as you lift your arm upwards. Keep your legs absolutely still and in the correct position. Repeat with the other arm.

With both arms outstretched at shoulder level, turn from the waist first to the right and then the left, so that your hands point to the horse's ears and tail.

Left: An excellent exercise for both lessening your reliance on the stirrups and improving your general coordination and confidence is to ride as this rider is with legs stretched out straight from the horse. Eliminating the use of your legs will show you how much you need them to give the aids.

heavy bags of shopping – one in either hand – which by definition require you to be evenly balanced.

To maintain a balanced position, all parts of your body must be perfectly relaxed and supple. Even though your back is straight and your shoulders are pulled squarely back, they should both still be relaxed and so should your hips and pelvis. Your knee, hip and elbow joints should all be supple. It is essential to co-ordinate body movements – that is, moving one part of the body in harmony with another – but you must also be able to move one part of your body independently of the other parts. To begin with, you will probably find this extremely hard to do; as you use your legs, your hands will automatically jerk up or make you lean backwards, but, as you think about it and practice it, you will find it becomes easier.

Every lesson or schooling session should include some exercises, for they are invaluable in developing the position in the saddle. They will help you to co-ordinate your body movements as well as use each part independently; they will help to supple you and reduce stiffness; and they will help to develop the correct riding muscles.

Some of the exercises pictured here are designed to help you learn to move one part of your body independently. Providing the assistant is still leading you, you can do them at a walk as well as at a halt.

Riding without stirrups

From an early stage, you should get accustomed to riding without stirrups. This will help you with your balance; it also teaches you not to rely on your stirrup irons to help you maintain your position.

With the horse halted, take both feet out of the stirrups and cross the leathers over in front of the saddle, the irons resting on either side of the horse's neck. The usual order from your instructor for this will be to quit and cross your stirrups. Ask the horse to walk on in the normal way and let your legs hang down in a relaxed fashion for a few paces. Put your legs in the correct position, then raise your toes, letting the weight fall down to the heel again. Keep your hands on the pommel initially, but when you feel secure, take up the reins as you would normally. You must be even more careful now not to rely on your reins to balance you; if you feel tempted to do this, take hold of the neck strap.

A good exercise to do while riding without

To quit and cross stirrups, take both feet out of stirrups and pull buckle down a short way from the bar.

Cross leathers in front of saddle.

Right: Riding without stirrups is excellent training. Try to remember to keep your legs in the usual position.

EASY EXERCISES WITHOUT STIRRUPS

Swing your legs backwards and forwards from the knee.

Keeping legs still, circle each arm from the shoulder.

stirrups is to swing your legs from the knee backwards and forwards, either together or alternately. Alternatively, try swinging one leg forward and the other back at the same time, making sure you keep your hands still and do not bounce in the saddle. This helps to supple your knees.

Always remember that, as the majority of exercises are designed to develop muscles, to always repeat those that involve just one side with the other one. By the same token, it is very important to ride evenly at the same pace on both reins, otherwise both you and the horse will develop a preference for riding one way. Largely because they are ridden by so many

Mistakes - Without Stirrups

Hanging on to the reins to maintain balance.

Moving out of position while doing exercises.

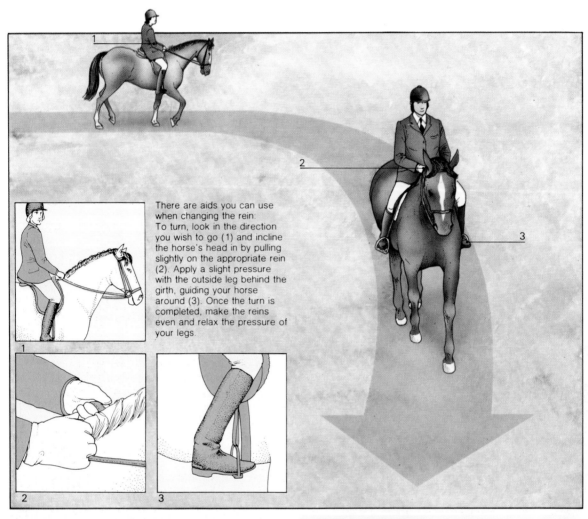

There are aids you can use when changing the rein: To turn, look in the direction you wish to go (1) and incline the horse's head in by pulling slightly on the appropriate rein (2). Apply a slight pressure with the outside leg behind the girth, guiding your horse around (3). Once the turn is completed, make the reins even and relax the pressure of your legs.

people, most riding school horses do have a preference for one side and you will soon feel this; they will always be a little stiff and more reluctant to co-operate on the other rein.

Changing direction

Changing direction is also known as changing the rein. To change the rein, look in the direction you mean to go as you approach the point of turn. If you fail to look in the right direction, your horse will not know which way to go. With a slight pressure on the appropriate rein, guide your horse around by closing your outside leg slightly further back than usual against his side. When the turn is completed, make the reins even again and relax the pressure of your leg, looking straight ahead between the horses ears.

When you reach the other end of the school, turn him in the opposite direction to the one you have been riding, giving similar signals. If you have turned right down the school, you will

Mistakes - Changing Direction

Hauling on the horse's mouth in the direction you want him to turn while looking down at your hands.

A frequent mistake, moving the right hand outwards, away from the neck, in direction of turn.

want to turn left when you rejoin the track, so incline the horse's head to the left and squeeze with your right leg.

The rising trot

By now, you should be confident enough in the saddle to learn how to rise at the trot. From your previous experience, you will know that the trot is a very bumpy pace, so, to avoid any unnecessary damage to the horse's mouth, take hold of the neck strap before moving.

At first, it helps to practice the technique of

Mistakes - Rising Trot

Rounded shoulders and elbows and tensed wrists will all limit your flexibility.

Rising with a hollowed back throws the shoulders forward and the seat back.

Rising too high out of the saddle, and so falling behind the movement.

the rising trot while the assistant holds the horse still. Gently stand up and sit down again in the saddle, using your knees as hinges to push you up rather than relying on the stirrup irons to support your weight. Thinking of this action as a forwards and backwards movement from your hips helps resist the temptation of rising too high. As you rise forwards and backwards count 'one, two', keeping the counting, and the rising, as even and regular as possible.

This may seem easy, but transferring it to the actual action is more difficult, though it soon

The rising trot may be difficult for you to get used to, However, once grasped you will find it to be a comfortable and non-tiring pace both for yourself and your horse.

comes with practice. Therefore, if you find you are rising in time with the movement for a few strides and bumping for double the number, you can be pleased, for it shows you are making progress. In these early stages, only trot for short distances at a time – down one side of the school, for example. The trot is a very tiring pace for you until you get used to it; if you get overtired you will find it even more difficult.

Riding on Your Own

Check List

(1) Check the girth to see that it is buckled tightly enough before pulling the stirrup irons down the leathers.

(2) Hold the reins lightly in your left hand as you mount your horse to discourage him from moving forward.

(3) Run through the things you learned and practiced at your last lesson before moving off around the school. Think particularly about the rising trot.

(4) Remember to sit in the deepest part of the saddle, your weight distributed evenly across the horse's back.

SOONER OR LATER the day will come when the instructor will dispense with the helper and you will no longer be led round the school. There is no need to be apprehensive about this; by now, you and your horse will be old friends and riding him around the school on your own should present few difficulties for either of you.

As usual, spend the first few minutes of your lesson re-establishing and correcting your position. Stretch your legs down to the ground and then settle as deeply into the saddle as you can. With the benefit of the experience you have gained, you can now try an additional exercise, which is designed to help to get you deep in the saddle and also to help develop the thigh muscles and supple your hips. The exercise does demand perseverance, for it can be quite difficult to do. However, it does become easier.

With your feet out of the irons, point your

Some of your time will be spent in the group practicing and exercising at a halt. Do not become discouraged if other members progress more quickly than you; remember that everyone will learn at different rates. Work on your position.

EXERCISES TO DO AT HOME

There are many exercises you can do in the saddle to improve your general physical tone and coordination and some which you may wish to do at home as well. **Left:** Sit in a hard chair and, bending at the waist, touch your right hand to your left foot with your other arm stretched out straight behind you. Repeat with the opposite arm and leg. **Below:** Sitting again in a hard chair with arms stretched out at shoulder level, turn your arms and upper body as far to the right and left as possible, keeping your lower body still.

toes down to the ground and make a very positive effort to stretch your legs. Then, keeping your legs straight, take them outwards away from the saddle and backwards from the hip. Do not let your upper body tilt forward; it should remain quite still. Repeat the exercise two or three times.

If you have been having group lessons and you find that the other pupils are progressing quicker than you at this point, try not to be discouraged. Like any sport, riding has to be worked at continually and people progress at different rates. It is not necessarily those who find it easy in the early stages who will make the best riders later. Keep working at the position; concentrate, too, on getting the feel of being on horseback. It is very difficult to teach a feeling, but it is this you must learn to

recognize – to feel if the horse is moving correctly beneath you. Try to feel him picking up and putting down each foot separately – and his back and spine moving beneath you.

If your instructor is lunging the horse, try the following exercise at a walk and trot. Put both hands on the pommel, then lift your knees up in the air, so that you are balancing only on your seat bones. This is an excellent balancing exercise; as your only point of contact with the horse are your seat bones, it is quite impossible to grip at all. Also practice all the exercises previously described (see pp. 26-27).

The art of control
Now that you are riding without a leading rein, you must also think more about controlling your mount. The time has come when the

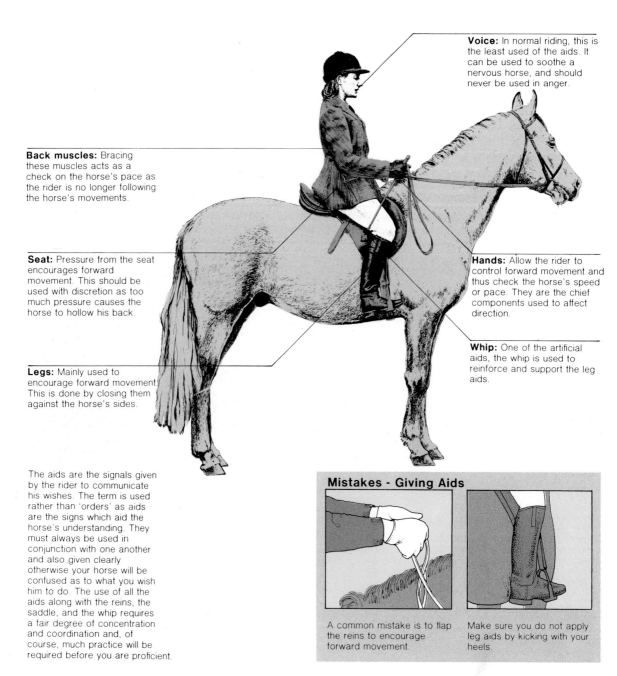

Voice: In normal riding, this is the least used of the aids. It can be used to soothe a nervous horse, and should never be used in anger.

Back muscles: Bracing these muscles acts as a check on the horse's pace as the rider is no longer following the horse's movements.

Seat: Pressure from the seat encourages forward movement. This should be used with discretion as too much pressure causes the horse to hollow his back.

Hands: Allow the rider to control forward movement and thus check the horse's speed or pace. They are the chief components used to affect direction.

Whip: One of the artificial aids, the whip is used to reinforce and support the leg aids.

Legs: Mainly used to encourage forward movement. This is done by closing them against the horse's sides.

The aids are the signals given by the rider to communicate his wishes. The term is used rather than 'orders' as aids are the signs which aid the horse's understanding. They must always be used in conjunction with one another and also given clearly otherwise your horse will be confused as to what you wish him to do. The use of all the aids along with the reins, the saddle, and the whip requires a fair degree of concentration and coordination and, of course, much practice will be required before you are proficient.

Mistakes - Giving Aids

A common mistake is to flap the reins to encourage forward movement.

Make sure you do not apply leg aids by kicking with your heels.

position you have worked so hard at perfecting has also to be effective in making the horse obey and work for you. Combining correctness of position with effectiveness is often one of the hardest aspects of learning to ride.

The signals that have been devised to help a rider transmit his wishes to his mount are known as the aids. They fall into two groups – natural and artificial. The natural aids are those given with parts of the rider's body. The chief ones are the hands and the legs; in addition, shifting the body weight slightly or bracing

muscles are included. The voice also counts as a natural aid, though this should be used sparingly and never in anger. The artificial aids are the additional items of equipment a rider can use to help encourage or control the horse. These consist of a cane or whip, spurs and ancillary items of tack, such as a martingale, which are used for specific reasons to do with control.

The most important point to remember about aids is that they should always be given firmly and decisively, but never roughly. A half-

USING A WHIP

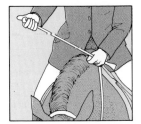

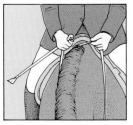

Above: When riding in a school, the whip is usually held in the inside hand. When the rein is changed, the whip is transferred to the other hand. To do this, take hold of the whip and reins in one hand. With the free hand, pull the whip through the rein hand, then take up the rein with the whip in this hand. **Above right:** Use the whip firmly, but not roughly, just behind the leg.

Mistakes - Using/Holding a Whip

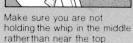

Make sure you are not holding the whip in the middle rather than near the top

Avoid rounding the wrists so that the whip is tucked under the elbow.

The whip should never be used on the horse's neck or hindquarters.

hearted aid is useless and the horse will not understand what he is to do. Aids should be given together, that is, a leg aid should be supported by a hand aid.

If, for example, you want your horse to move forward more quickly or alertly, you would tell him by squeezing his sides with the inside of your leg. At the same time you must relax or yield with your hands in order to give him the freedom to move forward. Equally, if you want him to slow down, you push him forward with your legs so that he gathers himself together, then stop the forward movement by resisting with your hands and bracing your back muscles.

At this time, you should learn to carry a whip during lessons. Choose either a cane or a short, fairly rigid riding crop. Hold it in your hand along the rein so that the top emerges from the crook of your thumb and forefinger. The remainder of the whip rests across your lower thigh.

When riding in a school, a whip should generally be held in the inside hand. This is because a horse will automatically move away

5

6

In turning, the rider should try and see
the eye of the horse on the side to
which he is turning (right eye, right turn).

from it when it is used and he should move
always towards the outside of the school, not in
towards the center. If you are carrying a whip,
therefore, you must remember to change it to
the other hand when you change the rein. Do
this as you cross the center of the school.

Refining the turn

With a greater knowledge and understanding of
the aids, you should be able to produce
smoother, better turns from your mount.
Instead of just indicating the direction you
want him to go with the rein and applying
pressure with the opposite leg, you can now
progress to slightly more refined aids.

As you approach the point where the horse is
required to turn, look in that direction and then
incline the horse's head very slightly towards it.
Apply pressure with your outside leg – a little

further back than normal – and also close your
inside leg against his side in the normal position. This has the effect of bending him round
your inside leg, so that he executes a smooth
turn in which his shoulders, body and hindquarters follow in an exact line.

The pressure of the inside leg maintains the
forward impulsion and gives the correct bend.
Without it, the horse will fall into the inside of
the turn, his body will be incorrectly bent and
impulsion will be lost. The outside leg helps to
balance and guide the hindquarters, keeping
them in the correct line as well.

Besides turning to change the rein on the
center lines of the school, practice leaving the
track at the three-quarter marker, having just
turned down one long side of the school, and
rejoining it at the three-quarter marker just
before the corner on the opposite long side. Try

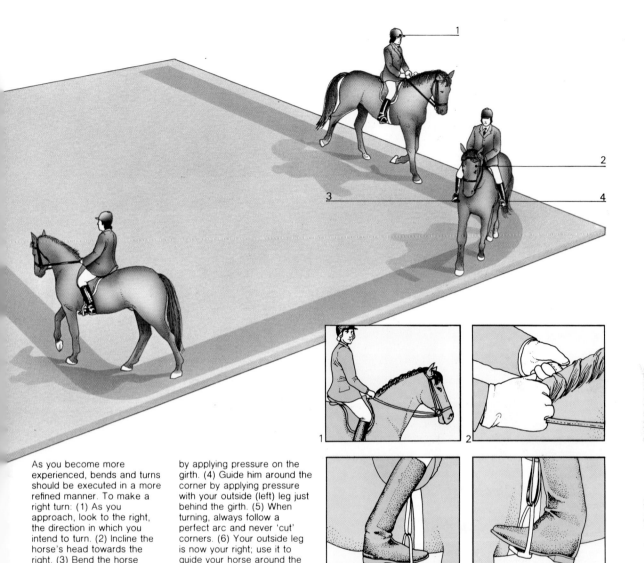

As you become more experienced, bends and turns should be executed in a more refined manner. To make a right turn: (1) As you approach, look to the right, the direction in which you intend to turn. (2) Incline the horse's head towards the right. (3) Bend the horse around your inside (right) leg by applying pressure on the girth. (4) Guide him around the corner by applying pressure with your outside (left) leg just behind the girth. (5) When turning, always follow a perfect arc and never 'cut' corners. (6) Your outside leg is now your right; use it to guide your horse around the corner.

Mistakes - Turning Corners

Above left: Moving the outside hand forward and the inside hand in towards your body. **Above right:** Collapsing your inside shoulder and hip and looking at the ground. **Right:** Pulling too hard on the rein so that the horse turns his head and shoulders too sharply and 'overbends' the turn.

to ride straight from one marker to the other. Fix your eye on it as soon as you begin the turn and steer the horse straight to it. If you are carrying a whip, remember to change it over to the opposite hand, so that you will be carrying it on the inside when you rejoin the track.

By now, too, you should be perfecting the rising trot, so that you are no longer bumping for any strides. It is better not to carry a whip for this, as it may well get in the way. If you have been using the neck strap for balance, practice taking your hands off it for a few strides and then moving back to it, holding it again. Try to let the movement of the trot throw you forwards and backwards from the hips, rather than trying to rise consciously. A good exercise to make sure you are not using either the reins or neck strap as a balancing aid is to practice trotting with your arms crossed.

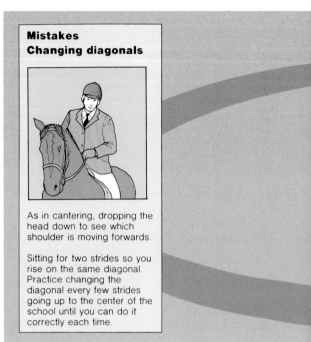

**Mistakes
Changing diagonals**

As in cantering, dropping the head down to see which shoulder is moving forwards.

Sitting for two strides so you rise on the same diagonal. Practice changing the diagonal every few strides going up to the center of the school until you can do it correctly each time.

Do this by cupping each elbow with the opposite arm, rather than actually crossing your arms through one another.

The sitting trot

Once you can maintain the rising trot around the school, you can begin to learn the sitting trot. For this, as the name suggests, you sit in the saddle all the time; this is far harder than it sounds, particularly if your horse has a very springy action. Try sitting for a few strides and then going back to a rising trot, gradually increasing the amount of time spent sitting as you begin to feel more comfortable. Relax your body, sitting deep into the saddle, but sit even more upright than for the rising trot. The tendency sometimes is to become sloppy in an attempt to relax into the movement, but you will find, in fact, that this throws you out of the saddle even more vigorously.

The sitting trot is a tiring pace for horse and rider, particularly when you are learning it. Therefore do it only for short bursts at a time. Rise to the trot down the long sides of the

school and sit along the shorter ones. Remember with all trotting exercises – both sitting and rising – to work evenly on both reins.

Changing diagonals

All riders should be aware of a further refinement about trotting and put it into practice. As discussed previously, when a horse trots, it moves opposite diagonal legs – that is, the foreleg on one side and the hind leg on the

Mistakes - Sitting Trot

Drawing the legs up and dropping your toes so you lose your stirrup irons.

Letting your hands fly upwards when you are bounced out of the saddle.

At a rising trot, the rider may either rise as the horse's left leg or the right leg moves forward. As the horse moves around the circle, his outside leg will cover more ground than the inside. You should make an effort to rise equally on different diagnoals.

other – simultaneously. At the rising trot, therefore, the rider may rise either as the left or the right shoulder moves forward. This is known as riding on the left or right diagonal.

The importance of riding equally on both reins has been emphasized on a number of occasions; it is just as important to rise equally on different diagonals. If a rider always rises on the same diagonal, both horse and rider will develop an unbalanced and uneven trot. A horse that is always ridden on one diagonal has a noticeably rough and uneven trot when ridden on the other one. This is because his muscles have not been allowed to develop evenly.

When riding in the school, you should rise as the outside shoulder moves forward. Thus when you are trotting on the right rein (clockwise around the school), you should rise as the left shoulder moves forward. As a horse trots in a circle, his outside legs cover more ground than his inside legs. By rising as the outside shoulder moves forward, the rider relieves the muscles on that side.

When changing the rein, you should change the diagonal as you ride across the school before rejoining the main track. This is done by sitting for one extra stride. Instead of the rhythm being 'up-down, up-down' (more accurately forward-backward, forward-backward) with the horse's movement, it is 'up-down, down-up'. Learn to recognize which diagonal you are riding on by glancing down quickly at the horse's shoulder.

When riding on a hack, it does not matter which diagonal you rise to as you trot along a road or a track. The important point is that you change the diagonal regularly so you ride equally on each one.

From trot to canter

Once you have truly mastered the sitting and rising trot, the next pace upwards is the canter. This is executed by the horse in quite a different way from a walk or trot and has a very different feel from the paces so far discussed. It is a pace in three-time in which one hindleg strikes off, to be followed by the diagonal of the opposite hind leg and foreleg, and then by the

At the canter, the horse moves forwards in a series of rhythmic bounds. In one complete stride, three distinct hoofbeats should be heard. A canter is described as being a left or right canter depending upon which of the forelegs lead the pace. On a circle, the inside foreleg should lead.

Mistakes - Cantering

Sitting humped over the front of the saddle, with legs up and toes out.

Getting left behind the movement so your hands fly up in the air.

Allowing the horse to trot faster, rather than breaking into a canter. Discourage this by closing your hands on the reins to prevent the faster movement.

Bumping so violently in the saddle that you lose the reins.

Forgetting that you still have to steer and control the horse: When cantering around the corners of the school, for example, do not let him fall into the corner. Instead, push him right into the corner by strongly using your inside leg.

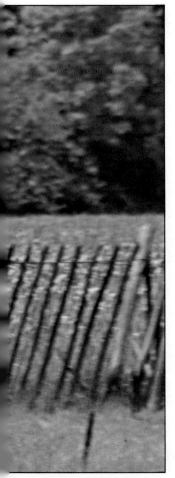

FROM TROT TO CANTER AND BACK AGAIN

To move from a trot to a canter, make sure your horse is attentive by sitting for a few strides and then pushing him forwards strongly with your legs. Close your hands on the reins to prevent him from going into a faster trot.

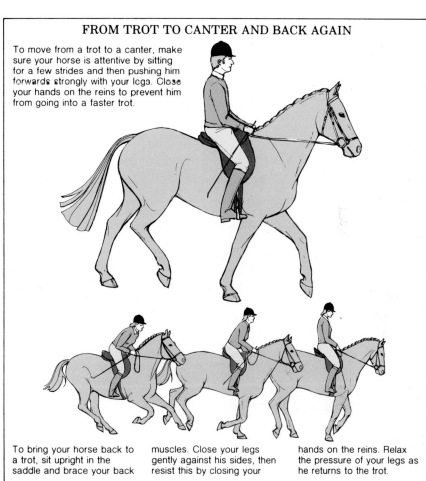

To bring your horse back to a trot, sit upright in the saddle and brace your back muscles. Close your legs gently against his sides, then resist this by closing your hands on the reins. Relax the pressure of your legs as he returns to the trot.

opposite foreleg. There follows a point of suspension when all four legs leave the ground before the pattern is repeated.

To go from trot to canter, sit deep in the saddle, close your hands slightly on the reins to prevent the horse going into a faster trot, and press both legs against his sides. Lean forward slightly from the waist to counter the horse's movement, but this should be barely perceptible. Leaning too far forward is a bad habit to get into and a hard one to break.

As the horse breaks into a canter, try to sit deep in the saddle. Make no conscious effort to move; let the rhythm of the pace move you.

Avoid using your hands to balance as at the canter, more than any other pace, you need to let your hands move with the horse to give his head the freedom it needs.

To return to the trot, slow the horse down by pushing forward with your legs, then resisting with your hands and bracing your back muscles. Then try to pick up the rising rhythm as soon as he begins to trot. This is easier than trying to go straight into a sitting trot.

Only attempt the canter for a few strides at the start. Work at relaxing into the saddle and then performing smooth transitions from a trot to a canter and a canter back to a trot.

Outside the School

HAVING ACHIEVED MASTERY over the sitting trot, the rising trot and the canter, together with confidence in your ability to control your horse and use the aids properly, there is no reason why you should not take a break from the formality of the school for a ride or two. Bear in mind, though, that this is going to be completely different from the conditions you have so far encountered. Riding on roads, or even across tracks and fields, is very different from riding around a school under the constant watchful eye of an instructor – even though a qualified person will accompany you.

Most situations you will meet with can be dealt with by your riding experience coupled with common sense, but this is something that people often seem to lose when on horseback.

Remember, first and foremost, to be constantly alert. This does not mean that you cannot relax and enjoy yourself, but you must be ready for the unexpected. Somebody may suddenly emerge from a concealed drive or something may flutter in the hedge, taking you by surprise and making your mount jump or shy. Control him gently, talking to him to reassure him, and turn him to see whatever has startled him.

Do not underestimate the size of your horse when going through gates, or when skirting around parked vehicles. The latter should be given a wide berth, but not so wide that you end up riding in the middle of the road. In the same vein, it is wise to ride around man-hole covers, which can be both slippery and potential hazards for the horse to trip over, but do not

Riding in public is a very different experience to riding in a school or in the country and there are some points which should be remembered: As any number of accidental or surprising incidents may arise, inexperienced riders should never venture out on their own but always be accompanied by a more experienced rider. Especially when riding in traffic, always maintain a watchful and alert attitude as not everyone around you will know or understand horses, and pedestrians can be as dangerous as a car or truck.

take this to extremes by going to the other side of the road. Remember you have to steer and control the horse at all times; he will do what you tell him to do and, if you do not steer him around a stationary truck, for example, he may well either walk into the back of it or just come to a halt behind it. Try not to get into the habit of expecting him to get you both out of difficulties; you are the one in control.

Coping with falls

Something you are bound to experience sooner or later in your riding career is falling off. It may have already happened during one of your school lessons, or it may be that the ignominy will occur when you are out for a ride. Ignominy is what it is – nine times out of ten when you

THE RULES OF THE ROAD

There are eight golden rules that should always be observed when riding on a road. These are:

1 To ride in single file, close to the curb if there is one – but not so close the horse knocks his fetlocks against it. The only time you should ride two abreast is if one rider is on a leading rein, or riding a horse that is traffic shy. In both cases, that person should ride closest to the curb.

2 To ride on the appropriate side so you are moving with the traffic.

3 To stop at road junctions and look both ways before proceeding.

4 To signal clearly when turning left or right by putting your arm out in that direction. Do this whether overtaking a parked car or actually turning into another road.

5 If motorists have slowed down, wave them past as soon as the opportunity arises and remember to thank them.

6 To obey traffic lights and other road instructions, just as you would if riding a bicycle.

7 If you are riding with others and you intend to stop, give them due warning, so the person behind does not ride into the back of you.

8 To avoid riding at dusk or nightfall, unless absolutely necessary. If you have to, wear something light that will reflect in a vehicle's headlights and attach proper stirrup lights to your stirrup irons.

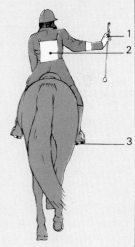

No rider should venture out on to the road without first acquainting himself with the rider's highway code. The numbered points in the illustration show: (1) Rider giving clear hand signals to turn. (2) Rider wearing a luminous back cloth, with, (3) stirrup lights attached to the stirrup irons. These are essential when riding at dusk or twilight, which should be avoided, if possible.

Riding through pleasant country-side with companions is one of the great joys of being able to ride. Schooling sessions for both horse and rider should be frequently interspersed with less exacting hacks, although lessons learned in the school should not be forgotten on these occasions.

Above: The correct way to go through a gate should involve the use of the rein back which will allow you to go through without dismounting. Bring your horse parallel to the gate and unlatch or unhook it. Holding on to the gate, give the aids for a rein back and use your leg to push the horse's quarters around. Walk forward through the gate being careful that it does not shut on the horse's quarters. Once through, turn the horse around parallel to the gate and shut it.
Right: This rider has obviously not used the right aids to maneuver through a gate. You will find yourself in a very awkward position unless the right ones are used.

fall off a horse, the only thing to be hurt is your pride.

Falls occur in all sorts of ways. They may be no more than a gentle slide to the ground when you have lost your balance in the saddle and have reached the point of no return. They may be caused by not ducking low enough or in time to avoid an overhanging branch so you get swept off, or they may be a seemingly dramatic toss and tumble as the horse trips, halts unexpectedly, or throws you off his back as part of a display of high spirits.

Whatever the cause or type of fall, try to get up as quickly as possible if you are not hurt, to show your instructor or companions that you are alright. Then, no matter what your personal feelings and wishes are at this moment, get back up into the saddle immediately. This is important for your confidence as well as from the point of view of establishing who is master. If a horse senses you are reluctant to remount, it will bring out the worst in him and he is likely to behave badly. It may help you to analyze the reasons for the fall; was it that you lost your balance, for instance, or was it the result of some other cause that could equally well be worked at and so avoided in the future?

Experts differ on whether you should or

Left: The instant you mount your horse to the moment you dismount, you should never lose either your awareness of your surroundings or of your horse. The riders shown are under the mistaken belief that if they are relaxing or letting their horse graze, they may also relax their attention. Riding does not require your attention only when you are moving, but when you are at a halt as well, and you should always be in complete control of your horse and yourself. Major accidents and injuries may otherwise result

should not make a conscious effort to hold on to the reins when you fall. Often, you have no choice, as they are wrenched from your hand; equally, you sometimes have no time to think. Within the confines of the school, it is generally better to drop them; the horse is not able to escape, as he might do in the open, and letting go of the reins lessens the risk of the horse trampling you.

If a companion falls off when you are out for a ride, the whole ride should stop and wait for him to pick himself up, regain composure and remount. Help to catch the horse, if necessary, and hold it still for the fallen rider. If a loose

horse decides to turn the escapade into a game and refuses to be caught, never chase after him. This will only heighten his excitement and make him even more determined to evade capture. Instead try to corner him; when he realizes all escape routes are blocked, he will soon give in.

Even though a hack is obviously less formal than school work, do not let your riding deteriorate as a result. Concentrate on maintaining the correct position at all times and on making the horse go well for you. Practice smooth transitions from a walk to a trot, a trot to a canter and back to a trot and walk again. Make sure the horse does only what you want him to do at the times you ask him to do it. If he displays whims of his own – perhaps to canter at a spot where he usually does – you must correct him. You are still the boss.

Across country

Just as there are rules to observe when riding on the roads, there are rules to follow when riding across the countryside. Also there are elementary codes of good manners to observe towards your companions on a ride and any pedestrians you may encounter.

In the country, always close gates behind you whether the fields they border contain livestock or not. Always pass single file through a gate, making sure you leave sufficient room for your knees – a rap on a gatepost can be extremely painful. It helps if one person on the ride holds the gate open for the others, but remember to return this courtesy by waiting on the other side until the gate has been closed and everyone is ready to proceed.

In many country areas, you are the 'guest' of a farmer, in that you are riding over his land. Behave as you would if you were a guest in someone's house by observing basic good manners. Do not canter or gallop across a sown field; indeed, you should not ride at speed across any field, particularly if the ground is very wet. You could cut it up and damage it considerably. If by any chance you do some damage, knock down a fence, or inadvertently let some animals out, find out whose land it is and tell them what has happened. It is unpardonable to leave someone else to discover the damage whatever it is; by the time they do so it might have got considerably worse.

Show consideration for the others on the ride. The pace should always be tempered to the least experienced and most nervous rider. Never ask or expect your fellow riders to do things they neither want to, nor are ready to do. It would be like asking you to jump a gate or hedge at this stage. Later, when you have learned to jump, never jump every obstacle in sight; if you do, you will become the farmers' enemy, rather than friend. If, you want to jump, jump only those obstacles that you know you are allowed to and which, should you crash through them or knock them down, will cause no serious damage – for example, knocking down the boundary fence of a field containing livestock.

When riding through wooded areas, lean well forward – not back – when passing beneath low

overhanging branches. This may sound obvious, but you would be surprised at how many people forget to do it. Equally, if you encounter a swinging branch that has to be pushed back, do not release it so it flies into the face of the horse or rider behind. If you meet pedestrians on a narrow track, slow down and go past them at a walk – never faster.

If your horse goes lame for any reason, get off immediately and see if you can determine the cause. The most likely reason is a stone

Check List

Points to consider when out for a ride include:

(1) Never canter on the road. A horse is not only likely to slip or trip, but cantering will cause considerable jarring to the legs.

(2) Similarly, do not ride fast on hard tracks, stony ground or muddy land.

(3) Do not ask your horse to canter or gallop when he is blowing hard and tired.

(4) Show consideration for any pedestrians you meet by walking past them - not cantering or trotting. Also, when any pedestrian moves into the side of a track for you, or motorist slows down to overtake you, be sure to thank them.

(5) Always walk your horse for the last part of a ride so he has time to cool down. Never return to the stable with your horse in a lather.

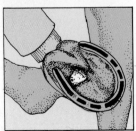

A stone lodged in the hoof is a common problem.

If you do not have a hoof pick, a twig is a useful tool.

lodged in his hoof. If this is so, remove the stone and he will probably be quite sound again. If you cannot find out the reason and the horse continues to be lame, run the stirrup irons up the leathers, take the reins over his head and lead him home.

As you will see, all the points mentioned have been no more than common sense and good manners. Do not lose sight of either of these just because you are on the back of a horse rather than in a more familiar situation.

49

Back in the School

Check List

Your check list should now begin to become more sophisticated. Besides the usual points, such as patting your horse and checking your girth before mounting, concentrate your thoughts on the finer points of position and control:

(1) Is your position in the saddle effective as well as correct?

(2) Are you supple and relaxed without being sloppy?

(3) Are you giving aids discreetly and in conjunction with one another?

(4) Do you notice any difference in the way your horse is beginning to respond to you? Are *you* now the one in control and able to make him obey your wishes?

(5) Do some exercises at the start of the lesson to loosen you up and get you deep into the saddle.

FROM NOW ON, hacks outside will probably be mixed with formal lessons in the school, for you still have much to learn and practice. When you return to the school, think about your position. Are you sitting on your seat bones in the deepest part of the saddle? Are you sitting up straight with your head held high? Are your legs pulled back beneath you with your weight down in the heel? Are you showing suppleness through your waist and hips, knee and ankle?

Try a few exercises to limber and supple you. Lift your legs in the air and kick them down hard which will pull you deeper into the saddle. Then put one hand on the pommel, and one on the cantle, and pull your seat bones beneath you, lifting your knees up and away from the saddle. Swing your legs backwards and forwards to help supple your hips and circle alternate shoulders to make sure they are relaxed. With your feet in the stirrups try taking your knee right away from the saddle.

Your instructor may now feel it is time for you to try a different horse, perhaps one that needs more conscious or decisive riding. Take it around the school a few times at a walk and trot on both reins to get used to each other. Later, when you ride your first mount again, you will get an idea of how much you have improved.

By now you may well feel the need to lengthen your stirrup leathers. This is an indication that you are settling deeper into the saddle.

Do some work without stirrups. Walk around the school first, perhaps doing a few exercises, then try a circuit of sitting trot. Once they are used to it, some riders actually find it easier to sit to the trot without stirrups. This certainly helps to draw you deeper into the saddle; it also ensures that you cannot rely on the irons to support your weight. Once confident of this, try a few strides of rising trot without irons. This is very tiring, but extremely good for strengthening muscles and improving balance.

Try riding for a few strides at a walk and trot down one long side of the school with your eyes shut. This will help you to understand more about that elusive 'feel' of the horse moving beneath you. No instructor can ever teach you this. You must experience it for yourself and, until you do, you cannot be sure you are getting the best from your mount.

Perfecting the canter

You are now at a point in your school work when you can take work at the canter a stage

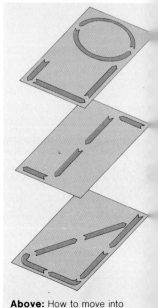

Above: How to move into riding a 20m (65ft) circle, and different ways of changing the rein across the school.

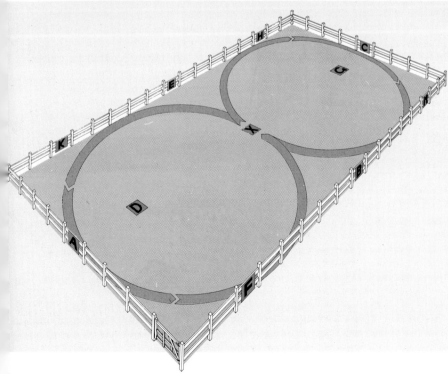

Above:
The rising trot without stirrups is a good exercise for strengthening muscles and improving balance. **Left:** Most riding establishments will have a coventional school or mènage which measures 6 X 12m (20 X 40ft) and is tradionally marked out with a series of letters. X marks the center of the school; A and C, the center points of the short sides and B and E the center points of the long sides. K, H, F, and M are known as the three-quarter markers, and are opposite D and G which are on the three-quarter points on the center line of the school. A circle ridden with D or G as the center point and A and X or C and X as opposite points on the circumference will have a diameter of 20m (65ft).

Transitions from one pace to another should always be executed as smoothly as possible. The rider is shown moving from a trot to canter with the right foreleg leading.
(1) Moving forwards at an even trot, sit for a few strides and incline the horse's head slightly to the right.
(2) Apply pressure on the girth with your right leg.
(3) Apply pressure behind the girth with your left leg.
(4) As the horse breaks into a canter, glance down (without bending) to make sure he is leading with the correct leg.

1

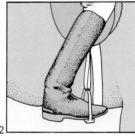
2

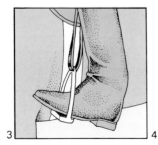
3

4

further. Instead of just giving the aids to canter (see p.40-41), you should now give some thought to which leg the horse leads with at this pace. If you watch a horse cantering, you will notice that one foreleg appears to lead, although it is in fact the last leg to move in the sequence. When cantering in a circle or around the school, the lead leg should be the inside foreleg in order to balance correctly. Thus, if you are riding on the right rein, it is the off-fore that should lead. Until you get used to the feel, you can tell which leg is leading from your position in the saddle by observing which shoulder moves forward most prominently.

You can ask your horse to lead with a specific leg by applying slightly more sophisticated aids than those previously used for the canter. Note that it is easiest to ask a horse to canter out of a bend or corner, so think about preparing for the canter – gathering up the reins slightly and sitting down in the saddle – as you approach the end of the school. If you are on the right rein, incline the horse's head very slightly to the right by gently squeezing that rein and push him forward by closing your right leg almost on the girth and your left or outside leg behind the girth. Again, you are maintaining impulsion while bending him around your inside leg and guiding his hindquarters with your outside one. As the horse strikes off into the canter, sit deeply in the saddle and try and resist anything but a cursory glance down at the shoulders to see which leg is leading.

If your horse strikes off on the wrong leg, bring him calmly back to a trot, balance him for a few strides, so that he is not trotting down the school uncontrollably, then re-apply the aids. As soon as he canters correctly, relax the aids and sit with the movement, but keep riding him forward or he will soon drop back to a trot again.

Try to resist any temptation to push forward with your seat bones as you give the aids. This will result in the horse hollowing his back, thereby restricting his free forward movement.

When you have cantered a few circuits of the school, change the rein and practice striking off with the other leg. Try a few circuits without stirrups, too; it will help you to sit deeper in the saddle.

Circles and serpentines

A recognized riding school measures 12 x 6m (40 x 20ft) and is usually marked out with a standard series of letters (see diagram). So far you have concentrated on riding around the outside and changing the rein across the center of the school or from the three-quarter markers, but there are other ways in which you can use the school.

The first school figure to practice riding – at a walk then a trot and finally a canter – is a 6m (20ft) circle. The command to ride a 6m (20ft) circle and then to return to the outside track from your instructor will be: 'At C (or A) go forward into a 6m (20ft) circle. As you return to C (or A), go large.' Leave the track at the center of the short side of the school (C or A) and ride in a perfect arc to a point between the three-quarter points and the center of the school – between H and E, K and E, or M and B and F and B according to which way you are going. Then go on to X (the center of the school) and next to a point between the other three-quarter marker and the center of the school. Finally go back to C or A.

Riding a perfect circle is not easy, so concentrate and make sure your horse is properly bent round your inside leg all the time. Bear in mind his body should be bending round the arc of the circle – at no point are you attempting to turn him. Watch that he does not 'fall in' to the center of the circle so the circle becomes imperfect. It is helpful to ride on soft ground as you can check hoofprints to measure the accuracy of the circle.

When you have ridden a few circles, change the rein and ride in the opposite direction, so both you and the horse do not favour one side. Also try riding smaller circles remembering that your aim is to form the horse's body into a perfect arc throughout the exercise.

The serpentine tests your control and ability to ride accurately to the full. This involves riding down the school from C to A making four perfect loops, the extreme point of which is about 3m (10ft) from the side of the school. The whole movement should be smooth and

Mistakes - Cantering/Circling

Leaning forward and looking down to see which leg is leading. Learn to tell by feel, or you will throw you and your horse off balance.

If the aids you give are not clear, the horse may end up cantering 'disunited.' This means that his legs are not following the correct canter sequence, the leading foreleg appearing to be on the opposite side to the leading hind leg. Instead of a smooth rocking pace, the canter will feel uneven and rolling. Bring the horse quietly back to a balanced trot and reapply the aids.

As you become more relaxed and familiar with riding the canter, there is sometimes a tendency to relax into the pace, collapsing your shoulders and thus becoming sloppy. On the other hand, if you are tense you are apt to confuse your horse and lose control.

Leaning into the circle will make the horse do the same and 'fall in' towards the center. Your hips and shoulders should remain square to the horse's shoulders.

Raising the inside rein in a misguided effort to keep the horse on the track.

'Overbending' the horse by applying too much pressure on the inside rein with the horse's head and neck forced into the center of the circle. Remember you want to achieve a perfect arc Conversly, in attempting *not* to 'overbend', the rider may force the horse's head out of the circle.

fluid, not jerky or uneven. Try the exercise at a walk first, and then progress to a trot, checking your tracks in the school to see how accurate you have been each time.

If you are riding with others in the school, there are several exercises and movements you can perform together, which will help to improve your skill, control and accuracy. Such manoeuvres include, for example, being told to position yourself at a letter by your instructor and then changing places with another rider standing at a different letter. If there are several of you in the school at one time, this manoeuver can be quite a test of your riding. The code in passing other riders head-on is to pass right-hand to right-hand.

In addition, practice riding holding both reins in one hand, so that this will not present a

20m (65ft) circles

Change of rein

10m (32ft) circles and
figure of eight

Serpentine
Half-volte and
reverse

6m(20ft) volte

problem to you should it ever be necessary on
a ride. If you are holding the reins in your left
hand, for example, hold the left rein normally,
then bring the right one across the top, so that
it enters your hand between the thumb and
forefinger, crosses the palm, and emerges
beneath your little finger. When riding like this,
you must control the horse more actively with
your legs, bending it round your inside leg if
you want to turn corners. Do not attempt to
guide it too accurately with your hand – inevitably, this will lead to confusion.

To help you think less actively about the
hand holding the reins, put your reins into one
hand in order to allow you to do something else
with your other hand – such as blowing your
nose, doing up a button on your coat, or
adjusting the length of a stirrup leather.

As you progress with your
lessons, you will learn to use
the school more actively by
executing figures-of-eight,
small circles, serpentines, and
other school figures. A
serpentine is a series of
evenly-sized loops executed
down and across the school.
Another school figure is the
half-volte in which the rider
leaves the school at a three-

quarter marker, changes the
rein by describing a
semicircle, and rejoins the
track going in the opposite
direction. A volte is a full 10m
(33 ft) circle executed at this
point so the rider rejoins the
track where he left it, to
continue on the same rein.
Far left: when passing other
riders in the school, pass
hand-to-hand.

Jumping

JUMPING IS A FORM OF RIDING which appeals to some riders more than others. Some are anxious to learn to jump; others do not want to achieve anything more than to be able to clear a small obstacle if it blocks their path out on a hack. No rider, however, should start to jump until he or she feels secure and confident at a canter and can perform the basic school figures discussed so far.

All riding horses can be taught to jump. Some will do it better than others – just as their riders will – and some will enjoy it more, but all have the natural aptitude to do so. For this reason, it is necessary to look at the horse's jumping action in order to understand the position the rider takes to jump and how he assists his horse to jump more easily by adopting it.

The elements of the jump

Although the aim is always to produce one continuous flowing movement, the horse's jumping action can be broken down into five elements – approach, take-off, suspension, landing and recovery. During the approach, the horse, having seen and summed up the obstacle in front of him, will balance and prepare himself for the jump by stretching his neck and lowering his head. He may begin to lengthen his stride, but, particularly if the fence is only a small one, he should continue at the same even pace, without altering his speed.

At the point of take-off, the horse brings his head up as he lifts his forehand off the ground. The power for the leap forward comes from the horse's hocks, which are tucked well beneath him to act like a spring. During the moment of suspension, the horse's body forms an arc over the jump with the head and neck stretched forwards. As the descent begins, the horse extends his forelegs, his head and neck down towards the ground and tucks his hindlegs under him, so that they will clear the jump. As the forelegs touch the ground – usually one just in front of the other – the horse balances himself by bringing his head up and shortening his neck. The hind feet touch down immediately behind the forefeet, one forefoot often moving into the next stride before the hind feet land.

Throughout this, the rider's aim should be to do nothing which will impede or restrict the horse's movement in any way. At all times, therefore, he or she must remain in complete harmony with the horse, taking particular care not to interfere with the free movement of the animal's head. The jumping position described

All riding horses can be taught to jump, although few will reach top competition standards.
Above: The horse in the picture has been trained as an eventer, that is, it must be bold and courageous, as well as highly skilled in order to jump large, solid fences at speed. **Right:** The horse's movements as he approaches, jumps over the fence, and lands on the other side.

56

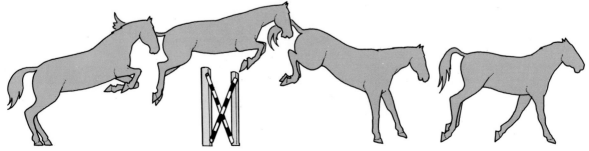

Above: A rider in the correct jumping position. Her legs hang down with the stirrup leathers perpendicular to the ground. The knee and ankle are slightly more bent than usual to prevent jarring as the horse lands. The upper body is inclined forward from the waist with the back straight. The reins are held further forward than usual, but a straight line from the elbows, hands, and reins to the horse's mouth are maintained.
Right: The first stage is to trot over poles maintaining the jumping position.

in the following section has been designed to fulfill this aim.

If jumping is to be included in a lesson, it should come towards the end or the latter half. This will give the horse time to loosen and limber up and ensure that the rider is sitting deep in the saddle and loosened up enough to be riding at his or her best.

The jumping position

The first thing to learn and practice until it becomes second nature is the jumping position. Assuming that you will have dropped your stirrup leathers a hole or two for general school work by now, you will need to take them back up again for jumping. The stirrup leather should still remain vertical to the ground, which means that your knee and ankle will be bent a little more deeply. This allows them to do their work as 'hinges' and 'shock absorbers.'

In the jumping position, the rider's upper body bends forward in a folding movement from the waist. The back remains straight and supple – there should be no slouching or rounding of the shoulders – while the head is still held high, looking straight between the horse's

Stirrup leathers should be shortened one or two holes from the usual riding length.

ears and never down at the jump. The seat should remain in light contact with the saddle throughout the approach, although it may lift up during take-off. The body weight is taken on the knee, thigh and heel, but resist any temptation to straighten the knee and so stand up in the stirrup irons. There should still be a straight line from your elbows, which are bent and remain close to your sides, through your arms and hands, along the reins to the bit. Your shoulders, elbows and fingers have to be even more supple in order to follow the movement of the horse's neck. In fact your hands should stay

in the usual position throughout a jump and it is better to move them forward rather than run any risk of jabbing the horse in the mouth.

In the early stages of jumping, make sure a neck strap is buckled around the horse's neck and hold on to this. It will make you feel more secure as well as guarding against you jerking the horse's mouth. Practice moving into the jumping position and then returning to the usual position in the saddle, first at the halt and then at a walk and trot. When you can bend forward and sit up straight again without losing your balance at a trot, try doing the same

Cavalletti are a type of
equipment that are invaluable
in teaching a horse or rider to
jump. In this picture a rider is
demonstrating an early stage
in learning to jump and is
asking her horse to trot over
cavalletti. Cavalletti are
spaced in such a way that the
horse will trot over one with
each stride taken. Note that
the rider is not, in fact, sitting
forward in the jumping
position. When learning to
jump, it will help to establish
the jumping position if you
lean forward as you trot over
the cavalletti; do not, however,
look down at the ground.

exercise at a canter. Your aim is to achieve a smooth rhythm that will correspond with the horse's smooth jump.

After this, the first positive step towards learning to jump is to adopt this position as you ask your horse to trot over some solid poles placed on the ground. Position them reasonably far apart at the start. Then trot towards one and move into the jumping position a stride or two before the pole. A stride or two after it, resume your normal position in the saddle.

When you can trot over the pole, shifting forwards and back into the correct position, move three or four poles closer together, so that

the horse steps over one with each stride he takes. Remain in the forward jumping position as you progress down the line of poles. This will require even greater balance to ensure you do not upset the rhythm, but remember that the most important thing is not to interfere with the horse's head. Hold on to the neck strap if you feel even slightly insecure.

The first jump
The next step is to hop over a small jump, which should be no more than about 25cm (10in) high; you can use proper jump supports or extemporize by using stout poles on wooden

The basic aim of the rider when jumping is to avoid interfering with the horse's natural movements at any point. **Left:** Jumping cavalletti, or jumping any low jumps without stirrups is excellent exercise and helps you to develop an independent seat which is not supported by your feet in the stirrup irons. Make every effort to keep your legs and feet in the usual position. **Below:** Taking the above exercise one step further by relinquishing your reins will show you just how much you have been using your reins and stirrups to maintain your jumping position as your seat is now totally dependent on your ability to balance.

COMBINATION JUMPING

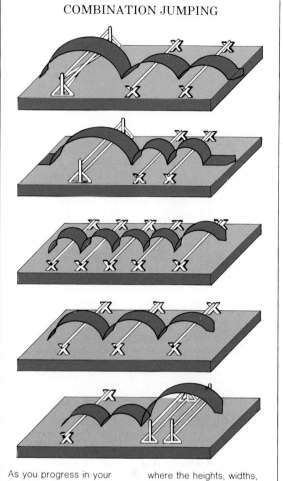

As you progress in your jumping, you may want to begin practising what are commonly known as 'combination jumps'. This particular type of jumping requires great skill and, it makes sense to say that if the jumps are all of a type and equidistant it will be less difficult than a series where the heights, widths, and distances vary, as the horse's strides will be determined by all of these points. The one crucial factor is that the first jump be perfectly synchronized with the horse's gait, otherwise all subsequent jumps will be missed.

boxes or barrels. Most riding establishments, however, will probably use a type of pole known as a cavalletti. If you do not use cavalletti, make sure the poles are thick and solid with no rough parts or sharp nails protruding. Horses show far more respect and jump better and more boldly over solid objects, rather than flimsy, unimposing ones.

Even though the horse is quite capable of stepping over the cavalletti at a trot, he will probably prefer to hop over it, so make sure you are prepared. The first 'jump' you take is bound to throw you off balance; remember to hold on to the neck strap, so that you do not jerk the horse's mouth by mistake. When you are reasonably confident and able to maintain your balance and rhythm at the trot, approach the cavalletti at a canter. Keep the pace calm and let the horse bounce over the jump, offering no interference so he can take it in his stride.

After this, try placing another cavalletti or low jump, perhaps slightly higher, several strides further on, so you have time to return to the normal position before resuming the jumping position for the next one. If you have approached the first one calmly and quietly, there should be no need to check the horse between jumps. It is better not to interfere with

As a horse approaches a jump, it will balance its stride and drop its head and neck. The rider should sit still, keeping her seat in light contact with the saddle and ensuring that the position of her hands is allowing the horse complete freedom of his head. The upper part of her body may be inclined slightly forward.

At the moment of take-off the horse brings his head and neck up and the hocks are gathered beneath him to give him the force to push him off the ground. The rider should lean forward making sure again that he is not restricting the horse's head and neck movement by holding the reins too short.

Mistakes – Position

Standing up in the stirrup irons so that the knee is straightened out and weight is placed on the balls of the feet instead of the heels.

Leaning forward which will lessen your control and make you less able to feel the horse's movement beneath you.

the reins between jumps if you can help it, as this will probably throw both of you off balance.

Having achieved good rhythm and balance over a couple of small jumps positioned some distance from each other, bring them closer together, so that they are separated only by a couple of strides. Again, allow your horse to judge the take-off points and distance between the obstacles; you should concentrate yourself on keeping your balance and not interfering with his movement in any way.

Starting to circle
So far your jumping has been in a straight line. Change this now by positioning three or four cavalletti in a circle. Place them so that the center of each cavalletti coincides with the circumference of the circle and jump at this point each time. Jumping in a circle is good exercise for you and the horse. It tends to excite him less than jumping in a straight line; it also makes him bend and supple his back and it helps you to ride more accurately – or at least point out the weak spots if you are not.

Whether jumping in a straight line or on circular course, always aim to jump any obstacle in the center. To help you judge this, use a simple jump made from two poles, one end of each balancing on a support and the other end resting on the ground. Provided the poles are supported at an equal height, the point at which they cross will be both the center and the lowest point of the jump.

Types of jump
From this point, the only way to improve and develop your jumping is to practice it over as

The horse traces an arc over the jump with his head stretched forward and down and legs tucked up beneath him. The rider maintains the jumping position, leaning well forward.

The horse stretches his front legs down while bringing his head up and shortening his neck. His hind legs are tucked beneath him and land just behind the forelegs. The rider should remain in the jumping position and not attempt to assume a more upright position until a few strides after the fence.

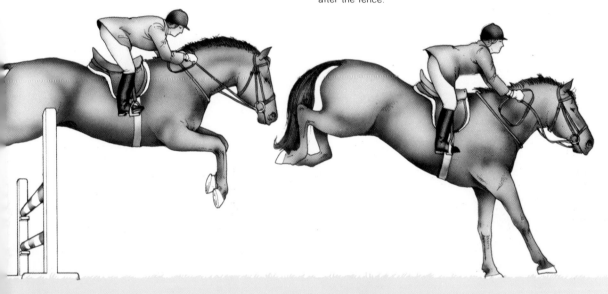

many different types of obstacles in the greatest number of different conditions as possible.

Jumps fall into two basic categories. These are uprights, such as walls, gates, hurdles, narrow hedges and poles placed in a vertical line on top of one another, and spreads, such as parallel or triple bars and oxers. In addition, ditches and banks should also be included in your practice jumping sessions. In the early stages, concentrate on jumping low jumps well, rather than raising the poles ever higher and jumping badly. Practice jumps – you can easily construct these yourself with a little imagination – should not be more than about 90cm (3ft) high and many should be smaller. It is far better to increase the width of a fence, so that the horse has to stretch himself over it, than to keep testing his high jump ability by raising the height – better for him and better for you in getting the feel of the jumping movement.

A ground line placed in front of a jump, particularly an upright, will help you and your horse to judge the take-off point more easily. The take-off point should be approximately the same distance away from the jump as the height of it. This will vary according to the height of the fence and the speed of the approach; a horse approaching a small jump quite fast, for

Mistakes – Flight/Landing

Losing the position of your legs against the horse so that they either jerk forward or backward.

Getting left behind the movement. If this happens, try and let the reins slip through your fingers.

Sitting too far back in the saddle will lessen your control and bounce you out of the saddle.

In landing, sitting up too quickly. Wait until the horse is at least one stride beyond the fence.

Not folding enough at the waist so the horse's movements pull you out of the saddle. You cannot balance if sitting upright.

Do not jump on a horse that has not been sufficiently loosened up first.

Try and alter the position of fences to avoid churning up the ground.

As they begin to include jumping in their regular riding routine, a horse and rider will be faced with all manner of varying obstacles. There are basically two types of fence – uprights and spreads. Uprights concentrate on the height of the fence, while spreads are designed to test the horse's ability to jump widths.
Above and right: The pictures show some of the jumps a rider can expect to encounter as he ventures into competition jumping.

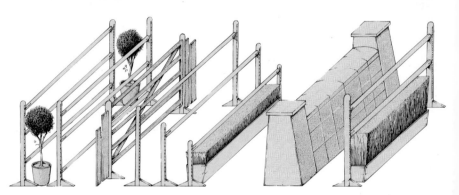

example, will take off far further in front of it than the height of that obstacle.

If the establishment where you are learning to ride has a jumping lane, or if you are jumping in the confines of a school, a useful exercise is to negotiate a line of low poles with your arms crossed and the reins knotted around the horse's neck. This will show you how much you are relying on the reins to balance you. Pick up the reins quickly at the end of the line; then try riding it again without holding the reins, but this time doing something like buttoning your coat or knotting a piece of string. This helps to encourages you to ride by 'feel' and instinct.

An even more testing exercise is to quit and cross your stirrups as well as riding with no reins, so that now you can only rely on the balance of your position to keep you sitting correctly. This is a useful and practical exercise since there are few riders who never lose their stirrup irons at some time in the middle of a jumping course. It is comforting to know that, if this happens to you, you will not be unseated immediately.

Coping with a refusal
Generally, horses jump badly or refuse to jump for one of two reasons – either they have been

If a horse refuses a jump, it is often because the rider has not ridden him correctly. Turn away from the fence in a small circle and ride at it again immediately, urging him forward strongly with your legs. Never finish with a refusal; always jump another fence, no matter how small.

badly schooled or they are being badly ridden. At this point, it is more likely that the latter reason will apply. Always try to analyze what it is that you are doing wrong and work at putting it right. Have you interfered with his stride on the approach, jabbed him in the mouth on take-off, or shifted back into an upright position too quickly on landing, for instance? Any of these errors might make him reluctant to jump for you. If he refuses or runs out, is it because you were uncertain yourself and did not ride him at the jump as if you really meant him to go over it?

If a horse refuses a jump, ride him in a small circle and come straight into the jump again. Horses that constantly run out at fences can often be discouraged from doing so by building high or elaborate wings on either side of the fence.

Always finish with a good jump from both you and the horse – however small it may be. This is the one you and your mount will remember for the next session.

Whether a show jumper or eventer, a horse trained for jumping must be a very special animal indeed as the requirements are many and strenous. While the type of horse may vary greatly, all jumpers have in common strong hindquarters and hocks needed for the power to get them over the jump. Besides this, they must be capable of powerful and sudden forward propulsion with little incentive except the rider's aim to get his mount over the obstacle as smoothly and successfully as possible. Also, because many shows take place indoors, it is necessary that the jumper has a calm and unexcitable temperament and not be affected by small spaces, many people, and bright lights.

Advanced Riding

ONCE YOU HAVE MASTERED the basic points and aspects of riding and horsemanship so far discussed in this book, you will have covered basically all you need to know in order to become a competent leisure rider – that is, one whose ambitions reach no further than to enjoy riding for pleasure. However, even if you do not want to progress to more advanced riding, it is still a good idea to have professional 'refresher' lessons from time to time; bad habits develop very easily and are hard to recognize, let alone break, without expert guidance.

Do not let the fact that you have become reasonably confident and competent in the saddle become an excuse for abandoning school work. Your riding should regularly include schooling sessions, for these keep both you and your horse up to the mark. Aim at perfecting your aids, making them more refined – positive, but discreet. Ask a knowledgeable friend or colleague if he or she can see the signals you are giving with your hands and legs at any given time. The aids you give should be indiscernible to anyone standing watching.

Work, too, at maintaining a steady contact through the reins to the horse's mouth. Now, you should concentrate even more on using your hands independently from the rest of your body. Instead of thinking of the reins as delicate lengths of thread as previously suggested, think of them now as pieces of elastic which will stretch as the horse's head and neck move, thus keeping the contact steady. It is your hands, of course, that must move to accommodate the horse's head movement; but as ever, it is his head and neck that move your hands – your hands should not move consciously.

If you are still riding at a school, try to ride as many different horses as possible. Each horse will have a different 'feel', as well as his own idiosyncratic quirks of temperament and movement. Each one, too, will require something different from you. One of the marks of a good rider is that he can adapt his or her technique sufficiently to get the best from whatever horse is being ridden.

Basic dressage

One advance movement which all riders should know how to execute accurately is the rein back. It is described as a dressage movement, but it probably has greater day-to-day application than most dressage exercises. It requires practice, as it is considerably more difficult to carry out correctly than might be imagined.

If a horse is being ridden properly, it should

Above: Horse and rider demonstrate a rein back. This should always be done from a halt, with the horse standing square. He then moves back in two-time, that is with diagonal front and hind legs moving together. After three or four steps, aids should be given for him to walk forward, and to ensure that the idea of moving backwards does not become instilled in his mind.

Above: The leg yield is the first of the more advanced school movements that are performed on two tracks – that is the forelegs and hindlegs moving on separate lines. The horse is bent round the rider's inside leg in such a way that he is facing the direction in which he is to travel. As can be seen, the outside fore leg and inside hind leg (in this instance the off-fore and near-hind) follow the same track.

move back in two-time – that is, by moving the opposite diagonal legs in unison. The commonest mistake is to allow a horse to move back in four-time, each leg taking a step in turn.

To perform a rein back, first make sure your horse is standing square – that is, with forefeet and hindfeet evenly positioned beneath him. Then apply pressure with the inside of your legs, as if asking him to move forward. Instead of giving with your hands to allow the movement, however, resist with them, squeezing the reins as if asking for a halt from a walk. The impulsion you have built up in the horse with your legs has to be dissipated, so he will take a step backwards. Maintain the leg pressure together with the resistance with your hands until he has taken about four steps backwards. Then yield with your hands and ask him to take the same number of steps forward.

The turn on the forehand

The other 'dressage movement' which is useful to include in your riding is the turn on the

The shoulder-in is a slightly more advanced lateral movement. Again it is performed on two tracks, but in this instance the horse is bent away from the direction in which he is travelling. The shoulders move in towards the centre of the school, so the forelegs describe a new track inside, the hind-legs stay on the usual track.

forehand. This has many practical applications, such as when you want to turn your horse around an open gate.

In the turn on the forehand, the horse moves in a semi-circle by pivoting on one or other foreleg (depending whether the turn is being executed on the left or right). No forward steps are taken, so, in theory, the movement can be performed in a space no bigger than twice the horse's length. In a right turn on the forehand, the pivoting leg is the off-fore and the hindquarters move to the left. To achieve it, you must again create impulsion with your legs and then control it – and stop the horse moving forwards or backwards – with your hands. Sit evenly and centrally in the saddle and apply strong pressure with your right leg behind the girth. The horse will move away from this pres-

An international dressage rider demonstrates a beautiful, flowing trot. In this pace, the horse covers the maximum amount of ground possible with each stride by stretching his legs forward so they are 'extended' to their fullest. It is a very attractive pace to watch because of the apparent moment of suspension that follows the trotting strides. An extended trot, however, is not necessarily a fast one.

The turn on the forehand is a useful movement that has regular application. Out hacking, for example, it is used to turn the horse around an open gate as he passes through to the other side. Some trainers, however, do not include it in their training program feeling it to be a somewhat unnatural movement as well as one that could instill bad habits in the horse. In the movement, the horse's hindquarters describe a semicircle around the forelegs, one of which acts as a pivot. The hind legs cross over, one in front of the other, during the movement. It is done from a halt and may be made through a half or full circle. You must both create impulsion with your legs and control it with your hands. By constantly using your right and left legs you can turn the horse with no forward movement.

The turn on the haunches is a similar movement to that of the turn on the forehand but includes forward movement. Ask the horse to move forward with your inside leg, moving your outside shoulder forward with your hands slightly on the inside. Take care that you do not pull harder on the inside rein, thus bending the horse's neck too much. As your horse moves to the inside, slide your outside leg well behind the girth. When a half turn is completed, move forward by reversing the aids, as your opposite leg is now on the inside. Be careful not to lean backward as the horse needs forward impulsion from the haunches. If you can perform this easily, try it coming from a walk. If you have problems, take only one step at a time, pausing in between.

sure, thereby moving his quarters to the left. Maintain the impulsion and also stop him taking a step backwards by keeping your left leg against his side close to the girth. Keep a steady contact on the reins and apply slightly more pressure to the right rein so his head is flexed, rather than turned, to the right.

Continue these aids until the horse has pivoted round his off-fore and is facing in the opposite direction. To execute a left turn on the forehand, reverse the procedure.

The importance of impulsion

The term impulsion is an important one for riders to understand. It refers to the energy created in the horse's hindquarters which leads to his forward movement. Think of it as the energy of movement similar to the tension trapped in a coiled spring. This energy is created by the rider's legs and should be controlled by his hands. It is very important to achieve; a pace that lacks impulsion lacks discipline or precision and the horse is certainly not giving of his best. Its proper use allows a rider to lengthen his horse's stride. This means that more ground is covered with each step, without increasing the speed of pace. Extension can be asked for a walk, trot or canter – always by creating more impulsion with the legs and then controlling it with the hands.

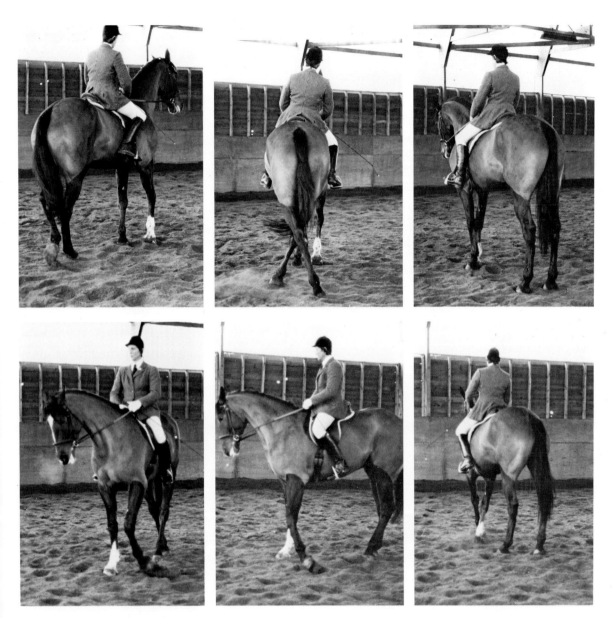

Another term that you may hear your instructor use is free forward movement. This, in effect, is the movement you are trying to achieve from your horse at all times. He should be able to move forward freely unhampered or unimpeded by you. This does not mean that you should be a passenger on his back, however, for he needs your help to get the best out of each pace. As an example, in a free trot, the horse will 'swing' his back and use his hindlegs to achieve the springiness of the trot. He can only do this if you are correctly positioned in the saddle and maintaining the steady contact that allows him the freedom to use his head, back and hindquarters to proper effect.

As you move on to more advanced work and become a more active rider, perhaps learning to execute some of the movements pictured here, make sure you resist the common temptation to look down at the horse's legs to see if they are performing the specific movement correctly. As it is natural to want to check yourself, most people have a tendency to do this, but it will throw horse and rider off balance, which in turn makes it impossible to execute the movements with the precision they demand. The rule of the very first lesson still applies – the head must always be held high and the only place to look is straight between the horse's ears. Remember also to keep your back straight, not rigid.

A selection of dressage movements are demonstrated by the experts. **Above:** Horst Koehler of Germany. **Left:** Miss A Van Doorne of the Netherlands. **Right:** Mrs. C. H. Boylan of Canada. **Below:** The Spanish Riding School of Vienna are mounted on white Lippizzaner stallions.

Western Riding

CONTRARY TO THE POPULAR IMAGE of Western riding conveyed by the cowboys of the movie screen, galloping furiously across the prairie with legs straight in the stirrups and arms flapping, classical Western riding differs only fractionally from English or European classical riding. The two styles certainly come from the same historial roots, because before the Spaniards landed in Mexico in the sixteenth century – the first Europeans to reach the continent – the people who lived there had never even seen a horse. Thus the riding style practiced by the Spaniards – the style followed throughout Europe at the time – must have been the example which the inhabitants of the country learned or copied.

The differences that developed in riding styles came about through practical reasons. The early settlers of the Americas were faced with vast tracts of land which were largely uninhabited, uncultivated and unfenced, even by natural boundaries. These conditions were entirely new to them as nothing similar existed in their European homelands and so they were forced to adopt new riding habits. Now, they had to spend hours, if not days, in the saddle, working with their horses to establish farms and ranches. From the native Indians who soon mastered the art of riding on horses that escaped from the early settlements, they learned how to use the lariat to rope stampeding cattle. They soon practiced this technique from horseback and it is now an essential part of Western riding.

Classical Western riding today is still closely linked to the riding of the cowboys. The point to bear in mind, however, is that, to the cowboy, the horse is merely a tool, part of the essential 'machinery' of his work. As long as the animal allows the cowboy to do his work with the maximum speed, ease and efficiency, he is generally not concerned as to whether or not he achieves a classically correct performance.

Schools and differences

There are two recognized schools of Western riding today – the South Western, or Californian school and the Texan school. In general, the Californian style is more classical than the Texan, calling for somewhat more refined movements and precision in performance from the horse. Contact with the horse's mouth, although still very light, is more definite than it is in the Texan school. To this end, the reins are often very slightly weighted close to the bit – the weighting consisting of no more than a length

Above: One of the most popular rodeo events, saddle-back bronco riding, This requires not only skill, but persistance as well. **Below:** Here a rider is wearing a traditional costume and is shown riding a horse known as a Peruvian Paso. The wide stirrups show the Spanish influence which also plays its part in the evolution of Western riding.

Above right: Although this picture was taken some 100 years ago, the rider's clothes differ little from the working gear worn by cowboys today.

of braiding of the reins – to make this part fractionally heavier. The Texan school generally demands a little less collection from the horse through the paces, so, to the observer, the horse has a longer 'outline' – that is, it is less gathered together.

The most obvious difference between Western and European riding, is that, once horse and rider have been trained correctly, the Western rider holds the reins in one hand only. This means that the horse has to be trained to understand the aids associated with neck-reining, (See p. 88). In the initial stages, however, it is better for a beginner to hold a rein in each hand. This gives the rider a far greater opportunity to establish a correct and stable position in the saddle. Holding the reins in just one hand, tends to pull you out of the saddle and generally plays havoc with what is probably a none-too-secure and well-established position.

The commonly-held belief that the Western rider rides with a perfectly straight leg is incorrect. To do so would give him no flexibility in his knee or control over his lower leg, both of which are essential in any style of riding.

Clothing and tack

Western riding kit differs markedly from the European equivalent; like the style of riding itself, the kit is the subject of much misconceived criticism. Critics of Western riding claim the clothes are untidy and sloppy – a description which they also apply to the riding style. This is not necessarily so, however; apart from the traditional gear described here, specially designed riding suits are now being worn by more and more Western riders, particularly in the show ring. These are well-cut and tailored suits, designed in the traditional style of Western riding clothes, but with particular attention paid to matching and co-ordinating colours. Unlike traditional European gear, however,

79

Top: A bosal bridle. The term 'bosal' comes from an old Spanish word meaning noseband, which this bridle basically consists of. Used mainly in the training and breaking of horses, control, comes from both pressure under the chin by the bosal knot and on the nose itself.
Above: A Western bridle showing a curb bit. Most Western curb bits have long cheek pieces giving great leverage. The bridle characteristically has no noseband. Component parts are kept to a minimum on the Western bridle.

While Western riding may differ only slightly from English or European riding, it was developed much more for reasons of necessity than for aesthetic considerations. **Left:** Western saddles are unique as well in having a high horn, deep, wide seat and high cantle. **Right:** The rider also looks different from the European or English rider because of his riding outfit which would include a wide-brimmed hat for protection from the sun, a brightly coloured shirt, blue jeans, leather or suede chaps, and boots with high heels and pointed toes. Again, Western dress is often criticized by European or English riders as being informal and sloppy. However, when one considers the enviroment and conditions under which most of these riders must perform, the particular Western habit is well-suited to the type of riding.

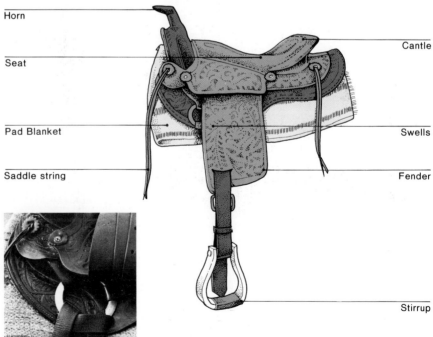

Horn

Cantle

Seat

Pad Blanket

Swells

Saddle string

Fender

Stirrup

Left: The cinch of a Western saddle shown properly tied in a knot. **Above:** the points of the saddle.

they are often very brightly coloured, which has also led to criticism from some traditionalists in the riding fraternity.

The tack worn by horses in Western riding is also different from that used in European classical circles. Once more it has evolved from equipment developed to suit the conditions of the Western prairies and to give the cowboy every possible assistance and comfort in his work. The bridle is generally 'skeleton' in design – that is, it consists of the minimum number of straps and other gadgets. This is partly because leather and metal do not mix well in burning hot conditions, tending to react badly with each other. Bridles traditionally associated with Western riding are either bitless or possess a spade or ordinary Western curb bit; many Western riders, however, prefer to use one of the Western snaffle bits, which is a type of jointed mouth curb bit. The English jointed Pelham is similar, but without a rein for a snaffle bit.

Both horse and rider need to be extremely well-trained if a spade bit is used. This bit has a high port, which moves fractionally in the mouth as the reins are moved. The horse feels this movement on the tongue, and also very slightly on the roof of the mouth. Such bits usually have a curb strap made of leather, rather than the chain one usually used in European riding. This, again, keeps the mixture of leather and metal to a minimum.

There are many different designs of Western saddle, the designs varying to suit the work the cowboy has to do. The type most frequently used for recreational Western riding is known as the Western Pleasure Saddle. This is lighter than most stock working saddles, but still possesses the traditional high horn.

Mounting

Getting to know the horse on which you are going to learn to ride Western-style is just as important as in any other riding style. Before attempting to mount, therefore, find out the horse's name and pat and make a fuss of him, before leading him to the school or paddock where your lesson is to be. When you are ready to mount, check that the rigging is sufficiently tight to prevent the saddle slipping.

Mounting Western-style is not very different from mounting European-style. Standing on the horse's nearside, hold the reins in your left hand sufficiently tightly to stop the horse from moving forward. Get into the habit of doing this from the start, even though someone will

be holding the horse's head during your early lessons. Face obliquely to the horse's hindquarters – that is, not directly towards the tail as in English equitation, but in such a way that a sideways glance over your left shoulder means you can keep an eye on the horse's head. Turn the stirrup towards you and put your left foot in it. Move your right hand over to the offside of the saddle and rest it against the swell; then spring up off the ground and throw your right leg over the horse's back and saddle. Remember that the extra height of the Western saddle means you will have to lift your leg slightly higher than normal. Settle into the middle of the saddle and put your right foot in the stirrup.

The advantage of putting your right hand against the offside swell means first of all that you eliminate any danger of pulling the saddle towards you, as you would if you took hold of the cantle. It also means that you can leave it in this position until you are sitting in the saddle. If you placed the hand further back, you would have to move it forward as you brought your leg across the saddle, which means that momentarily you would be balancing in space.

Such precautions as holding the reins sufficiently tightly to discourage any forward movement from the horse and placing your right hand in a way that you do not have to move it while you mount stem from the early days of Western riding. The worst thing that could happen to a Western rider on the range was to lose his horse. If, for example, it shot forward while he was mounting, so that he lost his balance and let go of the reins, he was often as good as dead. With the horse would go not only his transport, but also his canteen of water and his emergency food rations. If he was far from home in that arid country, his chances of survival were often minimal.

The Western seat

As in European equitation, the Western rider sits in the middle and center of the saddle, so that his or her weight is evenly distributed across the horse's back and directly over his center of balance. In just the same way, the rider's head is held high and the weight of the body falls down on to the seat bones. The residue falls down on to the knee and out of the heels; in other words, the rider's weight is all directed downwards. The feet should not be braced hard against the stirrups, as this lifts the seat upwards out of the saddle.

MOUNTING/DISMOUNTING — WESTERN RIDING

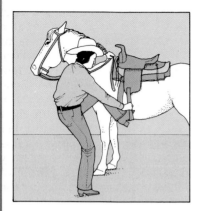

Mounting: Facing obliquely to the horse's hindquarters, put your left foot in the stirrup iron. Hold reins tightly.

Hop around to face the horse's side and put your right hand across the seat of the saddle.

Jump up off the ground and swing your right leg over the horse's back, settling gently into the saddle.

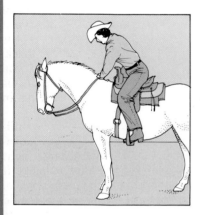

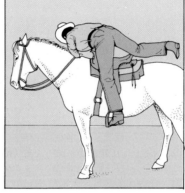

Dismounting: Take your right foot out of the stirrup iron, keeping a tight hold of the reins, resting your hand on the horse's neck.

With your right hand resting against the right hand side of the saddle, lean forward and swing your right leg up behind you.

Step down to the ground by the horse's side, then take your left foot out of the stirrup iron.

Mistakes

A common mistake is for the rider to take hold of the pommel when mounting.

Another similar mistake is to hold on to the cantle while pulling yourself up.

Take care to hold the reins tightly or you may very well lose your horse.

Certain exercises will help to ensure that you maintain the correct position in the saddle when riding Western. **Above:** By raising one arm, elbow bent and palm facing upward, gently push upward. Lower your arm without moving your back. This will help to maintain a straight back which is not hollowed nor rigid. **Right:** Initially, while learning the feel of the Western saddle and the correct position, it is better to continue to hold the reins in both hands. When more secure in the saddle, you will be able to switch to one hand.

Right: The rider's position in Western riding is similar to that of European or English: the rider sits evenly in the center of the saddle with the body weight distributed on either side and body weight and thrust directed downward into and out of the heels. As you will be lifting yourself out of the saddle, the stirrup leathers should only be slightly longer than normal dressage riding. Your head should be held high and straight, body upright, legs lying easily and hands positioned on the horn or holding the reins.

As mentioned earlier, it is often thought that Western riders ride with a perfectly straight leg. In fact, the stirrup leathers should be about the same length as that used for dressage; that is, slightly longer than for normal, European-style, recreational riding, but not so long that, if you stood up in the stirrups, your seat would not lift off the saddle. An exercise which initially will help you to find the right length is to put your feet in the stirrups and let the leathers down until your legs are hanging straight down on either side of the saddle. Remember, however, not to point your toes downwards too. Then, take the leathers up one hole – in most Western saddles, these are positioned about 5cm (2in) apart. If they are set closer together, take the leathers up two holes. Unfortunately, it is impossible to adjust the leathers on a Western saddle when mounted.

Dismounting

To dismount Western-style, put the reins in your left hand and place it just in front of the saddle. Put your right hand on the saddle horn and take your right foot out of the stirrup. Lean

Mistakes - Position

Bracing back leg muscles and pushing leg forward.

Here the rider's weight is off-centered to one side.

Pushing your feet forward, creating a straight leg.

The mistakes made when riding Western are also those common to other types of riding. However, there are some unique to this particular style. One is to reach for the saddle horn when feeling insecure. While better than reaching for the reins, this should be discouraged early-on in your riding. Another is to close your fingers on the reins rather than opening them when giving leg aids so that the horse comes to a stop.

forward and swing your right leg up behind you over the back of the saddle and across the horse's back. Looking towards the front of the horse, step quickly and gently down to the ground. As soon as your right foot touches it, take your left foot out of the stirrup.

The walk and the jog

As in all types of riding, the most important aspect of Western riding is to get the feel of the horse – to know the feel of sitting correctly in the saddle and to learn to recognize the feel of the horse's legs beneath you. Not only is this difficult to explain but very difficult to teach. The only way to understand even the meaning of this feel is to practice riding continually and extensively. Practice continually the walk, even before you move on to the jog, aiming to achieve smooth turns and perfect circles. Give the aids to turn in exactly the same way as you would normally, feeling gently with the rein in the direction you want the horse to move, with your inside leg pressed against his side close to the cinch and the outside leg applying pressure just behind this. Remember that the pressure you put on the reins should be no more than the slightest squeeze. Your aim is to achieve a smooth, flowing turn, with no jerkiness or violent head reaction from the horse. If you pull on the reins, rather than feel, your mount will inevitably react jerkily and violently.

The Western rider asks his or her horse to move forward into a walk from a halt in exactly the same way as a rider practicing any other style of equitation – that is, by closing or nudging the legs against the horse's side and opening the fingers to allow the horse to move forward. As the horse goes into a walk, the rider must follow the movement by allowing his body to move in time with the rhythm of the pace.

Above left: The walk in Western equitation is asked for in exactly the same way as in European riding. Ask the horse to move forward from a halt by gently tapping his sides with the inside of your legs and heels, at the same time yielding very slightly with your hands to allow the forward movement. He should move forward freely and smoothly, maintaining an even pace.
Above: The jog is the Western equivalent of a trot. Although the movement is the same as in European styles of riding, the pace tends to be rather more bumpy. The rider should sit deep into the saddle, keeping the waist and loins very supple in order to allow him to relax with the movement.
Right: Again, at a lope, the rider should follow the movement of the horse, by sitting deep in the saddle and relaxing the waist and loins.

In Western riding the trot is called a jog. The correct jog calls for engagement of the hocks, so the horse is coming from behind with energy and rhythm. Ask for it in the usual way, making sure first that your horse is walking out well and is attentive and obedient to your aids. Stay seated in the saddle, as for the sitting trot, relaxing your body so that you are able to follow the horse's movement. Do not brace your body against the saddle – if you do, you will inevitably bounce out of it – but, equally, do not relax enough to become sloppy. Sit up straight and let your loins and waist absorb the movement.

As with the walk, do lots of practice work at the jog, trying to maintain a completely even and steady pace for three or four circuits of the school at a time, and then through smaller 20m (65ft) circles and figures-of-eight. This is considerably more difficult to achieve than it sounds on paper, but it is extremely good practice. You should bear in mind constantly that the Western jog is a collected movement in which the horse's hindquarters are active and tucked well beneath him, giving an alert and active pace. The pace is not sloppy – and, as the rider, you should never allow it to become so.

Traditionally the Western rider always rides at the jog, and not rising like the European rider. However, particularly if you intend to go Western trail riding (pony trekking, Western-style) when you may spend many hours a day in the saddle, it is a good idea to be able to rise to the trot, too. On long rides, this is essential for at least some of the time; sitting in the saddle for very long periods is exceptionally tiring for both horse and rider. You will also find that practicing the rising trot will help you in recognizing feel, as you think more consciously about the legs moving in diagonal pairs beneath you.

Slowing down and stopping

Just as the aids for moving forwards, or going from a walk to a jog, are the same in Western riding as they are in other classical styles of equitation, so, too, are the aids for slowing down and stopping. To go from a jog to a walk, close the inside of your lower leg against the horse's side and squeeze on the reins to discourage the forward movement. You should think of 'walking' – this advice may sound strange, but, if you think consciously of what you want your horse to do, you are far more likely to transmit your wishes to him clearly. The phil-

osophy is just the same as looking ahead in the direction in which you want to travel, particularly when asking for a turn. Look where you want to go, think about the pace you want from your horse and the battle is half-way won.

The canter or lope

In Western riding, the canter is called a lope. It is exactly the same pace, although when it is executed correctly, with the horse moving very smoothly, it tends to look a little easier and more relaxed than the European version. Though there is a considerable amount of power coming from the hindquarters, it is a very light pace, so the contact with the reins should be similarly considerate. Such lightness, however, can tempt the horse to fall back into a jog, so the rider must ensure against this by urging him gently forward with the legs all the time.

The aids for the lope are the same aids as in the European canter (see p. 50). If you are moving counter-clockwise around the school, you would ask for a lope with the near fore leading; if you are riding round the school on the right rein, or clockwise, your aids should be directed towards making the horse's off-fore lead.

Ride at the lope in the same way as you

Left: The Californian way of holding the reins in Western riding. **Right:** The Texan method. In the first, the reins pass up through the heel of the hand and out of the top beside the thumb. The spare ends are hobbled together and frequently end in a braided and knotted 'romal'. They lie underneath the free hand on the thigh. In the Texan style, the reins are split and not fastened together. They pass through the top of the hand, under the thumb, first, with the forefinger sometimes placed between them. The ends come out of the heel or lower end of the hand. In contrast to the Californian method, they are not placed under the free hand, though this still rests on the thigh

would at a canter, sitting deep in the saddle with your loins and waist really supple, so that they can absorb the movement. Once more, you should be sitting bolt upright, your head held high and looking in the direction you want to go. It is also another pace in which the smoothness and evenness of rhythm can sometimes encourage the unwary rider to become sloppy. When you want to return to a jog, 'think jog' and give the aids for a downward transition.

More exercises
Many of the exercises described in the section on European-style riding also help the Western rider to establish an independent seat, develop and exercise the correct riding muscles and co-ordinate body movements to work together and independently, as necessary. Moving the shoulders up and around in a circle is a particularly good exercise, as tension here is a common fault among novice riders.It is also one that leads to problems and mistakes throughout the position. Another useful exercise is to swing your legs backwards and forwards from the knees and then swing the arm backwards and forwards from the shoulder in time with the rhythm of the pace. Try this in walk, jog and lope. Moving in time with the horse's movement helps the rider to capture and recognize the feel of the pace more easily.

In these early stages – when you are still holding the reins in both hands – practice riding at all paces – turning and circling – without stirrups. Remember your aim is to maintain the position in the saddle at all times, just as if you were riding with your feet in the stirrups.

Principles of neck-reining
So far, you have been riding holding a rein in either hand and you should continue to do this until you have established a really secure position and are thoroughly balanced in the saddle. Balance is of utmost importance, for holding the reins in one hand – in traditional Western style – can unbalance and unseat a rider very quickly. Make sure, therefore, that you are really competent and confident at all paces – able to maintain an even rhythm of stride from the horse and execute smooth turns and transitions – before moving on to ride with the reins in your left hand only.

The first essential to grasp is that you are riding a horse trained to understand the principles of neck-reining. All horses know what it means if direct pressure is placed on one or other rein; pressure on the left means turn or move to the left and vice versa for the right. Horses trained in Western equitation go one stage further. They respond to pressure placed on their neck by the reins by moving away from it. Thus, if a rider wants his horse to move to

NECK-REINING ON A TURN

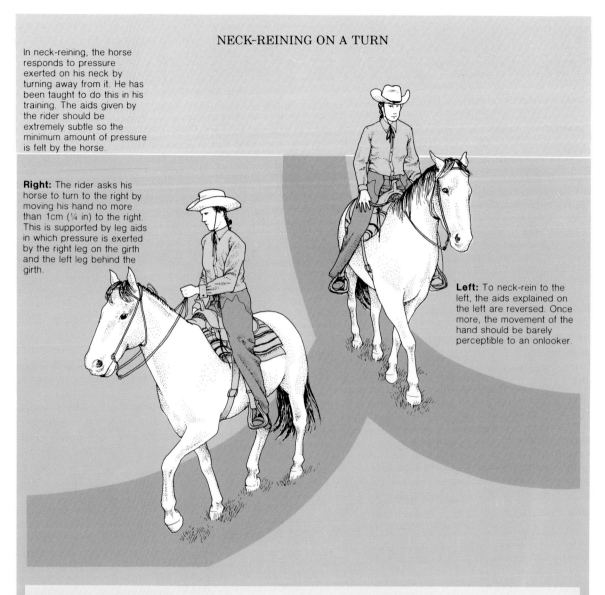

In neck-reining, the horse responds to pressure exerted on his neck by turning away from it. He has been taught to do this in his training. The aids given by the rider should be extremely subtle so the minimum amount of pressure is felt by the horse.

Right: The rider asks his horse to turn to the right by moving his hand no more than 1cm (¼ in) to the right. This is supported by leg aids in which pressure is exerted by the right leg on the girth and the left leg behind the girth.

Left: To neck-rein to the left, the aids explained on the left are reversed. Once more, the movement of the hand should be barely perceptible to an onlooker.

Mistakes – Neck-reining

Holding the reins in one hand will affect your position and handling of the horse, especially if you are used to riding with two hands on the reins. Some of the more common mistakes:

Holding the reins unevenly so one is much longer than the other.

Allowing the right hand to come off the thigh and wave in the air, clenching your fist as a sign of tension. The right hand must remain on your thigh at all times.

Holding the left hand too high and too far back.

Moving the rein hand too far to the left and right.

Moving the rein hand forward thereby putting pressure on the horse's neck making him bend back and head acutely.

Leaning into the rein hand, twisting to the right or left. You will eventually rise off the saddle and lose control.

the left, he moves both reins fractionally to the left, so the right rein is pressing against the neck. This is supported with the usual leg aids.

There are two accepted ways of holding the reins in one hand. Try both to see which you prefer and which gets the greatest and smoothest response from your horse. In the first method, the hand is held in the usual way, the wrist slightly flexed and the fingers pointing inwards with the thumb on top. The reins are then brought over the top of the hand between the forefingers and thumb. The other end emerges from the bottom of the hand and lies down the left side of the neck. In the other method, the hand is held in the same way but the reins are brought up through the hand from the bottom emerging between thumb and forefinger. This is a feature of Californian riding.

If the reins used are braided together into a romal (a knotted length of rein made by joining the ends together), this should be placed under the right hand which is laid on the thigh. If the reins are split, the end should be brought up through the hand to fall back over the thumb and the back of the hand, so they are out of the way. They should not dangle down in front, nor should they be held under the thigh.

Whichever method of holding the reins you adopt, your right hand should rest evenly and constantly against the thigh. Hold your left hand very slightly in front of the saddle horn – not behind it so it creeps back towards your body. If you take up this position, you will soon have no control over the horse.

Neck-reining in practice

Holding the reins in one hand inevitably tends to encourage various distortions – if not faults

– in the position. Therefore practice turning and circling at the walk thoroughly before attempting the jog and lope. Do not overemphasize the technique; although you are asking the horse to move away from pressure on the neck, that pressure should be no more than a whisper. A well-trained horse will respond to just the slightest feel; your hand should never move more than 7-14mm (¼ - ½ in) as you give the aid. If you move your hand more than this, not only will it affect your balance and position, but also probably lead the horse to respond by exaggerating the bend of his neck. He will move his head away from the direction of movement and if not reined hard to the left, he will be pulled to the right, or vice versa. Think of doing no more than fluttering the reins against the horse's neck, rather than trying to push or force him over.

Supporting leg aids are possibly even more important than usual when neck-reining. The horse must still move forward between your leg and hand, which means that you give the aids with your legs fractionally before the corresponding hand movement. The horse thus moves up to your hand.

When you have begun to master the principles of neck-reining at a walk, move on to turning and circling exercises at the jog. There is no need to exaggerate the aid because the pace is increased; you are still aiming to achieve the steady, even rhythm of the jog throughout all turns and circles.

To get your horse to lope on a given lead, the classic aids are used. Incline the horse's head very slightly in the direction of the lead leg, place your outside leg behind the cinch and apply pressure with your inside leg. The order

Left: Riding without stirrups but maintaining a correct leg position is a superb exercise for the Western rider. The position of the upper body and the rein hand should also remain correct, as it is in this picture. Practice riding without stirrups at all paces.
Right: An exercise to supple the loin and hip muscles. Keeping your legs in the correct position, lean over and touch the horse's point of shoulder with your opposite hand.

of the aids is vital! Although you are holding the reins in one hand, now ask for the bend of the head with the indirect rein – not the neck or direct rein. It will help your horse if you can learn to give these aids as the right shoulder moves forward. By the time the aid has been transmitted to his brain and back to his legs, his next stride will mean that he automatically moves into the lope with the off-fore as the lead leg.

Slowing down and stopping are carried out in the same way as when you are holding a rein in each hand. The action is a gentle closing or squeezing of your fingers on the rein as you ride forward with your legs. However, you must resist strongly the tendency to pull on the rein hand until you find it is almost back into your tummy. This will have no effect on your horse whatsoever.

Use of the legs

As well as controlling direction by pressure applied to the neck, you should also be able to make your horse move away from pressure

All the techniques used in Western riding today, including dressage movements such as the turn on the forehand and the rein back, were developed by cowboys for practical reasons. Here, a group of present-day cowboys are rounding up wild horses, a task calling for many such skills.

other horse. It also responds to the same aids. Try practicing this exercise to help to achieve a smooth half-turn (through 180°). Place a cavalletti (see p.62) about 1m (1 yd) away from the wall or fence of the school in the middle of one long side. Walk the horse on an inside track towards it – on the side nearest to the center of the school. When you reach the far end of the cavalletti, halt with the horse's front legs just clear of the end support. Now prevent forward movement by squeezing gently on the reins, but encourage your mount to move around the end of the cavalletti by bending him round your inside leg. If turning on the forehand, use leg nearest to the cavalletti in a series of nudges to push your horse's quarters away and so making the turn. When you have completed a 180° turn, walk around the school again to approach the cavalletti from the other direction. Then try the exercise again.

The rein back

You should also be able to execute a smooth rein back, which may be required on numerous practical occasions. As in European equitation, forward movement is encouraged by applying pressure with the legs and then restrained by not yielding with the hand. You may find that applying the aids in stages – squeezing very gently on the reins and then relaxing this pressure as the horse takes a step back – helps to achieve a smooth movement, in which the horse moves back evenly and correctly in two-time. In this instance, the hand aid is 'squeeze-yield', 'squeeze-yield', as each step is taken.

When the horse has taken three or four steps backwards, relax the pressure on the reins and encourage him to move forwards. This is to ensure that the impression of moving back does not become fixed in his mind and become a habit. This is important in dressage competitions, when a horse will be severely penalized by the judges if he takes a step back, except when required to do so.

When reining back, resist any temptation to sit down hard into the saddle in a misguided attempt to induce movement in the horse. This merely makes the horse hollow his back, making it almost impossible for him to step backwards correctly. Sit light and think light.

The sliding stop and quick stop

Although a horse should always respond to your aids instantly, even more emphasis than normal is placed on this in Western riding. Again, this originated for practical reasons. If, for example,

applied with one or other leg. The best way to practice this is through the turn on the forehand (see p.94), which is a useful movement to learn in any case for everyday recreational riding.

A Western-trained horse executes a turn on the forehand in exactly the same way as any

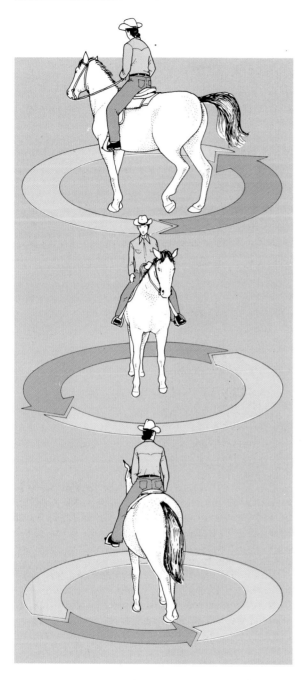

a rider in mountainous country found himself riding towards the edge of a cliff without realizing it, he would want his horse to stop instantly on a command when realization dawned, not three steps further forward. From this evolved the advanced movement known as a sliding stop, in which a horse stops dead in his tracks – even at a gallop – with his hind legs sliding right underneath him. This puts a tremendous strain on a horse's back and legs, so it should only be asked for very infrequently and then on a prepared surface. If this precaution is not observed, severe grazing of the hind legs can occur. The quick stop is a commoner movement. In this, the horse is required to stop as quickly as is physically possible after the aids have been given. He should do so in such a way that he is sufficiently balanced to move off again instantly at any pace.

Transition to the lope

Asking for a lope from a walk, halt or even a rein back, is a common feature of Western riding. It should be achieved with complete smoothness and precision. To ask a horse to go into a lope from a walk, make sure he is first walking out well and collectedly. Just before you reach a corner, give him a warning that you are about to ask him to change pace by squeezing a little on the reins at the same time as nudging his sides with your legs. Then, as you reach the corner, apply the aids for the lope – preferably as his right shoulder moves forward. Think 'lope', too. As you approach the corners in this instance, say to yourself 'ready' (attract his attention) and 'lope' (apply the aids firmly).

The same principle applies when asking for a lope from a halt. Make sure the horse is paying attention and knows you are about to ask him to do something. Tremble the reins slightly and nudge with your legs. Then give the aids firmly and definitely, using your legs strongly and yielding with your hands to allow the movement. The common fault is to scoop the reins up towards you, which has the reverse effect from the one you want to achieve. You must keep relaxed, so that your muscles do not tense, and yield with your hands. Such movements are impossible to execute properly if you are in a state of tension.

Western dressage

Reining patterns are Western dressage tests. Like their European counterparts, they are executed with great precision, but unlike the former, they are conducted at great speed. The

Top, center and bottom: The three stages of the turn on the forehand, as practiced in Western riding. The turn is a movement in which the horse's hindquarters move around his forequarters; in this case, the horse is describing a complete circle from right to left. Accordingly the rider's right leg is nudging the horse to the left, the pressure from the left leg controlling the speed of the movement. Direction comes from the legs alone; the reins merely restrain forward movement until the turn is completed. In the first illustration, the horse is stepping boldly to the left in response to the aids, though there is slight resistance as indicated by the tilted head and florished tail. In the second, the horse has moved through a semi-circle. It is nicely settled, with the rider's right leg encouraging the movement. The final illustration shows the completed turn, with the horse positioned at the halt ready to move forward.

movements called for will vary in order according to the individual test set by the judge.

The tests demand a highly trained horse and a similarly skilled rider. In addition to quick stops, moving into a fast lope from a rein back and flying changes of leg (changing the lead legs at a lope without altering the speed or pace), they also include movements known as pivots, spins and rollbacks.

In a pivot, the horse turns 90° from a halt by pivoting on his hindquarters. The front feet leave the ground at the beginning of the movement and do not touch it again until the pivot

is completed; in effect the horse 'rocks' around on his hindquarters. A spin consists of complete 360° turn on the hindquarters. In this the horse is usually brought to a sliding stop from a fast lope. He then executes the spin and immediately moves off on a given lead at the lope. The rollback is also asked for after a horse has been brought to a quick or sliding stop from a fast lope. He must roll around on his hocks, so that he executes a 180° turn with his forelegs coming down into the tracks he has just made. He leaves the turn straightaway on a given lead at a fast lope.

Side-Saddle Riding

UNTIL RELATIVELY RECENTLY, no lady rider would have dreamt of riding astride, considering such a position inelegant, unladylike and unsafe. It is perhaps questionable as to whether these very points account for the current revival in side-saddle riding; however, in recent years, more and more lady riders have returned to riding aside.

A side-saddle rider certainly looks extremely elegant to the observer. By and large, once practiced in the art, she also feels very secure, for the way the saddle is made is a guarantee of stability. Over long periods of time, side-saddle is generally considered to be a little more tiring than riding astride, but not sufficient, it would seem, to have stopped the ladies of yesteryear from enjoying a full day's hunting.

Most horses will carry a side-saddle and many actually appear to go better when ridden aside. This could well be because, by definition, the side-saddle rider has a more independent seat than her astride equivalent; she is not able to hold her horse in a vice-like grip, with her legs tight and tense around his middle. Providing she can develop light, sympathetic hands as well, she becomes infinitely preferable to the horse than the tense, astride rider. By bringing into play the emergency grip (see p.109), she

becomes almost irremovable from the saddle; this often allows her to manage strong horses which she might find more troublesome if she were riding astride.

The only type of horse that should not be ridden side-saddle is one that is known to rear. An astride rider can easily slip her feet out of the stirrup irons and slide off a rearing horse; the side-saddle rider cannot do so and may, therefore, bring the horse back on top of her.

Having said that most horses will accept a side-saddle, it is both kind and sensible to let them get used to the feel of it on its own, before having a rider on top as well. The side-saddle is considerably heavier than an astride saddle and its weight is obviously distributed differently. After putting on the saddle and leading the horse around for a while, he should then be lunged at a walk, trot and canter on both reins with the saddle still in place.

Apart from the obvious difference of sitting on just one side of the horse, the other main way in which riding aside differs from riding astride is that the rider is considerably higher off the back of the horse. The side-saddle is so constructed that the rider is about 10cm (4in) higher off her horse's back than the astride rider. Providing she sits and rides correctly,

To those who have never ridden side-saddle, while the rider looks very elegant; indeed, it might seem that she is precariously perched on her mount.
Most horses will accept a side-saddle largely because it does not allow the rider to grip and tense-up as the astride saddle does. As well, the independent seat allows for steadier grip and greater freedom of forward movement. **Left:** Recent years have seen a come-back of side-saddle riding and many riders are beginning to learn the techniques. **Right:** The romance of this type of riding becomes clear when the rider is in full costume like this one at the Seville Fair in Spain.

WHAT TO WEAR

The side-saddle habit definitely lends an air of elegance to the rider and her horse and cannot help but remind the viewer of days gone by when all 'gentlewomen' would ride only side-saddle. If you plan to be doing a lot of side-saddle riding, it is a good idea to purchase the correct habit. There are two types of material available but a double-weight, heavier one is preferable. It used to be acceptable only to have an either black or grey habit, but blue now seems to be equally fashionable. Whatever the color or fabric, it is essential that the skirt of your habit hangs correctly and covers the right boot. If you do a great deal of side-saddle riding, this could lead to the wearing of the fabric over your right knee and, for this reason, many skirts have a leather patch sewn in them. The correct dress for county or morning shows would include a tie, white or striped shirt, veil and bowler hat. For afternoon and evening events, the tie is replaced by a stock and the bowler with a top hat and veil.

however, she has just as much contact and control over her horse.

Most side-saddles now on sale are second-hand, as market demand over the last decade has not been enough to encourage saddlers to make them. Today with the revival of interest in riding side-saddle, new saddles are beginning to appear. Various designs are available, just as they are in conventional saddles, but all incorporate the same basic features. In the majority, the rider's legs will lie on the horse's near side, though a few allow the rider to sit on the off side. This is purely a matter of preference; as, in the past, most saddles were made specifically to fit the individual rider concerned.

Knowledge of the names given to the various points of the side-saddle is useful, as these differ from the usual astride saddle.

What to wear

The chief item of dress for side-saddle riding is the habit. This is expensive and usually has to be made-to-measure. Habits always used to be made of a material heavy enough to ensure that

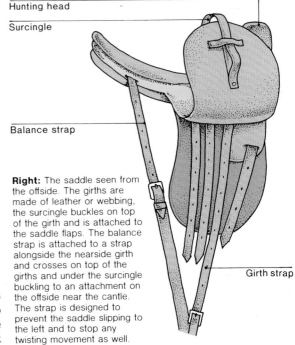

Hunting head

Surcingle

Balance strap

Girth strap

Right: The saddle seen from the offside. The girths are made of leather or webbing, the surcingle buckles on top of the girth and is attached to the saddle flaps. The balance strap is attached to a strap alongside the nearside girth and crosses on top of the girths and under the surcingle buckling to an attachment on the offside near the cantle. The strap is designed to prevent the saddle slipping to the left and to stop any twisting movement as well.

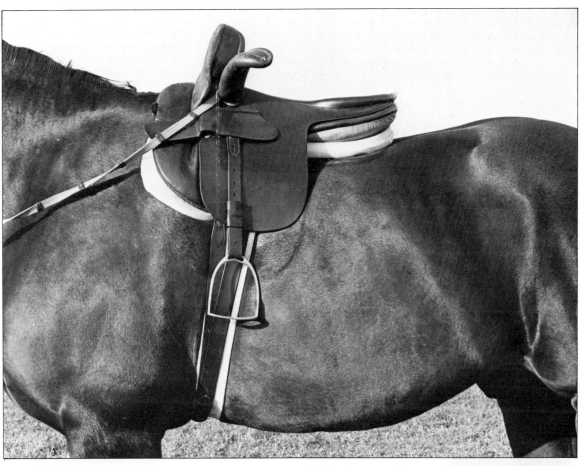

Above and below: From the nearside, the side-saddle is so constructed that the rider is necessarily higher off the horse than when astride. This in no way decreases control.

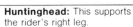

Seat: This is generally made of doe-skin or suede to give the rider a good grip.

Flap

Stirrup leather: This is adjustable at the lower end close to the iron, rather than next to the saddle.

Stirrup iron: This has a larger eye than normal to accommodate the leather.

Huntinghead: This supports the rider's right leg.

Leaping head: This usually has a screw fitting so its position can be adjusted.

Right: Most saddles have a quick-release safety catch for the stirrup leather. This remains in position while the rider's leg is pressed against the saddle, but if in a fall, the fitting releases dropping the leather and iron ensuring that the rider is not dragged on the ground. If this attachment is not fitted, a specially designed safety iron must be used. When the foot tips down hard against this, as it would in a fall, the foot-rest falls out to release the foot.

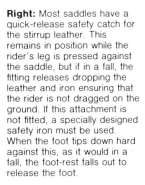

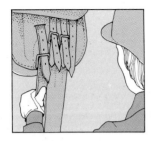

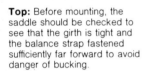

Top: Before mounting, the saddle should be checked to see that the girth is tight and the balance strap fastened sufficiently far forward to avoid danger of bucking.

Bottom: The stirrup leathers must be correctly fastened or an accident may occur.
Above: If you are mounting with an apron, put it over your left arm before mounting.

the finished garment would hang down over the foot and legs; modern habits, however, are sometimes lightweight, which means that weights often have to be sown into the hem of the apron to prevent it blowing up in a breeze.

Mounting side-saddle

You can mount to ride side-saddle in a number of different ways. Before doing so, however, it is essential to check that the girths and balance strap are reasonably tight. Make sure, too, that the stirrup leather is correctly attached to the saddle.

In the first method, you fold your apron over your left arm and mount in the same way as you would if you were riding astride, throwing your right leg across the saddle. Remember to stand clear of the pommels as you mount and that, as the stirrup leather is considerably higher off the ground, you will need to show slightly more agility. Once in the saddle, bring your right leg back to hook over the hunting head, taking care that your leg does not get tangled up in the reins.

In the second method, a helper gives you a leg up. With your apron hooked over your left arm as before, hold the reins in your left hand and stand near to the back of the saddle facing the front of the horse. Put the left hand (with the reins) on the hunting head and the right hand on the seat. Bend your left leg for your helper to support and spring off the ground as she hoists you up. This will require some

strength, as you have to be hoisted much higher than for an astride leg up. As you are hoisted upwards, twist your right hip forward to ensure that you land in the saddle facing to the left. Then swing your right leg up over the hunting head, making sure your helper moves first as otherwise you might kick her in the face. Alternatively, you can sit astride and then swing your right leg back over the saddle.

The most elegant way of mounting requires a considerable amount of practice to do gracefully; you also need an experienced helper. Stand facing the horse level with the cantle, your reins in your right hand which should be placed on the hunting head. Fold your apron over your left arm and place your left hand on your helper's shoulder. He or she then bends down, cupping hands one on top of another to suport your left foot. Then, at a given signal, the helper hoists you into the air, you springing off your right foot and straightening your left leg. Bring your right leg in front of your left leg, twisting slightly to allow you to slip it over the hunting head as you descend to sit in the saddle.

However you choose to mount, put your left foot in the stirrup iron once in the saddle and hook the elastic positioned under your apron on to your right boot.

Dismounting is perfectly straightforward. You unhook the elastic from your right foot and gather your apron clear of the pommels, folding it again over your left arm. Then remove your left foot from the stirrup iron, taking your reins in your right hand and resting it on the hunting head. Swing your right leg over the two pommels, so you are sitting sideways to the saddle, and slide gently down to the ground,

MOUNTING AND DISMOUNTING SIDE- SADDLE

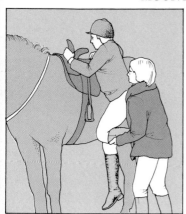

Take the reins in your left hand and face the saddle. With the loose length of the apron over your left arm, take hold of the fixed head with your left hand.

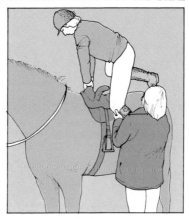

Push yourself up off your left leg as your assistant lifts you as high as possible. Remember that you have to clear the pommel.

Swing your right leg across the saddle so that you are sitting astride. Adjust your position and balance for the following steps.

Once in the saddle, bring your right leg up over the hunting head, first making sure that your assistant is well out of the way.

Once again, adjust your position and fix your legs and seat comfortably in the saddle. Shift your weight slightly to the left for the next step.

Leaning over to your left side, carefully and slowly, attach your skirt elastic over your foot. Your assistant may help you.

Dismounting: If wearing a skirt, first unhook the skirt elastic from around your foot and drape the material over your arm.

Bring your right leg around alongside the left and turn your body so that you are sitting squarely sideways on the horse.

Using your right hand and arm for support, push yourself up and off the horse as smoothly and gently as possible.

Inserting your palm between the leaping head and leg means the leathers are correct.

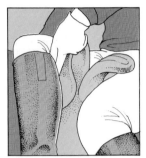

Two fingers should be capable of being placed between the right knee and the hunting head.

When hanging loosely by your side, your right hand rests on the balance strap.

Ask an assistant to check from behind to ensure you are sitting squarely in the saddle.

twisting slightly so you land facing the horse's head. Make sure you are placed towards the back of the saddle so that you do not catch yourself on the pommels.

Side-saddle position

The first important point about position on a side-saddle is that the rider should look exactly the same as the astride rider when viewed from behind, except for the lack of a leg on the right hand side. In other words, your weight must still be positioned centrally over the horse's back and your spine in line with his. To begin with, it will help greatly if there is somebody standing behind you to tell you if you are sitting centrally; it is much more difficult to feel

Until you get used to it, adopting the correct side-saddle position is initially more difficult than the astride position only because it is harder to determine whether you are sitting in the center of the saddle.

Your back should be straight and upright, as the rider looks directly between the horse's ears. The reins are held higher and further forward, with the elbows bent in a relaxed fashion, with a straight line running down from them, through the hands and reins to the mouth.

if you are sitting straight in a side-saddle.

Upper body and head Both should be held straight and upright, as in astride riding, with shoulders and hips level and square to those of the horse. Resist any temptation to hollow the back or to twist the hips.

A good test to see if your right shoulder is correctly positioned is to let your right arm hang down naturally by your side. It should be resting on the balance strap. The tendency always is to let your right shoulder move forward.

Seat You should rest slightly more weight on your right seat bone, so that the outside of your thigh is in contact with the saddle. Do not fall, however, into the temptation of sagging or leaning to the right.

Right leg This hangs almost perpendicular from the knee, the toe pointing slightly down and in towards the horse's shoulder. Brace the outside calf muscles against the saddle – this helps to tense your knee, which, in turn, pulls

you deeper into the saddle. The inside of your right thigh, not the crook of your knee should be pressed against the hunting head. You should be able to place one or two fingers between the back of the right knee and the hunting head.

Left leg The stirrup leather is the right length when you can insert the palm of your hand between the leaping head and your left thigh, with your foot in the iron and the leather hanging perpendicular to the ground. You will find that the same length is about the same as for riding astride. Keep your inner thigh and knee in close contact with the saddle, but do not grip firmly enough to tense your muscles . As with astride riding, let the weight fall down into the heel and turn the toe slightly out to the left, rather than trying to keep it parallel to the horse. This helps to keep the knee close to the saddle.

Hands Hold the reins in the usual way, the knuckles facing in towards each other and the

Mistakes – Position

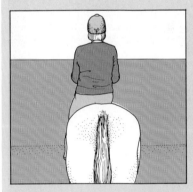
A mistake to avoid is collapsing the left hip and leaning to the side.

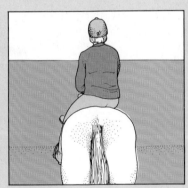
Sitting sideways with your right hip twisted in front of your left hip.

Riding with the leather too short so the knee is pushed against the leaping head.

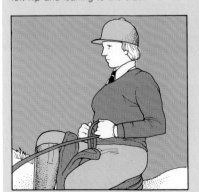
Pulling the reins too far back towards you making the reins totally ineffective.

Being jerked backwards as your horse moves; try to anticipate every movement.

When circling, letting the inside shoulder move forward and twisting body.

wrists very slightly flexed. You will find you have to hold your hands a little higher than in astride riding, because of the construction of the saddle and the position of your legs; however, a straight line should still run from your elbows, through the hands and reins to the bit. Place the hands on either side of the right knee slightly further back than in normal riding.

Moving forwards

Ask your horse to move forwards into a walk the same way as riding astride – that is, by applying pressure with the inside of the leg against the horse's side. The place of the right leg can be taken by the whip, although if you are only asking for a walk, it may not be necessary to use it. Horses ridden side-saddle will soon begin to understand that the whip is being used instead of the right leg aid and not correctively or as punishment, as it is generally used in regular astride riding.

As the horse moves forward into a walk, let your body relax and go with the movement. This means suppling your pelvis, so that it rocks very gently with the horse's stride. As in riding astride, this movement should be barely perceptible to an observer, although to the rider, it seems as if you are moving about in the saddle far more than you do when riding astride.

When riding side-saddle, it is particularly important not to tense your back and make it rigid. Bracing your back muscles is one of the main aids for asking the horse to slow down so, if you ride continually with a rigid back, you are actually aplying the brakes all the time.

When you want the horse to come to a halt from a walk, brace the muscles of your back and resist with your hands. Push very gently with your seat bones, so you are driving him forward into resisting hands rather than pulling him back.

Right: As with astride riding, the aids for side-saddle riding must be given in coordination, not contradiction, to one another.

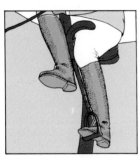

1. The left leg is the main aid to induce forward movement in the horse. It should be used easily, in the same way as astride riding.

2. The whip, held in the right hand, helps to compensate for the lack of the right leg. Use it in conjunction with the left leg, just behind the girth.

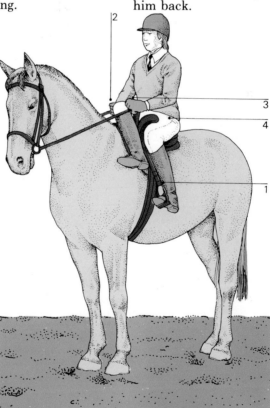

3. The hands operate in exactly the same way as when riding astride: they should be sympathetic and yielding. The novice side-saddle rider should be constantly aware of this as there is a tendency to rely on the reins for support.

4. The seat and back muscles are again used in the same way as astride riding. The seat can further be used to push the horse forward, inducing extra impulsion.

Mistakes – Aids

Trying to kick or give aids with the right leg. Think consciously of keeping the leg still until there is no temptation to move it.

Holding the right rein down by the side of the saddle so the right arm is straight. The wrist will lock and not be able to move efficiently.

At a trot, the novice side-saddle rider may well find herself being bounced around in the saddle. Try to sit still and move naturally with the horse's movement.

Trotting

Trotting is by no means the most comfortable side-saddle pace and, in times gone by, it was kept to a minimum. Ladies' horses were trained instead to execute a very slow canter, equivalent in speed to the trot of most gentlemens' horses.

To ask your horse to trot, make sure he is walking out well, so that he is both balanced and paying attention to your aids. If there is any doubt about this, make him pay attention by bracing your back muscles and very gently resisting with your hands, as if you were going to ask him to halt. This will make him a little more attentive. As he gathers himself together to stop, apply pressure on his left side with your leg and tap him lightly on the right with your whip. He should then move into a trot.

Make these aids very gentle, for it is far better if he moves first into a slow 'shuffly' trot, rather than a fast, long-striding one. When you want him to trot slightly faster, let your body bounce a fraction more energetically with the movement. The extra pressure from your seat bones will push him forward, encouraging more forward movement and a longer stride.

The most usual way to trot side-saddle is to remain seated rather than to rise. Two factors will determine how comfortable this is – the smoothness of the horse's trot and the suppleness of your waist and loins. There is not much you can do to make a very bumpy trot smooth, so it is essential that you are really supple. This will allow you to relax and follow the movement with your body. If you do bump around in the saddle, your horse will have a sore back in no time; bad side-saddle riding causes sore backs in horses very quickly indeed. You, too, will be exhausted.

Though the rising trot should be practiced – at least for short bursts – it is both difficult and tiring to maintain. You do not rise up and down, or forwards and backwards, in the same way as you do when riding astride; instead, it is a sort of roll forward on to the right thigh. Use your left knee very slightly as a pivot, but try not to put too much weight in the iron. If you do this, you will lose contact with the saddle and also pull it over to the left.

To slow down, use the same aids as when halting from a walk; that is bracing your back muscles and using your seat as you push the horse into a resisting hand.

Turns and circles

If you are riding on the left rein and want to turn off the track across the school, incline your

Above: The aids you give your horse to move into a trot should be given gently as it is easier to ask your horse to move from a slower trot than a fast and long-striding one. Push down in the seat to move him more quickly along.

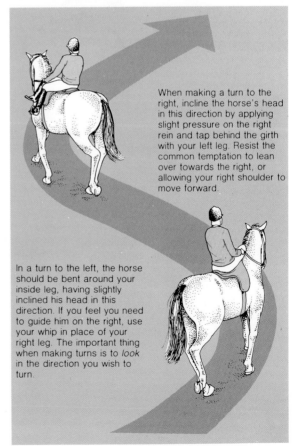

When making a turn to the right, incline the horse's head in this direction by applying slight pressure on the right rein and tap behind the girth with your left leg. Resist the common temptation to lean over towards the right, or allowing your right shoulder to move forward.

In a turn to the left, the horse should be bent around your inside leg, having slightly inclined his head in this direction. If you feel you need to guide him on the right, use your whip in place of your right leg. The important thing when making turns is to *look* in the direction you wish to turn.

horse's head in the direction you want to go, use your inside leg on the girth to bend him correctly and tap him on the offside behind the girth with your whip. Here, you must concentrate on putting your right shoulder back, for the tendency is always to twist towards the left.

To turn to the right, incline your horse's head in that direction and push him around with your outside leg. You can use the whip on the girth on the offside, but it probably will not be necessary. This time, avoid collapsing to the right.

The great thing when making turns or riding circles aside – just as it is when riding astride – is to look exactly in the direction which you

want your horse to go. As long as you look in the correct direction, the probability is that the horse will go there too. If you do not look there, however, there is no hope of him moving the right way.

Cantering side-saddle

A smooth canter is probably the most comfortable of all paces in side-saddle riding. It is certainly the most graceful to watch if both horse and rider are in complete harmony. Asking for a specific lead leg at the canter, however, is somewhat complicated until you get used to it, but if the horse has been correctly ridden in the past, he may well help you. Horses learn

Left: These three photographs show the transition from trot to canter in side-saddle riding.
Right: The result – a smooth, even canter. In the first photograph, the rider has brought her horse into a regular, balanced trot and is starting to apply the aids to ensure he leads into the canter on the correct leg. The process is continued in the second photograph. For a canter on the left rein, this means inclining the horse's head slightly to the left and closing the left leg to the girth. This is reinforced by pressure from the right seat bone, with a tap of the whip if necessary. For a right canter, the head is to the right, pressure is applied behind the girth with the left foot and the left seat bone from the saddle. In the third picture, the horse is responding by leading correctly. The rider is relaxing into the saddle, her waist and loins absorbing the rhythm of the movement.

106

quickly and generally realize what their rider wants them to do.

If you are riding on the left rein, you should canter with the left leg leading. Make sure first of all that the horse is attentive and going forward in a good balanced trot. To ask him to canter, incline his head very slightly to the left, apply pressure with your left leg on the girth and push with your right seat bone. Tap him behind the girth on the offside with the stick, if you feel this is necessary.

To canter with the right foreleg leading, it will help if you ask for the canter on a corner when the horse is naturally slightly inclined to the right. Try to give the aids – strong leg pressure behind the girth with your left foot and pressure from your left seat bone, with the horse's head inclined slightly to the right – when he is on the outside diagonal, that is when his off-fore and near hind are moving forward. The first step of the canter is taken with the off hind, which is free to respond to your aid.

Your loins and waist should absorb the canter movement and allow you to relax into the saddle. The upper part of your body remains still; do not let your shoulders become rounded.

The emergency grip
All side-saddle riders should be aware of and able to execute the emergency grip. As its name

There are no special rules or regulations for side-saddle riders out on a hack. They should be just as alert as an astride rider, ready to respond to any situation or cope with unusual circumstances. If riding with a companion, he or she would normally ride on the side-saddle rider's right side, so as to avoid being continually kicked with the rider's left leg.

suggests, this is only for use during emergencies – when your horse bucks or shies suddenly, say, or plays up and tries to unseat you by jumping sideways. In such a situation, bring the left heel up so the knee is pressed into the leaping head. Now your grip is tightened on the hunting head and your left knee is held secure by the leaping head. So long as you keep your right shoulder back you are irremovable.

General techniques

You will not find it always necessary to employ your emergency grip when your horse plays up. Often his antics will not be sufficient to unseat you and it is best to keep the grip for real emergencies. What is essential, though, is to once more make sure your right shoulder is back and has not come forward to point to the left. The tendency even in normal conditions is to turn to the left; this becomes even more pronounced if a rider is under stress.

Side-saddle riders, like those riding astride, must expect to take their share of tumbles, even though their seat is generally more secure.

The most common way to fall is backwards over the horse's right hand side. This sounds both more unpleasant and dangerous than it usually is; as the safety catch ensures that your stirrup iron comes free, there is no danger of your being caught up on the saddle or dragged.

If the horse falls forward, or if you feel you have reached the point of no return in overbalancing to the left, the expert advice is to free your apron and step off to the left. Do not worry about the stirrup iron, for again it will free itself. Though it is easy not to have the time or presence of mind to do this, it is essential to make a positive effort to do so. If the horse does fall to the left, he could trap you beneath him.

In the early stages of learning to ride side-saddle, it pays to concentrate on working at the walk and at a slow trot – ideally a sort of 'shuffly jog,' if your horse will do this. Remember that it will take a little time to get used to the aside position and to consolidate it and that until you do so, there is a strong likelihood that you will be using the reins as supports to balance you. This will obviously cause the horse great discomfort; if the habit persists, he eventually will become hard-mouthed, unresponsive and intolerant of a side-saddle.

To begin with, you will find that the muscles of your right knee and thigh ache very considerably. These are equally important in side-saddle riding as in astride riding, yet, because they are not used in the same way, they are bound to ache even if you are an experienced rider.

Other aspects of riding – riding on the road, going for a leisurely hack and so on – require no change in riding technique because you are riding side-saddle. As usual in these situations, you should let common sense be your guide to make sure you do not land yourself or your horse in trouble. Remember to give yourself extra clearance on the left side when going through a gate or riding along a hedgerow, for example. Be extra careful, too, when riding on the road. You are robbed of the use of your right leg, which is the one you would normally use to keep your horse into the curb, so make sure you guide him positively with the reins, keeping a firm, steady contact with his mouth. Tap him lightly with your stick if he begins to wander out into the road.

Jumping side-saddle

No special allowance need be made for jumping side-saddle; exactly the same obstacles can be tackled as when riding astride. In fact, horses are often said to jump better when ridden aside, not least because the rider is generally more

EMERGENCY GRIP

Falling off when riding side-saddle is obviously an occupational hazard, although it tends to occur less frequently than when riding astride. If circumstances and time allow, or if there is a likelihood of the horse falling to the left, try to step or jump clear, to avoid any possibility of being crushed under the falling horse. **Above, below right:** The normal side saddle position and the emergency grip position are shown. The left heel is brought upwards, so the knee is pressed tightly into the hunting head. The right heel is brought up towards the left shin, so tightening the grip here. The resulting 'vice-like' grip should help the rider to maintain her place in the saddle in most circumstances.

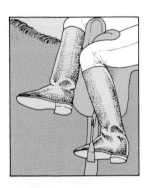

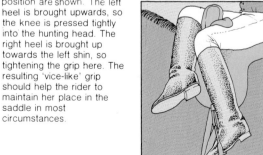

relaxed than the astride rider, particularly when she has gained a little confidence. When a horse being ridden astride rushes his fences, for example, it is often because the rider has tensed up and clamped his legs against the horse's side in a vice-like grip. The side-saddle rider simply cannot do this, so the horse is automatically more relaxed and unimpeded on the approach.

Unlike the side-saddle riders of yesteryear, the modern side-saddle rider adopts a forward position over a jump. Although her seat should leave the saddle a little, it is unlikely to move as far as when riding astride, since she cannot use her knees as pivots to the same extent. To compensate for this and for the fact that the rider's weight is fractionally further back, it is necessary to fold the top half of your body more considerably, closing the angle of the waist in order to lean further forward. Keep your weight positioned centrally, however, and resist strongly any temptation to look down to the left.

Until you are used to it, jumping side-saddle feels far less safe and secure than jumping astride. For this reason, it pays to put in concentrated practice over cavalletti and low jumps until you have really got the feel of the position.

The aims and techniques of jumping aside are exactly the same as when jumping astride. At all costs, the rider should not interfere with the horse's head as she lets the reins slip through her hands to accommodate his outstretched neck. Fold forwards into the jumping position as the horse nears the fence and do not attempt to return to an upright position until he has landed. For the rest, ride him straight towards the center of a fence, keeping the stride even and balanced throughout the approach. The rest can be left up to the horse.

Learning to jump side-saddle follows a similar procedure as learning to jump astride. The position is also similar in that the rider leans forward from the waist, while keeping her legs and hands in the normal position. As the knees cannot be used as a pivot in the same way, you must close the angle at your waist more acutely so that you lean further forward. **Top left:** The rider is attempting the first stage of trotting over poles. Note that she has relinquished her stirrup iron. **Below:** The rider is trotting over a cavaletti. Note the extreme angle of her waist, allowing her to keep her weight well forward. Next, she is shown in mid-jump. Here her position is basically correct, although she would have been more comfortable had she leaned a little further forward. The bottom picture shows landing after a jump. Note that she is still in the forward position where she will remain for the next few strides. **Right:** Practise without stirrups. Riding without stirrups, the rider is in the correct position for take-off, the top part of her body being folded well forward.

Mistakes – Side-saddle Jumping

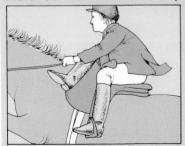

Being left behind the horse's forward movement and thereby being shot up in the air by the horse's spring.

Holding onto the hunting head while jumping rather than the leaping head.

Leaning too far forward or twisting the body while jumping. This will most likely unseat you.

A Horse of Your Own

MOST RIDERS ULTIMATELY AIM AT owning a horse of their own, but – even more than taking the decision to learn to ride – such a step demands careful thought – and thorough pre-planning. What sort of horse to buy does not depend only on how competent a rider you are, how much you can afford and how much riding you want to do; it also depends on how much time you can devote to looking after your horse and where you decide to keep it.

You should decide first whether you intend to keep your horse out of doors all the year round, or whether you are going to keep it stabled for part or all of the time. Keeping a horse at grass is both cheaper and less time-consuming than keeping it stabled, but it means selecting an animal that can withstand the rigors of the worst the climate can offer. This inevitably means you cannot choose a Thoroughbred horse, or even a Thoroughbred type; such horses are simply not tough and hardy enough.

If you decide to keep your horse out at grass, check carefully that the field you choose has all the necessary facilities. The facilities you will need are described on pages 130 to 149.

Keeping a horse stabled means spending considerably more time looking after him than if he were at grass and it will also cost more. However, a stabled horse is often fitter and in better overall condition than the grass-kept equivalent, as well as being more readily to hand. It also means that you can look for a somewhat better-bred animal, if such is your preference. Consider carefully, though, the amount of time you will have at your disposal before making this decision. Again, the necessary requirements and facilities are discussed in greater detail on pages 150 to 173.

An alternative to both of these courses is to keep your horse at a livery stable, where it will be looked after by experienced grooms. This relieves you of the responsibility and worry, but it is an extremely costly solution.

Choosing a horse

Where you are going to keep your horse and the type of riding you do are probably the main issues that govern the type of horse to look for. There are, however, other factors to take into consideration too – its height, age and sex, for example.

The height of the rider should always influence the size of horse to buy. If the rider is a

Owning a horse is a very different experience from simply riding one in a school, and will demand your constant attention. As well, it can be a great responsibility and you should be aware, before buying, of the time and effort which goes into owning a horse. Whether you intend to use your horse for competitive riding or simply for pleasure, owning a horse requires that you be organized and efficient and able to plan and follow a daily schedule of feeding, grooming, and exercise.

By and large, horse sales are a good place to stay away from when contemplating buying a horse unless you know a great deal about them as it is easy to find yourself with a horse that has some chronic disability, which has been cleverly disguised for the occasion. **Above:** Prospective buyers at a small, local sale in England bid against one another for rough mountain and moorland ponies. **Right:** A sale in America of quite a different type. These are bloodstock sales, where horses will change hands for enormous prices.

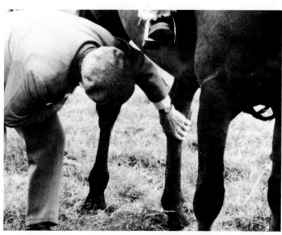

Above, top: Always watch any horse you are considering buying being ridden before you venture out on its back, much less buy it. Watch its actions carefully and the way it reacts to its rider.

Above: Take an expert along with you to check the horse's legs and general conformation. No horse should be bought without a vet's certificate which will guarantee that the animal is healthy and sound.

child, it is better to choose an animal that is slightly too big, rather than too small. Having to sell a horse because it has been outgrown can be a heartbreaking experience and it is best to put off this moment for as long as possible.

Shape is important as well as size. A broad-backed horse may not suit a short-legged rider, where a narrower horse of the same height may feel exactly right. A heavily-built rider needs a stronger, stockier horse than a very light rider, yet horses of the same height may well suit both individuals.

Unless a rider is very experienced, it is always best to buy a horse that is both physically mature and fully trained. This means one that is at least six years old, at which age it still has the ten best years of its life ahead of it. Most horses lead full and active lives, into their late teens or early twenties.

The horse's sex is usually of less importance. A mare can be used for breeding when she has been outgrown, although few riders have the facilities to cope with this. Geldings are said to be more reliable in temperament – and often in performance, too – than mares. Only the most experienced of horsemen will buy a stallion for riding purposes, as stallions tend to be unpredictable and excitable. Whether you are looking for a child's first pony or for a horse to carry you around a cross-country eventing course, temperament and reliability are both very important characteristics. Beware of any horse that is nervy or jumpy when you approach him or has a mean look in his eyes. A traffic-proof horse is essential for all riders, for no-one can escape riding on the roads. A horse that is easily frightened by cars and trucks is a danger to everyone concerned.

Where to buy
Having decided basically on the sort and size of horse you want, the search can begin. There are any number of places to find horses for sale; choosing the right one depends on how experienced you are in judging both horses and the people who sell them. Unless you are very experienced, the first rule is to always ask an expert to accompany you when you go to look at a prospective buy.

There are four main ways of finding a horse for sale. These are by word of mouth – hearing about it from a friend, for instance – going to a horse sale, looking at the advertisements in horse magazines, or approaching a dealer. The least suitable of these is usually a word-of-mouth buy. If you buy a horse from a friend and problems arise with it later, this can lead only to an awkward and embarrassing situation which is rarely resolved satisfactorily. There are, of course, exceptions; if you have watched the horse's progress for some time, it may be that you know he is exactly right for you.

Going to a horse sale should also be avoided, unless you are very experienced both in judging a horse from some distance off and are prepared to take a gamble. Advertisements are less of a risk, particularly if you take an expert with you. The majority of horses advertised in horse magazines are sold for genuine reasons, so you should always have the opportunity to examine them thoroughly.

Strange though it may sound, going to a dealer is probably the safest method of all, provided that you choose one with a reputation he is proud of and anxious to maintain. This being so, it will be in his best interests to sell you the horse best suited to you.

The other possible method is from the riding school where you have been taking lessons. In some cases, riding establishments also deal in horses and this can often be an excellent way of finding the right horse. Your instructor will know your capabilities as a rider and will be in

The type of horse you buy will be governed by your experience as a rider, the sort of riding you want to do, and the conditions and time you have for keeping him. **Right:** This attractive, useful type of horse would make an excellent recreational riding horse, and possibly a good eventer. It is not a Thoroughbred and could quite happily be kept our at grass for most of the year if provided with a New Zealand rug in the winter.

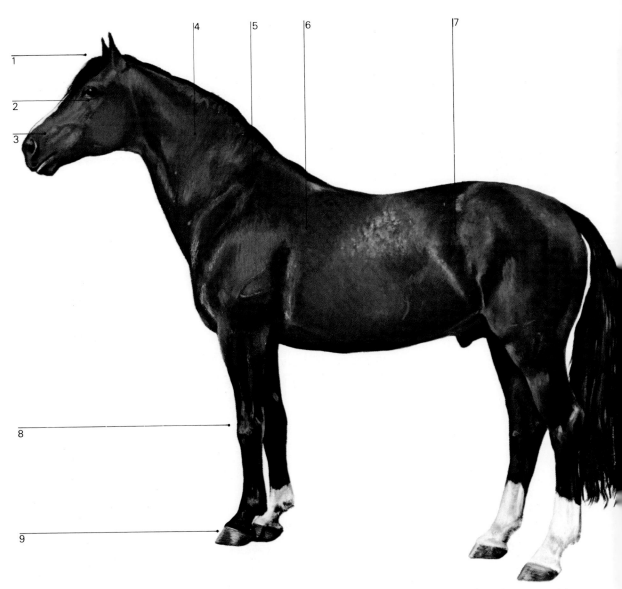

When buying a horse, care should be taken to note the following points and that they are as perfect as possible: 1) The ears should be pricked and alert, not pinned back so that the horse looks aggressive or bad-tempered. 2) The eyes should be generous and kind-looking not small and mean or rolling so that the whites are showing. 3) The nose is more attractive if slightly concave. 4) The neck should be gently arched and be in proportion to the size of the horse and head. Avoid those with a thick neck or with a convex bend from the throat to the chest. 5) The shoulder should slope evenly from the withers to the base of the neck. 6) The body must be deep enough to give the lungs and heart room to work, but not too long. 7) The hindquarters should look smooth, sleek, and well-rounded. Make sure they look strong enough for the rest of the body as well. 8) The legs should be strong and straight and in proportion to the body. Avoid a horse whose legs are covered with scars or bumps. 9) The feet should be neat, rounded and evenly shaped and distributing the weight evenly.

an excellent position to judge the sort of horse that would suit you best.

The trial ride

When you go to choose a horse try to see how it behaves in the stable while it is being tacked-up before watching it being ridden. Always let someone else ride it first, particularly on the road, before you get up on its back. Try it at all paces – over a jump, too, if this is to be part of your riding routine – and, above all, take your time. In the past, many owners would let a prospective purchaser have a horse on trial for a week or a fortnight, but, because of the expense of horses today, this is becoming a less frequent practice. See if the seller would be prepared to agree to this, for it is an excellent way of getting to know the animal.

Conformation should always be checked care-

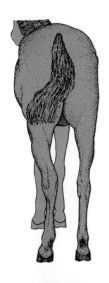

1

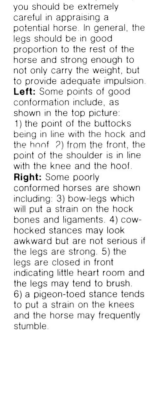

2

As good conformation is probably the most valuable asset a horse can possess, you should be extremely careful in appraising a potential horse. In general, the legs should be in good proportion to the rest of the horse and strong enough to not only carry the weight, but to provide adequate impulsion. **Left:** Some points of good conformation include, as shown in the top picture: 1) the point of the buttocks being in line with the hock and the hoof. 2) from the front, the point of the shoulder is in line with the knee and the hoof. **Right:** Some poorly conformed horses are shown including: 3) bow-legs which will put a strain on the hock bones and ligaments. 4) cow-hocked stances may look awkward but are not serious if the legs are strong. 5) the legs are closed in front indicating little heart room and the legs may tend to brush. 6) a pigeon-toed stance tends to put a strain on the knees and the horse may frequently stumble.

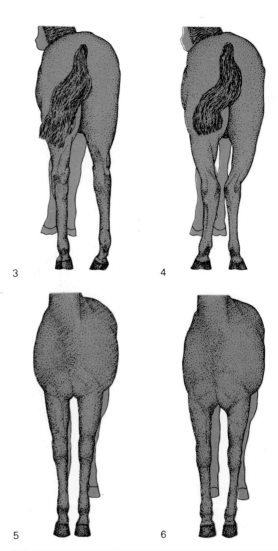

3   4

5   6

fully. Though you can, of course, judge these to the best of your ability yourself, never decide to buy a horse without having a veterinary surgeon examine it first. Some horses are offered for sale with a 'vet's certificate', meaning a vet has examined it and found it to be sound 'in wind and limb'. However, your vet will know the purposes for which you want the horse and can examine it with these in mind. Thus, his judgement will be just that much more valid.

Check each of the points outlined pictorially, individually, but look at the horse as a whole, too. He should look compact and well proportioned, as if each separate part or feature really fits with everything else. This will give the animal a good 'outline', meaning that he looks generally balanced and symmetrical, rather than un-coordinated and straggley if any one point is out of proportion, others will be as well.

BACK AND BODY POINTS

For obvious reasons, the horse's back is as important to consider as its legs. **Below:** A straight back restricts movement and the horse will probably lack power. **Top right:** A straight croup indicates little flexibility whereas an acutely sloping one means lack of power in the hindquarters. **Middle:** A shallow body indicates little stamina and lung power. **Bottom:** A hollow back lacks strength and usually indicates old age.

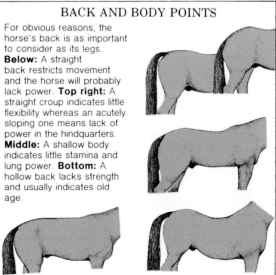

Types and Breeds of Horse

JUST AS THEIR ARE COUNTLESS different breeds of cats and dogs, so there are many different breeds and types of horses. In fact, there are more than 200 different breeds of horses and ponies in existence throughout the world. Many of these are indigenous to a particular country or area and have lived and bred there for countless generations. Over the years, they have changed little in physical appearance, for the characteristics best suited to their life style and survival were inherently established long in the past. These, therefore, have continued to predominate in successive generations.

An excellent example of the indigenous breeds are the nine different native ponies living in various parts of the United Kingdom, from the northernmost islands of Scotland to the southern counties of Devon and Somerset. Known collectively as the Mountain and Moorland breeds, some of them have lived in their particular region since prehistoric times. Other countries have similar breeds that have also inhabited their homelands for centuries. Striking examples are the hardworking little Icelandic ponies, first taken to that country over a thousand years ago by Norwegian invaders, and the pretty grey Camargue ponies. These live in the Rhône delta region of southern France and are almost as wild today as they were in the past.

The Arab

One of the most beautiful and important of all native breeds is the Arabian horse. This magnificent animal, considered by many riders to be the most exquisite of all horses, has lived in the deserts of Arabia for thousands of years; in fact, its origins are completely lost in antiquity and surrounded by romantic fable.

Nowadays, the Arabian is bred in almost all horse-loving countries of the world. The dif-

Exmoor

Iceland

Przewalski's

Pictured are some of the native ponies found around the world. **Left:** a small herd of Camargue ponies which have lived on the watery marshes of the Rhône delta in southern France, reputedly since prehistoric times. They are usually born black, and turn the characteristic grey as they get older. The strong, little Fjord pony is a native of Norway and is still used to assist farmers in remote, mountainous districts. It is generally a dun colour, with black legs, mane, tail and dorsal stripe. Its mane has a proliferation of grey hairs and stands erect and brushlike along its thick, crested neck. The Icelandic pony is another put to daily work by many of the inhabitants of this island. It is renowned as being extraordinarily hardworking and friendly and well able to survive the inhospitable characteristics of its homeland. Przewalski's horse is one of the oldest of all breeds of horse or pony and many people believe it to be one and the same as *equus caballus* – the prehistoric horse from which all others are said to descend. Few are left today, particularly in the wild, but those that there are, wander wild in the desert areas of Mongolia. The Welsh Mountain and Exmoor ponies are two of the oldest of the native breeds of Great Britain. Both have the usual characteristics of surefootedness, hardiness, and stamina and an ability to survive in a harsh environment. Both make excellent riding ponies for children.

Welsh   Fjord

ferent qualities that have emerged to aid survival in such widely different environmental conditions have resulted in there being a number of different types of Arabians, each of which displays some exclusive characteristics. For more than any other horse, the Arabian has been responsible for influencing and helping to create the many 'new' breeds of horse that are now firmly established in the horse world.

Selective breeding

These 'new' breeds – new is a relative term for many have existed for several hundred years – are those that have been produced and developed by man as a result of careful selective breeding. They were produced to fulfil a need, to answer a dictate of fashion or to satisfy a new whim or desire by some group or community. The superb riding horses found in the United States of America and those produced in most of the countries of Europe are all fine examples of breeds developed by man over the years.

The most famous of all created breeds is without question the Thoroughbred, which was developed in England in the late 17th century using three Arabian stallions as the foundation stock. By this time, the racing of horses, which had previously been frowned upon as the 'pastime of the devil' had become, instead, the 'sport of kings' and therefore respectable.

The Thoroughbred was developed solely to produce a horse of great speed over a comparatively short distance. Over any long distance, the Thoroughbred is still no match for its

Below: The Thoroughbred is the most famous of all breeds produced by man through careful and selective breeding. It has been in existence since the end of the eighteenth century and three Arabian stallions were used as the founding stock. **Right:** The Arabian is among the most beautiful of all horses and has bred in the deserts of Arabia for countless generations. Now bred in almost all horse-loving countries of the world, there are countless different types of the breed.

ancestor, the Arabian, which combines a fair turn of speed with considerably greater powers of endurance and stamina than those possessed by its descendant.

The world of the cross-breed

Most of the horses used all over the world for general riding – and many seen in competitive fields, too – are cross-breeds – that is, the offspring of two horses, one of which may be a pure breed or both of which may be cross-breeds themselves. The lack of pure blood in their veins generally means that cross-breeds are less expensive to buy than pure-bred horses; however, this does not detract from their performance as riding horses or from their temperament and disposition. Indeed, many cross-breeds have more equable characters and are considerably less highly strung than their pedigree relatives.

Horse types

In addition to the specific breeds and countless cross-breeds of horse, there are various recognized horse 'types'. In most cases, the type refers to the work for which the animal has been bred and for which it is the most suited.

One of the best known types of horse is the hunter, so-called because it possesses special characteristics that suit it for riding to hounds. Several different types of hunters are now recognized, this having come about as the characteristics required in a horse wanted for hunting in one part of the country became quite different from those that would be suitable elsewhere. For example, the strong, heavily built horse required by a large man riding heavy ground fenced into small fields would be of little use to the lightweight lady hunting across fast, wide-open grassland where there are few fenced boundaries. Various types of hunters have thus emerged – the main categories being lightweight, middleweight and heavyweight. All hunters, though, must possess the basic qualities of stamina, boldness and courage as well as being able to jump the obstacles they are likely to encounter during a day's hunting. They should also be resourceful or intelligent enough to cope with, or extricate themselves from, the unforseeable predicaments that can occur.

Show horses

As a result of the different types of hunter required, the 'show hunter' has come into existence. The show hunter is also categorized into different types. It displays the qualities that

Opposite: The spectacular Tennessee Walking Horse is particularly noted for its unusual 'running walk'. This is not in fact a natural pace, but is inbred and foals are said to perform it naturally. **Above:** The Morgan is one of the smallest breeds to come from the US and was bred at the beginning of the eighteenth century. Nowadays the breed is extremely popular among all members of the riding fraternity. **Below:** The Quarter horse was originally the work horse of the US, bred by the early settlers to help them cultivate and work their new homeland. **Bottom:** The spotted Appaloosa was established as a breed by the Nez Perce Indians who inhabited central Idaho and eastern Washington. The characteristic spotted coat appears in five basic patterns.

would be sought in any hunter, but it will probably never be ridden to hounds, or at least, not as long as its showing career continues. The reason for this is that one tiny little blemish – the result, perhaps, of a knock against an obstacle out hunting, or a tear from a vicious thorn bush that leaves the slightest trace of a scar – will immediately end its career in the show ring. Its value on the market would therefore drop considerably, which makes it understandable that few owners of these animals are prepared to take such a foolhardy risk.

Hacks and the pleasure horse
Another type of horse which exists almost solely as a show horse is the hack. Nowadays this is essentially a lady's horse, but the term is derived from the medieval French word *haquenai*, which literally meant riding horse and referred to horses of very lowly stature. Gradually, two types of hack evolved. The first was the park hack, which was the riding horse mainly used by ladies (but also by gentlemen to some degree) when going for a recreational ride or 'hack' through the grounds of their estate or the public parks of the cities and towns in which they lived. The second was known as the covert hack, which was the horse a man would ride to the meet of the hounds while his hunter (the more important animal that was to carry him through the day's sport) was taken along at a more leisurely pace by a groom.

It is from the park hack that the hack of today's show ring has evolved. Recreational

Opposite: No one breed of horse always makes an eventer. Besides great jumping ability, they must show boldness, speed, and stamina.

Above: Equally, many types of horse will be seen in the show jumping ring. Even more than the eventer, this horse must be a top-class athlete.

riding, after all, used to be the prerogative of the wealthy and the aristocracy, the lower orders using their horses in more practical ways to help them in their daily work. Thus, when riding through a park, the riders expected to be admired and they would choose their horses accordingly. Besides being attractive in appearance and conformation, the hack had to have graceful movement and flowing paces, as well as – and perhaps even more importantly – perfect manners, which would ensure it obeyed its rider's commands and did not suddenly indulge in a display of high spirits which unseat the rider. It is these qualities of impeccable manners and beautiful appearance that abound in the show hacks of today.

However, the word hack can actually be applied to any riding horse that is used for recreational riding – the term 'to go for a hack' meaning to go for a ride. But, though it still strictly applies to any riding horse, the term has become more commonly associated with the show animal. In the same way, the United States has its pleasure horse, for which classes are held at most shows. The term refers to almost any horse that is suitable for recreational riding as practised by its particular rider. Although many different types or cross-breeds of horse, as well as some specific breeds, will be

127

Above: Show horses in the US often wear elaborate tack and harnesses with riders dressed similarly. **Below:** Show ponies are not a specific breed of pony but are recognized as a type. Perfect in conformation and appearance, they must have faultless action and manners. **Right:** Always ridden by ladies, the hacks are usually Thoroughbreds and, like show ponies, must have superb manners and appearance.

found in the pleasure classes in American horse shows, they all have to conform to the various standards laid down in the specifications of that particular class.

The show pony
Another type of horse, or more particularly pony, bred almost solely for the show ring is the show pony. This elegant little animal is certainly not classified as a breed, but it is probably mainly produced by crossing small Thoroughbreds with extremely good quality (in terms of appearance and conformation) cross-bred or native ponies. The term show pony is used to describe any pony possessing a sufficiently faultless appearance, together with superb manners, to enable it to compete against others in the show ring. Movement and overall performance will also be taken into account by the judges as they make their decision.

Cobs
The cob is another type of horse. Although most major horse shows include classes for cobs, the animal is more generally considered to be a recreational riding horse, particularly suitable for those who want a calm, willing, but rather placid, mount. The cob is characterized by its stocky limbs and sturdy muscular appearance. It is usually smaller more compact and thick-set than a hunter, even when compared proportionally to the strong build of a heavyweight hunter. In the not-so-distant past, horses of a cob type were often used as harness horses; indeed, with the current revival in popularity of driving as a sport, they are again coming into their own in this field.

There is one cob – the Welsh cob – that is also an established breed. Like its relative the Welsh Mountain pony, it is a native of the hills of Wales and is said to be descended from horses that were the result of the inter-breeding of Spanish horses with the smaller native ponies. Whether this is historically accurate or not, the Welsh cob has continued to reproduce as a breed in this part of the UK for many hundreds of years. Another type of cob emanates from Ireland, where it, too, has been breeding for centuries. Called the Irish cob, it is not usually afforded the same breed status as the Welsh cob. Other cobs or cob types are usually the result of crossing a hunter with a small, well-built horse that may have some heavy horse blood in its ancestry. The riding cob, however, while strong and sturdy retains the pony characteristics of small ears, flowing mane and tail.

Show jumpers and eventers
The tremendous increase in popularity and participation in the competitive fields of show jumping and eventing have resulted in the emergence of types of horses known as show jumpers and eventers. These are not only not recognized breeds, but are also probably not even as uniform in appearance as the other types of horse so far discussed. In both cases, the term refers more to the animal's ability than its conformation or appearance.

More than any other type of horse, the show jumper has to be an athlete of outstanding talent, with the ability to jump large fences and willing to do so in cold blood – without the incentive produced, for example, by the thrill of the chase in the hunting field. A show-jumper must also be nimble and agile, particularly if jumping in an indoor competition where the smallness of the arena calls for sharp turns often to be executed at speed. Horses that do well in indoor competitions are generally those with a fairly calm temperament, not being easily upset by the bright lights and the often tense, electric atmosphere. Even a superficial look at the horses entered for an important show jumping competition will immediately indicate that horses of widely differing shapes, sizes and builds seem to make good show jumpers, in the same way that there is no such thing as a typical top-class athlete. The features that all show jumpers have in common, however, are very strong hindquarters and hocks, for the thrust and power needed to propel them upwards over the jump comes from these areas.

The eventer is perhaps the boldest, most courageous and most versatile horse of all, but, once more, successful eventers come in all manner of shapes and sizes. The three main aspects of eventing – dressage, cross-country jumping and show jumping – call between them for a horse with fluid paces and great precision of movement, considerable speed and stamina and a highly developed jumping ability. Above all, they demand complete obedience from the horse, who must constantly listen and instantly respond to his rider's commands. In general terms, the eventer – is probably well-bred – that is, with a fair amount of Thoroughbred blood in its veins, probably mixed with that of a hunter. It is these two types of horse that, between them, possess most of the qualities necessary in a top-class eventer – the hunter instinct providing aggressiveness and courage, and the Thoroughbred characteristics giving refinement, obedience, and poise.

Care at Grass

KEEPING A HORSE AT GRASS for all or part of the year is less expensive and less time-consuming than keeping him stabled. Not all horses are sufficiently hardy to live out throughout the year, however, and such animals therefore have to be stabled in the colder months – at least at night. Others that are required to work hard at certain times of the year – during the hunting season, for instance – may be turned out in the field for a well-earned rest at the end of their work period.

The same sort of grazing and facilities must be provided regardless of whether a horse is kept out at grass for just some months in the year, or whether it is out all the time.

How big the field should be depends in part on the quality of the grazing; in general terms, however, a horse needs at least 0.8 hectares (2 acres) of grass to sustain him for six months. While horses do not need the lush green grass necessary for fattening cattle, they are much fussier eaters and will eat nothing at all rather than touch grass they find sour or unappetizing. Thus, a field choked with weeds and nettles is unsuitable for grazing horses, unless it is treated

to turn it into suitable pasture. Areas where weeds are rife must be ploughed and reseeded with suitable grass seed. Grasses of the Fescue and Meadow types are generally popular with horses, as are the Rye varieties. These, however, tend to do well only on heavy ground.

The field must also be checked to ensure it contains no poisonous plants (see page 134), and also to ensure that it is not littered with harmful objects, such as discarded bottles and cans, polythene bags or similar debris. Check regularly for these items, particularly in the summer months if picnickers use the field.

Fences should be solid and secure. The material chosen must be able to withstand a horse leaning or rubbing against it without giving way or weakening appreciably. The best type of fencing is wooden post and rails, but it is also the most expensive. Strands of wire – never barbed wire – stretched taut between wooden posts are an acceptable alternative, providing the lowest strand is high enough for the horse not to get his foot caught over it if he tries to stretch through to reach the grass outside. Other types of fencing, such as stone walls or

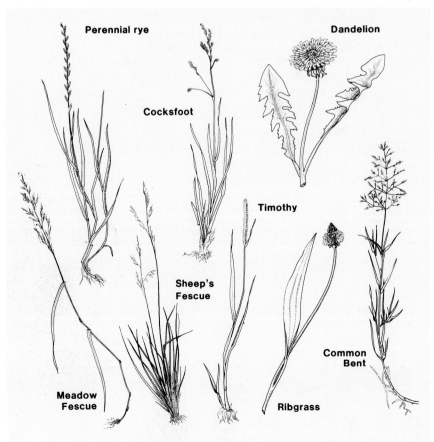

Perennial rye

Cocksfoot

Dandelion

Timothy

Sheep's Fescue

Common Bent

Meadow Fescue

Ribgrass

While keeping your horse at grass may prove to require less effort on your part, statistics have shown that more accidents are likely to occur with horses left at grass than those that are stabled. The fences should be solid, secure, and kick- and jump-proof. The field should be checked at regular intervals for both poisonous plants, which might be sprouting and dangerous, and items like broken glass or plastic bags. A horse kept at grass can be in an ideal situation to satisfy his rather choosy appetite if the field is well-maintained and cared for. **Left:** Some of the more common types of grasses and weeds which you horse will enjoy, including perennial rye grass, Timothy and Cocksfoot, both of which are highly nutritious and appetizing. Dandelion and ribgrass, although weeds, have a high mineral content. Water is also an essential item and if you are not lucky enough to have a running stream in your field, it should be supplied in water troughs. If there are any stagnant ponds or pools in the field they should be fenced off.

FIELD FITTINGS

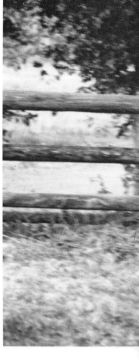

Left: Horses that live out at grass should always be provided with some shelter in the field. The most satisfactory type is a solid wooden construction that is completely open on one side, so the horse can easily wander in and out; the side should not face north or in the direction of any strong prevailing winds. Although a horse may use this shelter to escape cold or wet weather, it is more often used as a sanctity from troublesome summer flies. **Below:** Constant, clean water is another essential for grass-kept horses. This is best provided in a solid, galvanized, iron trough, which is linked to the main water supply by a ballcock system. When the water looks remotely cloudy or the tank slimy, the tank should be emptied and scrubbed out. Do not use any kind of detergent when doing this.

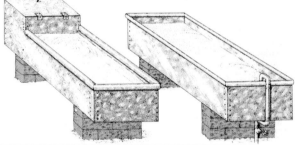

hedges, are perfectly acceptable, so long as they are kept in good repair and do not harbour any poisonous plants. Whatever type of fencing is chosen, it must be checked regularly to make sure it is safe and is showing no signs of weakness. If it is allowed to deteriorate, a horse will find the weak spots in no time at all and will soon push his way to freedom. Any damage he does to other people's property is his owner's responsibility; the owner can also be fined if the horse is found straying on the road.

Gates, too, must be solid and should operate efficiently. This means that any gate should open wide and shut securely without having to be tied up with bits of string or loops of wire. Wooden or tubular steel gates are the best; they should be wide enough for a horse and rider to go through side-by-side without either one of them banging against the gate post. Slip rails which slide through strong metal hoops are satisfactory, although not generally as convenient as a gate.

The importance of water

Fresh water must be constantly available, even if the horse is turned out only for part of the day. Though natural streams are probably the best and easiest way of providing this, the ground leading to them will often get very churned up and muddy. It is more usual to provide water by linking the field to a mains supply and having this piped into a trough. The best type of trough is one that is operated by a ballcock, so it fills automatically as the water level is lowered. Keep the ballcock mechanism enclosed so the horse cannot reach it with his mouth; if he can, he will play with it until it goes wrong. The trough should not have sharp

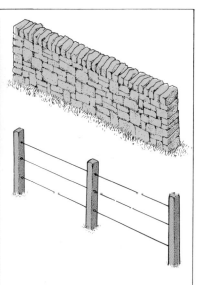

Left and above: Fencing around any field where livestock are grazing must be strong and solid. Being safe and long-lasting, wooden post and rails are the most satisfactory for horses, but are very expensive to install. Walls and strands of wire stretched between wooden posts are both satisfactory alternatives, but both should be regularly checked to ensure there are no holes or weak spots. **Left:** The gate is another important feature of the field. It should be strong and secure, and swing easily to and fro. It should fasten securely, without having to be tied up with pieces of string or loops of wire.

edges which could injure the horse's knees; if you have to use such a container – an old bath, for instance – box in the sides, so the sharp edges are enclosed. Check the water frequently to make sure the ballcock is operating correctly. When green slime begins to form around the edges of the tank, clean out the trough by emptying it and scrubbing it, using plain water, before refilling it.

Types of shelter

Grass-kept horses need to be provided with some type of shelter to protect them from cold winds and driving rain in winter and from flies in the summer. The best type is a three-sided shed, the open side of which should ideally be positioned opposite a line of trees or tall hedge. It should not face north. A wooden or brick shelter is ideal; if possible, the floor should be of hard material, such as roughened concrete. If this is extended to the area immediately outside the shed, it helps to prevent the ground from getting too muddy in wet weather.

The shelter should be big enough for a horse to turn around in and lie down in comfort. If two horses are turned out together, the shelter should be big enough to accommodate both of them, the opening being made wide enough to prevent them colliding. Put some straw on the floor of the shelter so a horse can use it to lie down and rest if he so desires. Do not be surprised if, in the summer, the shelter is mainly used as a refuge from flies.

Poisonous plants

Any field intended for grazing horses must be thoroughly checked over for poisonous plants. Those most frequently found are Yew, Deadly

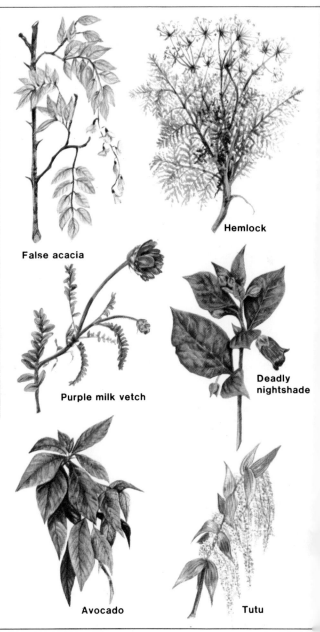

False acacia

Hemlock

Purple milk vetch

Deadly nightshade

Avocado

Tutu

Any field in which you intend to let your horse roam about should be very well checked, and frequently, for both man-made and natural objects which could do the horse damage. The more obvious dangers include broken glass, tin cans and litter. Plastic bags are for some reason attractive to horses and if swallowed could lead to suffocation and death. Poisonous plants in a field can make your horse extremely ill or even kill him. Every owner should be able to recognize on sight most, if not all, of the common types and the field should be checked frequently for new growth. Any toxic plants that are found should be completely removed as if left to die on their own they remain toxic and will simply regrow. As well, all hay and bedding should be checked and any harmful plants removed. Fortunately, most horses are not naturally attracted to the more toxic plants, however, some, like deadly nightshade will be eaten if the horse is very hungry. Yew and privet are more common and a horse will indulge if they are available to him.

Nightshade, Hemlock, Ragwort, Laburnum and Foxgloves. Privet and Laurel are also considered to be poisonous, although some horses can eat them and suffer no problems.

Trees such as Yew and Laburnum should be fenced off, so a horse cannot reach their branches. Horses seem to find dying Yew branches particularly appetizing. These are deadly. Have other poisonous plants pulled out by the roots, removed from the field and burned. Never leave them to wither and die in the field; their potency remains.

If you suspect your horse has eaten something poisonous, bring him into the stable, or lead him into the field shelter, and send for the vet immediately. Symptoms of this are obvious pain and discomfort, accompanied by the horse looking round or jabbing at his stomach with his mouth. He may also dribble streams of saliva or appear feverish.

Looking after and preserving grazing
Good grazing land is hard to come by so, having found some, it is worthwhile keeping it in good

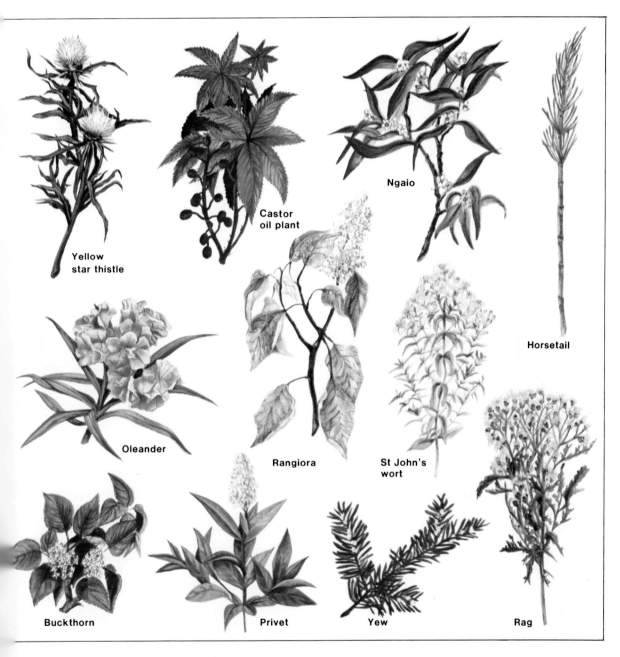

Yellow
star thistle

Castor
oil plant

Ngaio

Horsetail

Oleander

Rangiora

St John's
wort

Buckthorn

Privet

Yew

Rag

condition. The first essential is that it shall be rested for part of the year; if it is continuously grazed, it will become what is known as horse-sick. This means the grass is coarse and unappetizing and is also likely to harbour large numbers of the worms that live parasitically in horses.

The new grass begins to grow in the spring; it is at its richest and best in early summer. During this period, the field should be rested, both to give the new grass an opportunity to come through and to prevent the horse over-indulging himself on the lush pasture, which can lead to various disorders and obesity. If a horse is given the free run of a large area of good grazing, he will pick only at the best grass, trampling over much that he would find perfectly acceptable if his rations were slightly less prolific. The trampled grass then becomes inedible and the resulting wastage is immense.

If the field is large enough to divide into two, so that each half can be rested in turn, this can be easily and effectively done with electric fencing. A horse soon understands what will

135

Putting your horse out to grass requires just as much attention as stabling him. **Above:** This picture illustrates very poor conditions for a horse at grass. Letting your horse wander through muddy fields is dangerous as he could easily slip and a field with poor drainage is also not going to provide very much food. **Right:** One of the absolute requirements of keeping your horse at grass is that the field be cleared daily of any droppings; if these are not removed, vermin may develop and infect the horse.

happen if he comes into contact with the ticking wire and will keep away from it. If the field is not large enough for this, then an alternative field must be found. Remember if a field is divided into two, you must make sure that the horse still has access to fresh water and is provided with some form of shelter in whichever half he is grazing.

Day-to-day maintenance

Try to rest the field or fields alternately during the late spring and the early summer. This is the period of maximum growth. If the growth

While a horse at grass is able to take advantage of all the assets of living out in the open including a constant and healthy source of food, almost unlimited exercise space, companionship, and entertainment – he should not just be left to the elements or to fend on his own. **Left:** These horses are happily eating where they feel most at home, but have been carefully covered with New Zealand rugs to protect them from the cold. In summer it is wise to cover your horse with a light rug or sheet to protect him from flies and direct sun.

of grass during this time proves to be particularly prolific, you can have it cut to make hay to go towards providing winter fodder. The grass ceases to grow in mid-autumn; there is then no more growth until the following spring.

As mentioned briefly earlier, horses are notoriously fussy eaters. Besides shunning any grass they feel is not up to standard, they will also not eat the areas which they have soiled with urine or dung. In one way this is good, as it is these areas which generally harbour the most worms, but much good grazing can also be lost. It helps considerably if you go around the

field each day with a wheelbarrow and spade, removing the droppings. If this is impractical to do for any reason, spread them out more evenly by raking them over the ground at least once a week.

Pasture also benefits from being grazed by cattle every now and again. They will graze the whole field evenly, happily eating grass which a horse has rejected as inedible. Alternatively, the patches of long, coarse grass that are the inevitable result of horse grazing should be cut down to allow new growth to emerge. Harrowing and rolling the land also helps to give even and

137

improved growth, while applications of various recommended top dressings, such as lime, will help, too. If weeds begin to appear in quantity, they should be treated with weedkiller rather than left to multiply and stifle the grass, but obviously this must be done when the horse is not grazing the field. Alternatively, weeds can be cut down when the long, rough grass is being cut.

Establishing a routine

If you are turning your horse out for a rest, make the change-over gradual. For a week or two, turn him out in the field by day and bring him back into the stable by night, or vice versa. Particularly if it is springtime, this pattern will prevent him from gorging himself to excess on rich grass, which, after a winter of corn feed, could upset his digestive system considerably. Any change in a horse's diet should be gradual rather than effected overnight. The shoes can be removed, too, as he will be doing no work, but the farrier should still look at the feet at least once a month, to cut back excess horn and thus prevent the hoofs beginning to split. In order to avoid this, it is worth investigating the possibility of having the horse shod with special shoes known as 'grass tips' (see page 192).

Try not to choose the height of the summer to give a hard-working horse a rest. If it is very hot, the ground is not only likely to be hard and dusty and the grazing minimal, but the horse is also likely to be plagued by flies. Far from having a rest, horses can be driven to a frenzy by flies and they tend to lose condition by endlessly wandering around the field in a vain attempt to escape them. In such cases, it is far kinder to turn a horse out at night and

Most horses appreciate some company while in the field. This could be another horse and, as the picture on the right illustrates, like does not have to be turned out with like! Indeed a horse and donkey will soom become inseparable friends if they share a field, much to the chagrin of those around who have to listen to the wailings of a bereaved donkey whenever the horse goes out. If other horses or a donkey can not be found, some farmers will allow a horse to be turned out with cattle. This will depend on the type of horse and whether he is likely to excite the cattle to riot or turn them into a stampeding herd.

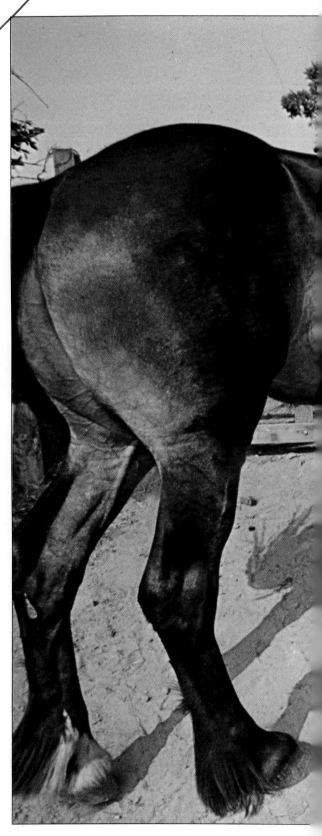

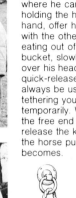

Catching a horse at grass requires patience, some food, and a gentle voice. Approach your horse quietly or stand where he can see you. While holding the headcollar in one hand, offer him some food with the other. Once he is eating out of your hand or a bucket, slowly slip the collar over his head. **Below:** These quick-release knots should always be used when tethering your horse even if temporarily. While a pull on the free end will immediately release the knot, the harder the horse pulls, the tighter it becomes.

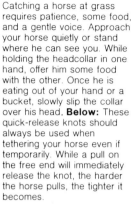

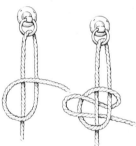

bring him into a stable, or to shut him into the field shelter during the day when the flies are at their most active.

Providing companionship

Horses may be turned out to grass for a number of reasons. They may be kept there permanently all the year because this is the most convenient or practical way for the owner to look after his horse. Or they may be turned out to grass to rest after a period of heavy work, such as hunting through the winter or competing in shows and three-day events during the spring and summer. Either way, they will appreciate companionship; horses are gregarious animals and tend to get bored and lonely on their own. Company of their own kind – or, failing that, a donkey – will help them to pass the time and can help to stop them seeking means of an escape to the outside world.

The combined system

Many people favour keeping their horse partly out at grass and partly stabled. In such a system, technically known as 'combined', a horse would normally be brought into the stable by night and allowed to wander in the field during the day wearing a protective New Zealand rug in winter. In the summer, this practice is usually reversed, so the horse is stabled during the day and turned out at night. This

helps to overcome the fly problem explained above and also reduces the likelihood of him over-gorging on summer grass, since horses eat much less during the hours of darkness than they do during the daylight hours.

The system involves the owner in more work than if a horse is kept permanently out at grass, but there are advantages that compensate for this. In summer, the horse is ready to hand in the stable during the day when you want to ride, but equally you do not have to ride as much as you would if he was stabled, because he will exercise himself when turned out in the night. Turning a horse out by day in the winter involves the owner in considerably less work than if the horse is stabled all the time and yet allows him to keep the horse fitter and more respectable in appearance than if he was turned out by both day and night.

Catching a horse

All horses at grass should be caught up once a day, even if they are not going to be ridden. Not only does this provide an opportunity to check them over to make sure they have not hurt themselves in any way; it also accustoms them or keeps them accustomed, to being handled. If a horse is only caught up when he is to be ridden, he will soon make sure he does not have to work by simply not allowing his rider to catch him.

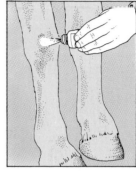

A habit you should get into is checking your horse for injuries. This is especially important if your horse is at grass as you won't be able to watch him. Whether done while he is still in the field, or in the stable, a thorough check should be made of his entire body, especially the legs and hooves as these are the most prone to cuts, sprains and infection. Having tethered the horse, run your hands up and down each of the legs, feeling for any swelling and watching to see if he reacts with pain. **Above:** If a minor injury is found, it should first be thoroughly washed with water and then sprayed or wiped with antiseptic. Never let a cut go unattended.

Particularly if they are treated properly and kindly, most horses present no problem to catch, but a few do remain shy and difficult to catch throughout their lives. The correct way to catch a horse turned out in a field is to walk straight up to him quietly but directly, perhaps talking to him softly to reassure him. Take a headcollar and some tasty titbit with you to entice him towards you. As he takes the food from you, slip the rope of the headcollar round his neck so you have hold of him and then put on the headcollar. Lead him either to the field shelter and tie him up or out of the field to the stable, making sure any companions do not escape through the gate. If you know a particular horse is difficult to catch, turn him out wearing a headcollar and place the titbit – a handful of pony nuts, say – in a bucket, so you can rattle it gently to attract his attention. This is usually successful even for the most stubborn of horses.

Checking for injury

The purpose of checking a horse over for injury is obvious. You must make sure the horse has not cut, scratched or bruised himself and check

Discharge from eyes and nostrils: This usually indicates a cough or cold.

Thin neck: As with protruding ribs, could indicate underfeeding and generally diminishing health.

A healthy and happy horse will always perform and respond better than one that has been left alone and not properly cared for. It will carry its head high, ears alert and eyes bright and attentive to its surroundings. Because a horse which you own, as with any pet, is totally dependent on you to recognize any signs of illness or injury, you should be very familiar with the different symptoms and always be on the look-out for them. If your horse is acting unusually or unnaturally and you are in doubt, do not hesitate to call your vet.

Coat: If in poor condition, this means the horse's general state or health is poor or the saddle is not fitting correctly.

Ribs: If protruding, the horse is either being underfed or suffering from a digestive ailment.

Tail: If tucked in, indicates that the horse is not feeling well. Call a vet.

Front legs: Check these often for obvious injury or swelling. Laminitis is particularly important to catch immediately.

Hind legs: If the horse is resting on one of these, there is an injury to the opposite leg.

that he appears to be in general good health. Run your hand over his coat to feel for lumps and bumps, paying particular attention to his legs. Bruises will manifest themselves by obviously tender or hot areas, or by swellings. Pick out each foot in turn to make sure no stones have lodged in the hoof, or that the sole of the hoof has not been bruised or pricked by stepping on something sharp.

Any small cuts you may find will generally need very little treatment. Wash them well, preferably using running water from a hose, to clean them and then check the extent of the injury. Dress them with antibiotic powder, which you can get from your vet – a supply of which should always be kept handy.

If a horse has sustained a more serious wound – from some broken glass someone has tossed into the field, for instance – do not hesitate to call the vet. Proper medical attention in such instances not only speeds recovery, but it often reduces the possibility of the horse being marked by an unsightly scar later.

Good and bad health
To know if your horse is feeling off colour or under the weather for any reason, you must first be able to recognize the signs that tell you whether he is in good health. These are obvious: the horse looks and appears alert, comfortable and happy; his coat – although possibly quite long and maybe muddy, is nevertheless healthy-looking, appearing sleek, rather than coming out in patches; his eyes should look bright and clear and his ears should prick backwards and forwards, indicating he is alert and taking notice of his surroundings. He should not be so thin that his ribs stick out through his coat, or so fat that movement is a strain. When at rest, he should stand evenly on all his feet, perhaps resting a hind leg (but never a foreleg).

An unhealthy horse contravenes some or all of these points. He may appear dull and listless, standing miserably in a corner of the field, his head dropping, his ears back and still, and his body looking 'tucked up'. His eyes may be dull, the lining around them coloured a livid red instead of a more moderate pink, and there could well be some discharge from the nostrils. The coat will look dull and the horse may be sweating and–or shivering.

Diagnosing what is wrong with a horse that is clearly unwell is usually a job for the experts. If it seems obvious that something is amiss, it is always wisest to call a vet. Bring the horse into the shelter or stable and keep him quiet and

warm until the vet arrives to help.

A horse out at grass is leading a more natural and healthy life than one in the stable, and may well suffer less from minor diseases and ailments as a result. Nevertheless, he is still at risk and there are bound to be times when he is not one hundred per cent fit and well.

Coughs, colds and colic
Coughs and colds can infect both stabled and grass-kept horses. The symptoms are exactly the same as those in humans suffering from the same complaints. The animal will sneeze, discharge will come from the nose and he may have runny eyes. He will be miserable, his coat will appear dull and he may be feverish. Do not ride him; and seek advice about treatment at once from the vet. He may advise bringing him into the stable, at least at night; however, a horse with a cough is better kept out in the fresh air than confined in a stable.

Colic is another complaint which can attack both grass-kept and stabled horses. This is a form of severe indigestion, resulting in a tummy ache which varies in its intensity and which can be caused for a variety of reasons. Among these are over-feeding; eating bad food – such as any which is old or musty; exercising the horse immediately after a heavy feed; watering after a heavy feed; and excessive amounts of worms in the gut. A horse with colic appears uneasy, fidgeting from foot to foot, swishing his tail and perhaps sweating. He may bite at his belly with his mouth or kick it with a hindfoot. The worst thing that can happen is if he succeeds in getting down to roll. This must be stopped instantly, as he could roll so violently as to knot his intestine so severely that it proves fatal. Try to keep a horse with colic warm and moving about *very gently*, while getting someone else, if possible, to call the vet. If you are on your own, tie the horse on a short rope while you telephone the vet yourself.

Other common illnesses
If greedy horses are allowed to over-gorge themselves on lush summer grass, they run the risk of contracting the disease laminitis. In fact, there are other causes of this disease, too; horses with flat feet are more prone to contracting it than others, while it can occur if an unfit horse is made to do a lot of strenuous work on hard ground. Laminitis is, in effect, a fever in the feet, in which the area immediately behind the wall of the hoof becomes infected. The feet become very hot and, as evidenced by the

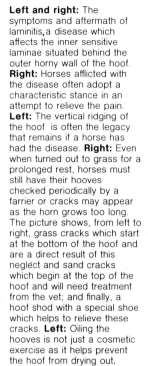

Left and right: The symptoms and aftermath of laminitis, a disease which affects the inner sensitive laminae situated behind the outer horny wall of the hoof. **Right:** Horses afflicted with the disease often adopt a characteristic stance in an attempt to relieve the pain. **Left:** The vertical ridging of the hoof is often the legacy that remains if a horse has had the disease. **Right:** Even when turned out to grass for a prolonged rest, horses must still have their hooves checked periodically by a farrier or cracks may appear as the horn grows too long. The picture shows, from left to right, grass cracks which start at the bottom of the hoof and are a direct result of this neglect and sand cracks which begin at the top of the hoof and will need treatment from the vet; and finally, a hoof shod with a special shoe which helps to relieve these cracks. **Left:** Oiling the hooves is not just a cosmetic exercise as it helps prevent the hoof from drying out.

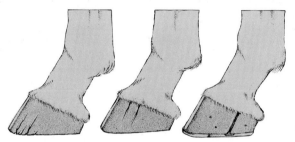

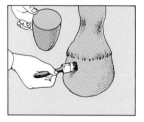

animal's reluctance to move and obvious suffering, they are extremely painful. Laminitis is certainly a case for the vet, who will recommend that the animal's shoes be removed and that cold poultices are applied to the feet to try to reduce the heat. Affected horses should be shut away from the summer grass for part of the day, but make sure they are in a loose box where there is plenty of room for them to move. The condition will be heightened, if they are forced to stand still for hours on end.

Grass-kept horses are perhaps more likely to suffer from insect bites and stings than their stabled counterparts. These usually show as large soft lumps, the swelling of which generally reduces after a few hours. If a bite or sting is bothering the horse, or is on his face, bathing it very gently with cold water may help to bring relief and reduce swelling

All horses suffer from girth or saddle galls. These more frequently occur in grass-kept horses which are out of condition because they have not been ridden for a while. Horses brought from grass after a spell of rest are likely candidates for saddle sores, unless considerable care is taken as riding recommences. Saddle and harness sores can occur anywhere on the horse's back or face touched by saddlery; girth galls are caused by girths that either pinch or rub the soft skin behind the elbow. A horse

with saddle sores of any type cannot be ridden until they have healed. As they are also signs of bad horsemastership – ill-fitting saddlery, bad riding or lack of consideration when riding – they are clearly best avoided.

If the skin has broken, the gall or sore should be treated like an open wound. Bathe it with salt and water and dab it with methylated spirit when it has healed. This helps to harden it.

Protective medicine

Worms are another constant source of trouble. All horses, whether they are kept stabled or at grass, suffer from worms that live parasitically in the gut. Although the damage they do is minimal, provided that they are only present in small quantities, they should always be kept under control. The way to do this is to give regular doses of anti-worm preparations – a procedure known as 'worming'. Various types of worm preparations are available; they include powders to be mixed in with the feed and liquids given by tube straight into the stomach through a syringe inserted into the side of the mouth. Always consult a vet before worming to see which preparation he recommends. New ones are constantly appearing on the market and it pays not to use the same type each time as otherwise the worms will build up an immunity to it and be unaffected.

Left: If a horse has displayed any of the symptons of colic it should not be allowed to lie down and roll as this could lead to fatal twisting of the gut. **Above:** Coughing is one of the most common of all ailments to affect a horse and there are myriad causes. Stop all but the lightest work and seek advice from your vet.

Grass-kept horses are more susceptible to worms than stabled ones, particularly up to the age of three. Ideally foals and young horses should be wormed monthly to ensure they are properly protected as a permanent disability can otherwise be the result. Statistics show that nine out of ten untreated horses have some permanent disability caused by the presence of worms for long periods of time.

After the age of three, grass-kept horses should be wormed every six weeks in the summer to fit in with the life-cycle of the worm runs over a period of six weeks. Stabled horses will need less frequent doses, but consult your vet about when to worm, and the preparation to use. Read any instructions carefully.

The importance of vaccination
All responsible horse owners should vaccinate their horses to protect them whenever possible against disease. The two main diseases that can be guarded against by vaccination are tetanus and influenza.

Tetanus is a fatal disease caused by infection setting in to a wound. Even a minor injury – one so small it is easy to miss in the daily examination – can lead to tetanus; for this reason, the wisest course of action is to make sure a horse has permanent immunity against the disease. Young horses are generally given a

course of anti-tetanus injections. This consists of an injection at the age of two months, followed by another a month later, and a booster after six months, though the exact timing may vary according to the serum and course of treatment favoured by each individual vet. Thereafter, a horse should have an annual booster, with an additional injection if he cuts himself badly. This must be given within twenty-four hours of contracting the injury. When you buy a horse, find out if he was given the course of vaccination when he was a foal; if not, ask the vet to do so at the time of purchase.

Influenza is the most infectious and contagious of all diseases; if not fatal, it is extremely debilitating. Protect your horse against it by a course of two vaccinations and then a yearly booster.

Supplementary feeding
Grass-kept horses will need supplementary feeding whenever the grass is not rich enough to provide them with sufficient nourishment. This means supplementary feeding must be carried out constantly throughout the winter months; it must also be done whenever the weather is so hot and dry that the grass becomes scorched and bleached.

Hardy horses may survive wintering out at grass with just hay as their supplementary feed.

145

Left: A haynet should always be tied to a ring in the stable or field, never hung over hooks which present a potential danger to a horse. When the haynet has been filled, pull up the drawstring at the top to close the net and then tie is to the ring using a secure, quick-release knot.

There are two types of hay – meadow and seed. The former generally contains a greater mixture of grasses, as it is cut from a normal meadow, while the latter is cut from pastures which were specifically sown for hay. Either kind is perfectly acceptable, providing that the hay itself is of good quality and in good condition. It should smell sweet and fresh, not old and musty; it should not be dusty or full of matted lumps and prickly thistles; and it should never have damp, mouldy patches. The colour will vary slightly according to type and may be a browny-green or golden brown. It should never be yellow or dark brown, both of which indicate that it is of bad quality.

Feeding routine

Horses should have at least two full haynets a day, one given in the morning and the other in the late afternoon. If they consume these avidly, give another one in the middle of the day as well. Most horses will also need some supplementary corn as well; this helps to keep them warm and in good condition. A grass-kept horse that is allowed to lose weight in the autumn or winter is unlikely to put on any flesh again until the following spring. It is the accumulated fat that helps to keep a horse warm and healthy; without it, he is vulnerable to cold weather and possible illness.

The concentrated foodstuffs most commonly given to horses are discussed on pages 163 to 167; of these, the best sort of concentrated food to give to grass-kept horses is probably horse nuts. These can be mixed with dampened bran to discourage a horse from bolting them down too quickly. When feeding oats, let your judgment and common sense guide you as to the amount you feed your horse. Too many oats are liable to make a grass-kept horse doing irregular

Above: Even though your horse may be put out to grass, he should be given at least two full haynets each day and if these are consumed quickly, another can be given in the middle of the day. Avoid putting the hay on the ground as your horse will trample it about.

exercise hot and excited. In general, observation is the key to satisfactory feeding. If your horse starts to lose weight and is obviously very hungry, step up the rations. Unless you are feeding very small amounts, it is best to give the daily rations in two feeds, one in the morning and the other in the late afternoon. Once these times are established, keep to them; a horse will begin to look forward to them and

will not understand if you decide to change the time for any reason.

Grooming at grass

If your horse is kept out at grass all the year, then naturally you will often be catching him to ride him, not just to check that he is healthy and uninjured. The procedure for catching is the same, after which there are certain essential things to do before you can go out for a ride.

In the summer, grass-kept horses should be groomed in the same way as stabled horses (see page 158) to make their coats shine and to generally smarten their appearance. In the winter, however, extensive grooming should be avoided. This would remove the natural grease in the horse's coat, which acts as protection against cold and rainy weather. It renders the coat waterproof, enabling the rain to run over it without penetrating through. If the grease is removed, any rain will soak the horse through to the skin, whereupon he is almost bound to catch cold.

It should be a matter of pride and common sense to ensure that your horse looks reasonably smart when you go out for a ride; there is

147

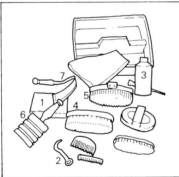

Above: During the summer, a horse at grass should be groomed the same as a stabled one. In winter, the grooming procedure should not be as extensive as the horse needs the natural grease in his coat to protect him from the cold. **Right:** All grooming equipment is shown for stabled and at grass horses, however the only equipment you will need for a horse at grass is: (1) a sponge, (2) a hoof pick, (3) hoof oil, (4) dandy brush, (5) body brush, (6) rubber curry comb, and (7) sweat scraper.

GROOMING AT GRASS

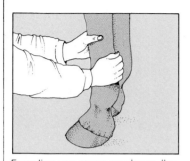

Every time you groom your horse, the entire body should be checked for cuts, swellings and injury. Pay special attention to the legs.

Use the dandy brush to remove mud and sweat from the saddle area, belly and fetlocks.

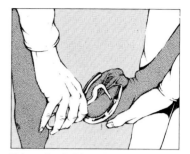

Using a hoof pick and working from frog to toe, remove any stones or debris lodged in the hoof.

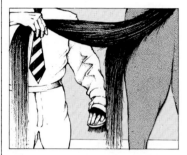

Groom the tail with the body brush starting under the tail with a few hairs at a time.

With a wet, warm sponge, wipe the horses eyes, lips, nostrils and muzzle. Use separate sponge for the dock.

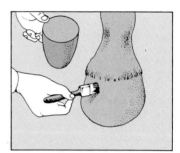

Paint the hooves with hoof oil to protect them from cracks and from drying out.

certainly no excuse for riding out on a horse whose coat is caked with mud.

Preparing a wet horse

If the horse is very wet when you go to get him for a ride, use the sweat scraper on his neck and body. Do not attempt to brush a wet, muddy coat or legs; rub them down instead with handfuls of dry straw, rubbing in the direction the hairs grow. If the back is wet, it must be dried before putting on the saddle. Cover it with straw and throw a large piece of sacking on top. Buckle with a surcingle.

Grooming after exercise

When you return from a ride, always try to walk for the last half-an-hour or so. This gives a hot and sweating horse a chance to cool down. If he is still sweating when you get back to the field, you must dry and cool him before turning him out into the field. Otherwise he is likely to catch cold. Again, this can be done by covering his back with straw and sacking for approximately 30 minutes. Pick out his feet, too, before turning him out in the field, in case he has picked up any stones during the ride.

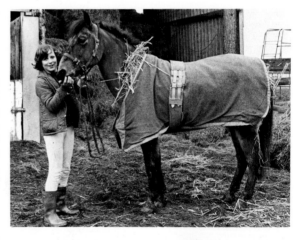

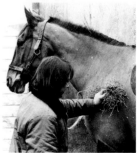

Your horse should be carefully attended to if you come in wet from a ride as if not carefully dried off and covered, he could easily catch cold, especially after strenuous exercise. First wipe the horse down with the sweat scraper to remove any excess water. Taking a bunch of straw, smartly hit him on the large muscles in the direction of the hair and cover him well with a rug.

Care in the Stable

THE ADVANTAGES OF KEEPING A HORSE in a stable have been already briefly mentioned. The horse is generally neater, fitter and more instantly at hand than those kept out at grass. The disadvantages are that the horse does not enjoy as healthy and natural an existence as one living outside, while it involves the owner in considerably more time and expense.

In the past, stabled horses were generally kept in stalls, that is, in a long building divided inside into several three-sided compartments in which they were kept tethered. Nowadays, it is more usual to provide stabling in the form of 'loose boxes'. These are individual, self-contained stables, in which a horse does not have to be tied up. They can be constructed to stand alone, if just one is required; or alternatively, several may be placed next to each other in a row if more than one horse is to be stabled.

Exterior Requirements

Roof Though expensive, tiles or slates are the best roofing materials. It is quite common, however, to use wooden roofs overlaid with waterproof felt, which is quite satisfactory. Avoid corrugated iron, if possible; it is a bad insulator, making the building hot in summer and cold in winter.

Walls Most pre-fabricated loose boxes (which are the most common type of building) are made of wood. They should be lined inside with strong boards to eliminate any danger of a kicking horse knocking his way through the wall itself. Brick or concrete breeze blocks are also suitable materials, particularly if they are lined with boards.

Windows At least one window is essential, as adequate ventilation inside the box is of paramount importance. The best windows are hinged along the lower horizontal edge, so that fresh air is directed upwards into the stable.

Door The doorway must be high enough to ensure that the horse will not bang his head if he lifts it suddenly when standing at the door. It should also be sufficiently wide to allow horse and owner to pass through without one or the other getting stuck. Stable doors open in two sections, the lower half generally being about 105-120cm (3-4ft) high. The top half should be permanently hooked back to the wall to pro-

The advantages of keeping your horse stabled are many: your horse will be generally healthier and happier and in better overall condition than his grass-kept neighbour. On the other hand, a stabled horse will require more of your time and effort, and can prove to be expensive as well. All of these points should be carefully considered before you decide whether to stable your horse or not.

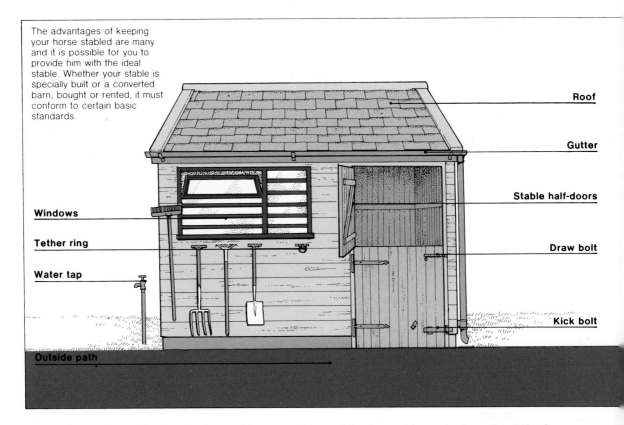

The advantages of keeping your horse stabled are many and it is possible for you to provide him with the ideal stable. Whether your stable is specially built or a converted barn, bought or rented, it must conform to certain basic standards.

Roof

Gutter

Stable half-doors

Draw bolt

Windows

Tether ring

Water tap

Kick bolt

Outside path

vide light and ventilation in the stable as well as relieving boredom for the horse, as he can look out into the yard. The lower door has two bolts or catches on the outside. The top one is a bolt which slides across and turns down, making it horseproof. A swing catch at the bottom of the door which can be operated by the foot is the most convenient type.

Ground by the door The area immediately outside the stable should be solid – roughened concrete and stone slabs are among the suitable surfaces – rather than bare earth, which will soon get churned up and muddy.

Aspect Ideally, the box should face south. Avoid one facing due north, if possible, which will make for a gloomy, miserable and often cold home for the horse.

Tethering ring To tie the horse up outside the stable.

Water tap The closer this is to the stable, the more convenient it is for refilling the horse's water bucket.

Interior Requirements

Electric light Positioned either high up on the wall or hanging from the ceiling, well out of a horse's reach. A protective wire cage should cover the bulb. The light switch should be

outside the stable, out of reach of the horse.

Floor This should be non-slip, non-absorbent, quick to dry, hard wearing and, ideally, slope to give better drainage. Old stables met these requirements by using stable flooring bricks, but these are expensive and hard to obtain today. Concrete is satisfactory, providing it is thick and the surface roughened to provide a hoof hold.

Tethering ring Positioned in one of the walls at a suitable height for tying up the horse when required.

Manger Some stables have a manger in one corner, in which the feed can be given. This must be wide enough for a horse to reach its bottom, yet deep enough to discourage him from scooping the food out on to the floor with his lips. Manger fittings, which hold a removable bucket or box, are better than fixed mangers as they make cleaning (both of the feed container and the stable) easier. If there is no manger fitting, a heavy box or bucket can be used. The disadvantage of these is that, if the horse tips the container over, the food gets mixed up in the bedding and is totally wasted.

Water bucket Stabled horses must have access to fresh, clean water all the time. This is best provided in a large rubber bucket, positioned in

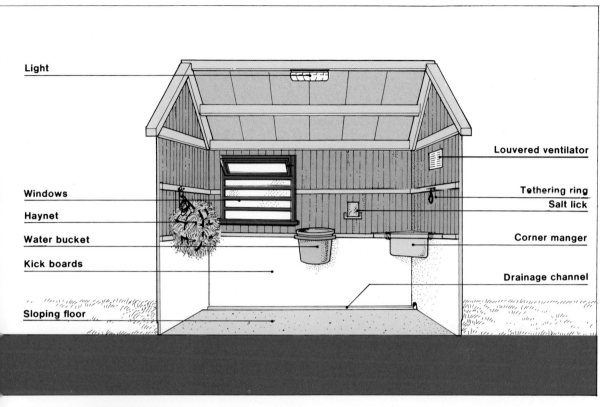

Light

Louvered ventilator

Windows

Tethering ring

Salt lick

Haynet

Water bucket

Corner manger

Kick boards

Drainage channel

Sloping floor

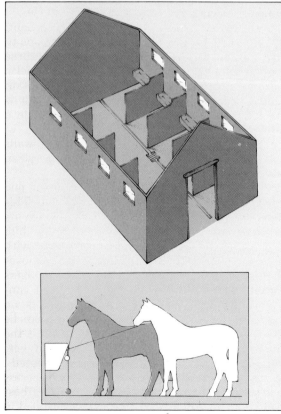

a corner of the stable and strong enough not to be knocked over. Some stables have hinged rings on the wall designed to hold the bucket securely. Automatic watering systems, which the horse operates when he wants to drink, are available; however, these are not easy to keep clean and must also be checked regularly to ensure they are working properly.

Hay nets The best and most economical way to feed hay is in a haynet which should be tied to a fitting in the wall. Ideally, another tethering ring should be used – not hooks which could cause injury to the horse – placed approximately level with the horse's head. Hay racks, positioned high on the wall, used to be the standard fitting. Now they are frowned upon, as their use means that dust and particles of hay fall into the horse's eyes as he feeds.

Salt lick A soluble block of salt, which slides into a small wall fitment in the stable, is appreciated by many stabled horses. This is particularly so if they are doing a considerable

Left, above: Traditional stalls take up less room than boxes and are thus cheaper to maintain and easier to clean. They are often used by schools where many ponies are kept. **Bottom:** The 'rope and ball' method is a safe way of securing your in a stall. The headrope is passed through a metal ring and a heavy wooden ball is attached. It must be long enough to let your horse lie down.

amount of very hard work and losing a lot of salt through sweating.

Walls If these are to be painted, make sure a paint that is non-toxic to animals is used. Many stabled horses fall into the habit of licking the walls as a relief from boredom.

The daily routine

A stabled horse needs extensive care and attention throughout the day – if you want to keep him fit and in tip-top condition, none of his demands can be skimped. The routine begins early in the morning with the first visit of the day. During this, he is checked over for injury, 'quartered' (see page 162), his rugs adjusted, fresh water and a full haynet given, and perhaps the worst of the soiled bedding removed. It ends late at night when his bed is made comfortable and clean for the night, the water and hay checked and the final feed given. In between, the stable has to be thoroughly mucked–out (after which the droppings are removed at regular intervals during the day), while regular feeding, daily exercising and strapping (see page 162) must all be fitted into the routine.

Types of bedding

Stabled horses must have a bed; the thicker and cleaner this is the more the animal will like it. If a horse were left to stand on the bare floor all day, not only would it be cold (a good thick bed provides insulation) and uncomfortable, but would also deny him sufficient rest. Most horses like to lie down from time to time; only by doing so do they get adequate rest. Standing on a hard surface for prolonged periods will also lead to swollen and jarred legs.

There are various types of bedding material. Straw is the most widely used, and the most satisfactory. Wheat straw is the best type to use – it is easy to obtain, relatively cheap and has good draining properties. Oat and barley straw are less satisfactory; the former tends to flatten thus providing a less comfortable bed and horses also find it tasty. The latter, too, packs down quickly to make a thin bed; it also tends to irritate the skin of many horses.

Peat is sometimes hard to obtain, and conversely, once used is not as easy to dispose of as straw manure. It makes a satisfactory bed, particularly for horses that are prone to eating straw, but it must be kept extremely clean. As it is both very absorbent and possesses 'deodorizing' qualities, it is not always easy to spot soiled patches; however, these must be found

DAILY ROUTINE FOR A STABLED HORSE

7:30 AM:	Your first chore should be to check the horse over for any symptoms of injury or illness. Next, give him fresh water, then tie him up and give him a haynet of fresh hay to keep him occupied while you muck out the stable and lay a fresh day bed. With the horse still tethered, pick out the hooves with a hoof pick and then untie him.
8:00 AM:	Give him the first feed of the day.
9:30 AM:	Remove any droppings from the day bed. Remove rugs from the horse, saddle him up and take him out for his daily exercise. After exercising, return to the stable, remove the saddle and bridle and rub the horse down if necessary and provide him with fresh water.
11:30 AM:	After returning from exercise, tie the horse up and groom thoroughly. Put on his day rugs, untie him and give him his second feed of the day.
5:00 PM:	Tie up the horse and remove droppings from the day bed. Pick out the feet. Provide fresh water and rug him up for the night. Give him his third feed. Clean saddlery.
6:30 PM:	Remove any droppings from the day bed, provide fresh water and a new haynet, give the horse his fourth and last feed of the day.

and removed and the peat forked over thoroughly each day to keep it soft and clean. It should be kept at a thickness of about 20cm (8in) and not allowed to rot in the stable. Keep an eye on the horse's feet; if they become packed with soggy peat and not cleaned out regularly, problems will soon develop.

Wood shavings are again useful for horses that eat straw bedding, but are not as good as peat. A top layer of shavings can be used with sawdust underneath (sawdust alone heats up when damp), but the bed will require constant attention to keep it clean. Close attention must also be paid to the horse's feet to make sure they remain disease-free.

Mucking-out

Keeping the bed clean and fresh is one of the most important daily stable chores and must never be neglected as your horse's health is concerned. Besides the major clean out of the stable – known as 'mucking-out'– droppings and soiled straw should be removed regularly throughout the day.

During your early morning visit, remove any droppings that have not been trodden into the

TYPES OF BEDDING

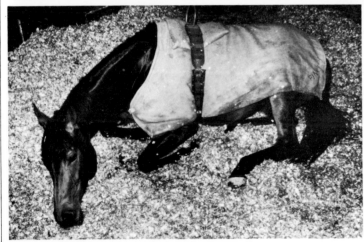

The types of bedding available are many and your selection should be largely determined by comfort and warmth provided, as well as practicality. **Above:** Straw is the most effective and popular type. **Center:** Wood shavings are ideal for horses who tend to eat other types of bedding, but are easily and quickly soiled. **Below left:** Wheat straw is ideal being easily obtainable, cheap, and hygienic. One drawback is that your horse may find his bed quite tasty. **Below right:** For the above reason, peat is often used, being, as well, absorbent and deodorizing.

bed, together with patches of soiled straw. This is known as 'skepping out' and should be repeated during the day. Remove the dung or straw with the pitchfork into the skep and empty into the dung heap. The more thorough mucking-out should be one of the morning chores, or the first skepping-out can be dispensed with and mucking-out done straightaway.

Tie up the horse and give him a full net of hay to keep him occupied. Remove the wet and soiled straw and put it either into a wheelbarrow, or on to a large piece of sacking, placed outside the door. As you do this, separate out the clean straw and stack it against one wall. When the straw has been sorted and separated, sweep the floor and shovel up the sweepings into the wheelbarrow. Leave the floor to dry.

Day bed and night bed

The floor should be covered with a thin layer of straw when dried, so the horse does not stand on the hard surface all day. In the evening, remake the bed. Spread the remainder of the used straw (stacked at the back of the box) on the floor, shaking it well. Add more clean straw, shaking it well with a pitchfork. This makes the bed light and 'elastic'; if the straw is matted together, the bed will be hard. Build it up higher round the walls of the stable to exclude draughts and lessen risk of injury if the horse knocks his legs against the wall as he lies down.

Some riders favour a system known as deep litter. For this, straw is the only satisfactory type of bedding. The droppings are removed from the stable in the same way, but the soiled straw is left. A layer of clean straw is placed on top each day and the wet straw left to pack

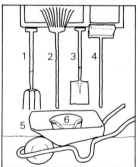

Equipment for mucking out: Keeping your horse's bed clean and fresh is a chore you must never neglect. A major clean-out should be done regularly as well as a daily removal of soiled bedding and droppings. The basic equipment you will need for mucking-out includes: (1) a four-pronged fork; (2) a wood or plastic rake; (3) a shovel; (4) a broom; (5) a wheelbarrow or piece of sacking; (6) a plastic or wicker skep.

On your first morning visit, it is a good idea to remove what droppings you can from your horse's bed, with any soiled straw.

In a thorough mucking-out, first remove wet and soiled straw with a four-pronged fork and put it in a wheelbarrow or sacking.

While doing the previous step, sort the fresh straw from the soiled and stack it against one wall banking it up as neatly as possible.

The day bed is a thin layer of bedding laid on the floor for use during the day; the night bed is thicker and more comfortable. Using peat or shavings is relatively simple whereas laying a straw bed is a little more difficult. As the straw will be compacted into a bale, it will first need to be shaken out and laid down to separate it and keep it from lumping. Some owners prefer to simply cover the soiled straw with fresh, allowing the under-layer to rot.

Ideally, the dung heap should be situated not far from the stable, down-wind, for convenience and hygiene. Keep the stack well-shaped and tidy at all times.

Sweep the floor clean and leave to dry, covering it with a thin layer of straw. The full bed should be replaced after the horse has been exercised.

DAILY GROOMING

Grooming equipment needed:
(1) one sponge for cleaning eyes, lips, and nostrils and one for the dock;
(2) sweat scraper for removing water and sweat; (3) stable rubber for final polishing; (4) soft body brush to remove dust and scurf; (5) hoof oil and brush to improve the appearance of and treat brittle feet; (6) rubber curry comb can be used in place of the dandy brush on the thick-coated horses; (7) soft water brush for laying the mane and tail and washing the feet; (8) hard dandy brush to remove dried mud and sweat; (9) combs for plaiting, trimming, or pulling the mane and tail; (10) hoof pick for removing dirt and stones; (11) metal curry comb for cleaning the body brush.

Concentrating on the edges and working frog to toe, dislodge any objects.

With a damp, warm, sponge, wipe the eyes outwards from the corners.

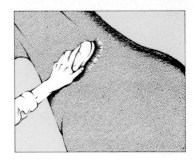

The dandy brush is used to remove heavy dirt. Do not use on the more tender areas.

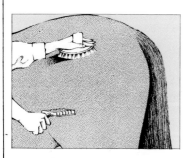

The body brush, with short, dense bristles, is designed to penetrate and clean the coat. It should be used with a fair amount of pressure in circular movements and frequently cleaned with a curry comb.

The head may also be cleaned with the body brush, but using gentler strokes. The water brush is used to lay the mane. Keep the brush flat and make firm, downward strokes leaving the mane to dry.

As well as cleaning the body and head, the body brush is used on the tail. Brush a few hairs at a time, starting from underneath. As a final step, the tail should be fully brushed from the top.

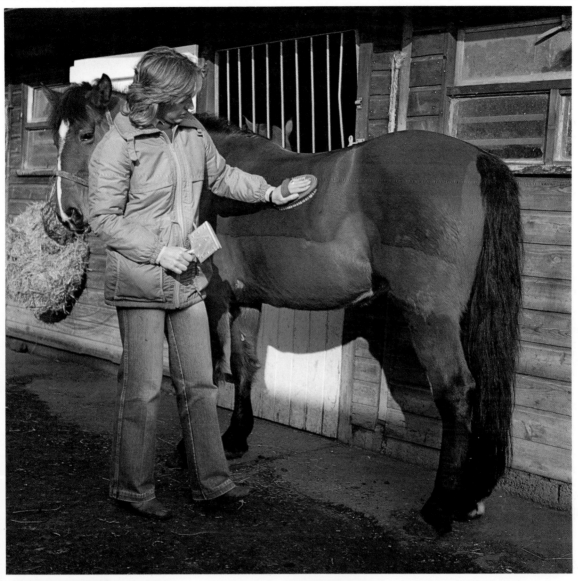

Take a smallish bunch of hay, dampen slightly and slap against the thick muscular parts of the horse's body in the direction of the coat. This helps tone the horse's muscles.

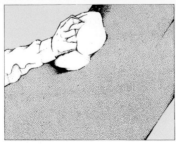

Folding a stable rubber into a pad, give the body a final polish, always moving in the direction of the coat. As a final touch, oil the hooves with hoof oil.

The aim of grooming is to keep your horse clean, massage the skin, and tone the muscles. Horses at grass generally require less grooming, but some is nevertheless essential. A good, complete grooming kit is necessary and should be kept clean and organised. If you are grooming more than one horse, each should have his own kit. Grooming can be divided into three stages, each for different times of the day. The first morning exercise is quartering. Strapping follows exercise, once the horse has cooled down, and is more extensive and thorough taking between half an hour to an hour depending on the groom's skill and experience.

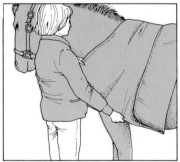

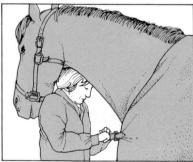

Rugging up: Swing the blanket over the horse to lie centrally along its back and high on the neck. Buckle the surcingle.

Check to make sure the blanket is not slipping and buckle the strap at the front but not too tightly.

A roller relieves any pressure on the spine, but use a pad underneath. Like a surcingle it should not be buckled tightly.

down and begin rotting. This is not really more economical than the conventional process, but it does save mucking-out each day. Every few months, however, the stable has to be cleaned our completely. This time, it should be disinfected and left for a day to air.

Rugs and clips

If horses are kept stabled during the winter, they usually need to wear rugs to keep them sufficiently warm. This becomes essential if the horse has been clipped – that is, if he has had his heavy winter coat removed. It is common practice to clip stabled horses in winter; the absence of a thick winter coat enables them to work harder without getting hot and sweaty and also makes them look smarter.

The extent to which the coat is removed by clipping varies considerably. It can range from a total clip, in which the whole coat is removed, to a small 'trace' clip, in which just a line of hair is removed from beneath the neck, under the belly and top of the legs. Horses mainly living out at grass are frequently trace clipped. This makes them somewhat easier to keep clean and prevents them from sweating too profusely

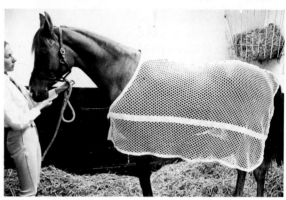

Left: Much like night rugs, day rugs are designed to keep your horse warm. Day rugs are usually of woolen material and bound with coloured braid. They are often used only for decorative purposes and are not as practical as night rugs.
Above: the summer sheet is usually made of cotton and is used instead of a rug in hot weather. It provides some warmth and protection from insects. The night rug, **above right**, is considerably warmer and sturdier than the day rug.
Right: The sweat sheet is made of cotton mesh and usually worn under a rug to keep the horse from overheating or cooling off too quickly.

if they are asked to do relatively hard work; however, it does not rob them of the thick coat they need to keep warm.

The night rug is the one most commonly worn in the stable. This is made of tough jute, lined with woollen material, and is usually bound at the edges with leather. It covers the horse's back, hindquarters and sides, and buckles in place across his chest. It is held in position around the middle either by a surcingle or roller. The latter is preferable to the former as it is padded on either side of the spine to reduce the risk of pressure being brought to bear on it. The surcingle is simply a long plain webbing strap which passes around the horse's middle. If one is used, it is advisable to put a pad of foam under it across the spine region.

Particularly at night, horses that are clipped out will need to wear blankets under their rug to ensure sufficient warmth. Special horse blankets, made of fawn coloured wool with contrasting coloured stripes down the sides, are obtainable. However, these are very expensive; an ordinary domestic blanket, provided it is not so threadbare it has no warmth left in it, is perfectly satisfactory. The blankets are thrown over the horse's back under the rug, well up to the neck and the front then rolled over the rug

CLIPPING

Choosing to clip your horse's coat in winter allows him to work harder and keep him looking smart. The types of clips vary considerably. The trace clip removes just a line of hair from beneath the neck, belly, and tops of legs. The blanket clip is the same as the trace clip but with all hair removed from the neck. The hunter clipped horse must be kept inside in winter or turned out with a warm New Zealand rug.

Blanket clip

Trace clip

Hunter clip

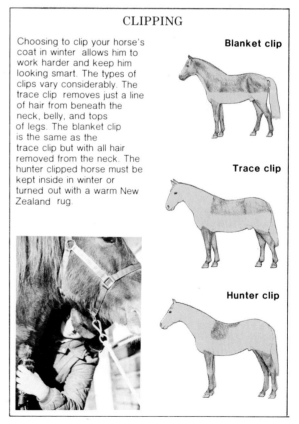

like a collar. The number a horse needs depends on the temperature, the type of horse (some, like people, are more prone to feel the cold than others) and the extent to which the coat has been clipped. You can tell if a horse is cold by feeling his ears; if they are cold, the rest of the body is. Day rugs are also available. These are designed in the same way as night rugs, but are made of woollen material only and are usually bound with coloured braid. They are considerably smarter than night rugs, but they are not as practical; they are neither as hard wearing, nor as resistant to stains from soiled bedding. For this reason, night rugs are often worn by stabled horses during the day and day rugs kept for special occasions, such as for use at an autumn or winter show.

If night rugs are worn night and day, each horse should have at least three – one for day use, one for night use and a clean one kept in reserve. If the day is sunny and warm, hang the rug used during the night out in the fresh air.

Quartering and strapping

Stabled horses must be thoroughly groomed every day; this is another chore which should never be skimped. Not only is grooming important from the point of view of appearance; it also helps to keep the horse in good health by toning the muscles, stimulating the blood circulation and massaging the skin.

The first grooming of the day is known as quartering. It should be done during the early morning visit. The purpose of this is to make the horse respectable for exercising; it is better to leave the full grooming, or strapping, until after exercise, when the heat generated in the body will have made the dust come to the surface of the coat. Quartering consists of picking out the feet and sponging the eyes, nose and dock (as described on page 158). Then without undoing the rugs, lift them up at the back and brush the exposed parts of the body with the body brush, working with the hair. Any stains caused by the horse lying down on wet bedding can most likely be easily removed with the dampened water brush.

The full grooming or strapping takes an experienced rider about an hour. The horse should be dry and cool after exercise – you cannot properly groom a horse that is wet either with sweat or rain. If he is in this condition, dry him by covering him with straw and loosely buckling a rug on top. Any mud on his legs or tummy should also be completely dry before you begin strapping.

Types of food

Permanently stabled horses are denied the opportunity of eating their natural food – grass. Whatever time of year a horse is stabled, therefore, he must be fed at regular intervals throughout the day to compensate for this.

There is a variety of foodstuffs fed to horses: the choice depends on individual preference, the horse's condition and what is available. The most common are detailed below, but, in addition to these, a stabled horse should also be provided with hay. This should be constantly

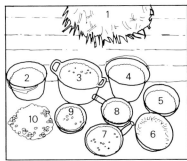

Horses at grass have an advantage over stabled horses in that they easily and naturally obtain food which is essential to their health and well-being. Stabled horses, however, must be carefully and conscientiously fed a varied and nutritious diet, to be determined largely by personal preference, the horse's state of health, and the availability of foodstuffs. Because the horse has a small stomach, it is essential that you do not overfeed your horse, but incorporate frequent feedings of small quantities into your horse's daily regime. (1) Hay should always be available for your horse, and can be used in conjunction with the following: (2) Sugar beet (cubes) are an excellent source of bulk; however, be sure they are soaked before feeding as there is danger of the horse choking. (3) Maize should be fed flaked and is energizing but low in protein and minerals. (4) Oats are a highly nutritious source of Vitamin B and protein and should be fed shredded or crushed. (5) Barley should not be given to horses involved in long, fast, work. It contains Vitamin B and should be crushed and fed raw. (6) Chaff is poor in food value but gives bulk and helps mastication. (7) Linseed has laxative properties and helps give a glossy coat. (8) Bran is rich in protein, Vitamin B and salt. (9) Peas are rich in protein and should be fed sparingly. (10) Pony nuts contain all essential nutrients and can be fed in place of oats.

available to him. A horse at grass grazes continually – a stabled horse should be able to emulate this. The animal has a very small stomach for its overall size, which is at its most comfortable if it is partially filled all the time rather than completely full at certain times. For this reason, one of the golden feeding rules of horses is to give small feeds frequently.

Concentrated foods

Oats are the best of all concentrated foods. They are easily digested, high in nutritive value and liked by all horses. They can be fed whole or crushed, the latter being the easiest to digest; however, crushed oats should be eaten within a fortnight of being crushed and should not be so heavily treated that all the floury content is lost. The oats should look clean and smell sweet and there should be no sign of mould or dampness.

Bran is a by-product of wheat milling. Bran with broad flakes – known as broad bran – is preferable, as it tends to be less dusty. However, it is not always easy to obtain. All bran has a reasonably high nutritive value, although not as high as oats. Bran is often used as a diluent with oats; to give an equivalent quantity of pure oats would cause over-heating and excessive excitement in most horses. It should smell sweet and there should be no clotted lumps when you run your hand through it.

Besides being mixed with other feedstuffs, bran can also be fed in mash form. This is ideal for sick, 'off-colour' or tired horses, as it is easy to digest and has laxative properties. Fill a bucket two-thirds full of bran, add a spoonful of salt and pour boiling water on top. Stir this thoroughly and leave the bucket covered with a cloth until the mash has cooled enough to feed.

Flaked maize has about three-quarters the equivalent nutritive value of oats and is often given to excitable horses as a replacement for oats, normally as part of the daily diet, mixing with a few oats, some bran and other foodstuffs.

Barley is usually given to horses in poor condition as it has good body-building properties. It should be soaked and boiled until soft as otherwise the horse finds it very indigestible.

Pulses, such as beans and peas, are extremely nutritious but have a very heating effect on horses, inducing great high spirits – hence the expression 'full of beans.' They are good for horses doing a considerable amount of hard work or for those in poor condition that need building up while being worked. Again, they should be fed as a regular part of the diet, small

RULES FOR FEEDING
The rules for feeding are clear and simple.

Give small feeds frequently. A stabled horse needs a minimum of three feeds a day and four is infinitely preferable.

Offer water before feeding. If a horse takes a long drink after he has eaten a feed, the food will be washed through his stomach before digestion is completed.

Feed the best food you can buy and feed lots of bulk with corn feeds. A horse will often reject old or musty food, even if he is hungry.

Be guided in the amount you feed a horse by his condition and the work you are asking him to do. A thin horse, or one doing a lot of work, needs more high-energy food, such as oats, than a horse in good condition doing light work.

Give the horse plenty of time – at least an hour before riding – to digest a feed and always allow him to eat his feed in peace.

Below: Because horses are choosy eaters, it is desirable to keep all food in a simple food store where it can be measured and mixed only at feeding time. Scales are a useful item and all grains should be kept tightly covered to prevent vermin. **Right:** Your horse's condition will be reflected by his diet: a carefully fed horse is a happy horse.

Below: The suggested feeding chart is only given as a rough guide, for in reality, how much a horse is fed at any time of the year will depend greatly on its age, work, temperament, size and condition. Besides the feedstuffs mentioned, a tablespoon of salt should be added to every feed, and whenever possible add some succulent food such as carrots or apples. All stabled horses should have a bran mash once a week, preferably given the night before their rest day, and on this day of rest the hard feed ration (i.e. oats) should be halved.
The over 16 h.h. hunter/eventer in hard regular work should receive vitamin supplement with his feeds each day and on return from the hunt or an event, will appreciate a bran mash with boiled barley, salt and glucose.

SUGGESTED FEEDING CHART

	7.30 a.m.	Midday	5.00 p.m.	7.30 p.m.
13.2 h.h. pony, being lightly ridden at week-ends. Turned out at grass (winter feeding).			4.5 kg (10 lb) hay 450 g (1 lb) bran 900 g (2 lb) nuts	
14.22 h.h. pony turned out in New Zealand rug. Being lightly ridden and hunted at weekends.	450 g (I lb) bran 900 g (2 lb) nuts		5.5 kg (12 lb) hay 900 g (2 lb) oats 450 g (1 lb) bran 900 g (2 lb) nuts	
15 h.h. horse, clipped out and stabled all the time. Being ridden and hunted regularly.	1.8 kg (4 lb) hay 450 g (I lb) oats 450 g (1 lb) bran 900 g (2 lb) nuts	900 g (2 lb)oats 450 g (1 lb) bran 900 g (2 lb) nuts	1.4 kg (3 lb)oats 450 g ((1 lb) bran 900 g (2 lb) nuts	4.5 kg (10 lb) hay
15.2 h.h. horse, turned out by night, stabled during the day. Being ridden regularly (summer).	450 g (1 lb) oats 450 g (1 lb) bran 900 g (2 lb) nuts	1.8 kg (4 lb) hay (this is not necessary if horse is in good condition)	450 g (1 lb) oats 450 g (1 lb) bran 900 g (2 lb) nuts	
Over 16 h.h. hunter/eventer, clipped out and stabled. Regular hard work (winter).	3.6 kg (8 lb) hay 900 g (2 lb) oats 450 g (1 lb) bran 450 g (1 lb) nuts	1.4 kg (3 lb) oats 450 g (I lb) bran 450 g (1 lb) race-horse nuts	1.4 kg (3 lb) oats 450 g (1 lb) bran	4.5 kg (10 lb) hay 1.8 kg (4 lb) oats 450 g (1 lb) bran 900 g (2 lb) racehorse nuts

amounts being mixed with other feedstuffs.

Linseed is also extremely nutritious, but must be cooked before it is fed. It is available in various pre-cooked forms, or can be bought 'loose', in which case it must be boiled to turn it into a jelly. Only small quantities – no more than about 225g (8oz) cooked – should be fed to a horse per day and then only if he is in poor condition.

Horse cubes are one of the most convenient foodstuffs; the cubes contain a balanced diet of proteins, roughage, carbohydrate, minerals and vitamins. Various types are available, specially prepared for different types of horses. Their disadvantage is that you lose the ability to vary how much you feed of the various ingredients, but this is not a serious drawback.

Chaff is chopped hay. It is often mixed in with corn feeds, such as oats and bran, to add bulk and roughage and to discourage a horse from bolting his food. Some form of roughage and fiber is essential in a stabled horse's daily diet in whatever form readily available.

How much food and when
There are other foods fed to horses for specific reasons – to build them up if they are in poor condition, to warm them when tired or cold, or provide extra energy. By and large, however, horses are satisfied and stay healthy on a diet containing a balanced mixture of the foodstuffs mentioned. In addition, try to feed something fresh and succulent each day – such as green vegetables, carrots or apples – which help to make up for the lack of grass in the diet of a stabled horse.

How much to feed a horse is a perennial problem and one for which there are no hard and fast rules. However, various points are of paramount importance. Having complied with these, judge whether your horse needs more or less food by his general condition (is he too thin or fat?); his performance (does he seem sluggish and tired or too headstrong and excitable?); and his appetite and hunger (does he gobble his food down as soon as you give it to him and then eat his bedding, or does he not finish each feed and seem uninterested?)

The exercise routine
A stabled horse needs daily exercise to keep him in good condition. This not only keeps him fit, but also helps keep him healthy, by making

A group of young riders combine necessity with pleasure. By going for an enjoyable ride in the country, they give their horses the exercise they need.

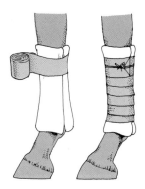

Right: Exercise bandage gives support to the area between the knee and fetlock, protect it from injury and help prevent too much jarring. A cotton wool or gamgee should be placed under them. Begin winding the bandage at the top, fitting it firmly, but not too tightly around your horse's leg and tying it at the side of the leg. **Far right:** a finished exercise bandage.

his lungs and breathing apparatus work efficiently. If a horse is left to stand day after day in the stable, he soon loses condition. His legs begin to swell from standing perpetually in one position, he develops kidney disorders and he becomes stiff, dull, lethargic and bored.

If the horse is being kept in the stable for a specific reason – perhaps because he is being hunted, ridden in competitive work, or is getting regular schooling – the exercise routine will need to be planned around such factors. As a rule, a stabled horse needs about two hours exercise a day, but do not confuse exercise with work. If he has been hunted, ridden around an event course, or given an extensive and exhausting bout of schooling on one day, he will not require two hours exercise the following day. Indeed, he will probably appreciate a rest, perhaps with just a short session of walking around outside to get a breath of fresh air and to take away any stiffness he may be feeling as a result of his previous exertion.

Routine exercise should be conducted at a brisk walk and a slow jog. Both of these are ideal for building up muscles and either getting a horse fit and into condition or keeping him that way. If you have only recently brought him into the stable and are trying to get him fit, build up to the two hours gradually, doing no more than walking for the first couple of weeks. Riding at a steady, controlled pace up hills is marvellous exercise for building up a horse's muscles and getting him into condition.

When riding out on exercise, try to vary the route taken each day. A horse will soon anticipate where he is going if he is regularly taken the same way and he will cease to concentrate or listen to your instructions. It helps to relieve boredom, as well as making for a more obedient horse, if you occasionally substitute a light schooling session in the paddock or manège for the full exercise period. This, however, should not be for two hours continuously.

Detecting lameness

Horses asked to work after a long period of rest or those being worked hard daily are more prone to lameness than their less hard working colleagues, unless the rider is very watchful and careful. Lameness in a horse is easy to detect in general terms, but often very hard to pin down to any particular leg. It is easiest to detect in the front legs; these are the more likely to become lame as they carry the greater proportion of the horse's weight. If a horse rests or points a foreleg, this is a clear indication he is feeling pain in that foot. However, doing the same with a hindleg does not carry a similar significance, for a horse will rest one or other hindleg when he is standing quietly.

Note from the start that the causes of lameness in horses are numerous. Simple ones can be treated by the rider, but, in most cases, the wisest course of action is to consult your vet.
Thrush An inflammation of the frog, generally caused by a horse having been left to stand for

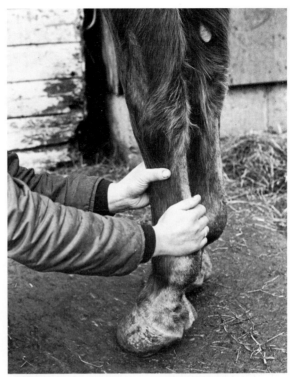

Left: Racehorses are given their daily exercise in the early morning around a marked-out track. These horses are given a strenuous and carefully planned exercise routine; however, all horses, especially if stabled, should be given daily exercise, at least once a day.

Above: Lameness is the most common disability and can be permanently debilitating if not attended to. To detect lameness, run your hand gingerly down the horse's leg feeling for any heat, pain or swelling. In all cases, treatment is best left to your vet.

protracted periods on wet, heavily soiled bedding. The frog becomes soft and diseased, giving out an unmistakeable, extremely unpleasant smell. It must be thoroughly cleaned and treated with antiseptics. The vet must be consulted.

Windgalls Puffy swellings that form above the fetlock on either side of the leg and caused by excessive work on hard ground. Although they are not serious – and may not even cause lameness – a horse should be rested until they have disappeared.

Broken knees Usually caused by a fall on the road or other hard ground; if the skin is broken and the wound ugly and bleeding, the vet must be called instantly. Proper treatment may result in there being no permanent scarring (although the new hair will grow white over the healed wound); ineffectual or non-instantaneous treatment could mean a permanent unsightly lump on the knee.

Sprains Sprains to the leg ligaments are caused by excessive riding on hard ground, particularly if the ligament is already slightly strained from a blow, say, or a twist. The chief site for a sprain is the forelegs. Its presence is indicated by heat in the affected area, which may be accompanied by swelling. Hosing the leg with cold water for about ten minutes several times a day will help to relieve this. Rest is essential; if the sprain is severe, causing acute lameness, the horse may have to be rested for a month or two.

Over-reach Wounds caused by the horse striking the heel or back of the coronet on the forelegs with the toes of the shoes on the hind feet. Severe over-reaches may cut the flesh, in which case the wound must be cleaned and treated with an antibiotic powder. If the horse is lame, it should not be worked until it is sound again. If a horse has a tendency to over-reach it should wear protective over-reach boots on the forelegs.

Brushing Like over-reaching, this is a self-

169

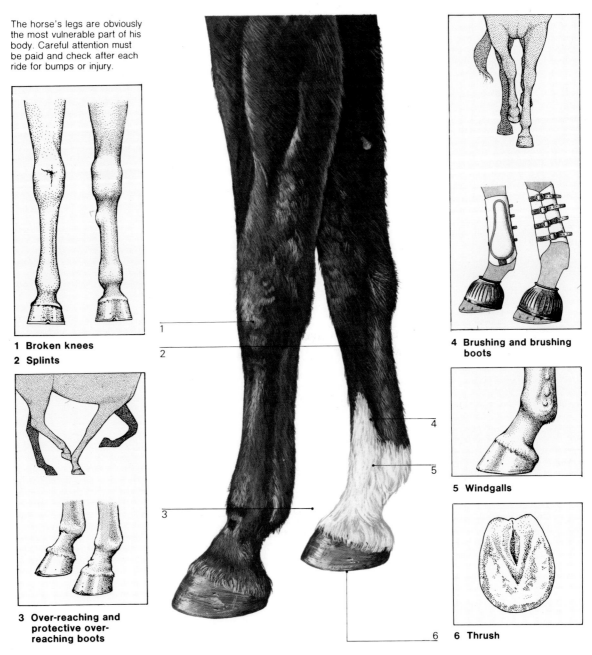

The horse's legs are obviously the most vulnerable part of his body. Careful attention must be paid and check after each ride for bumps or injury.

1 Broken knees

2 Splints

3 Over-reaching and protective over-reaching boots

4 Brushing and brushing boots

5 Windgalls

6 Thrush

inflicted wound, occurring if the horse hits the inside of one leg with the opposite foot. Again, if an open wound results it should be treated accordingly. Special brushing boots are available for permanent protection.

Cracked heels Sore patches, often suppurating in the heels caused by an irritant in the soil. An ointment containing cod liver oil or poultices of dry warm bran are effective treatment.

Splints These bony enlargements are commonest just below the knee on the inside of the foreleg and are frequently seen in young horses. They are caused by the legs being jarred on hard ground. The horse goes lame while they are forming, but, though they remain as swellings, there is no pain. If detected in their early stages, rest and hosing with cold water may eliminate them.

Capped elbows and hocks Unsightly swellings to the point of the elbow or hock are usually caused by bruising from hard stable floors not covered with enough bedding. They can also be caused by the horse kicking or hitting himself

170

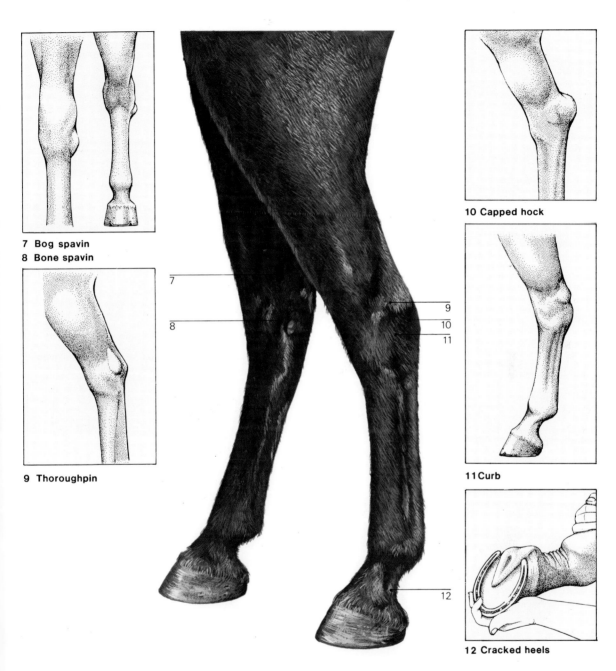

7 Bog spavin
8 Bone spavin

9 Thoroughpin

10 Capped hock

11 Curb

12 Cracked heels

against the wall. Ask the vet to treat them and check that no abscess has been formed.

Curb An enlargement or swelling of the leg. Situated just below the hock, and the result of spraining the ligament. One common cause is making a horse jump on heavy ground. The animal may not go lame immediately; if the curb is left untreated, however, it may lead to constant bouts of lameness. Consult your vet. He may advise shoeing with a special shoe, which helps to relieve the strain, but sometimes more drastic treatment is necessary such as

blistering the leg; this draws the blood to the affected area, so helping to speed the healing process.

Spavins There are two conditions – bog spavin, which is a puffy swelling on the inside joint of the hock, and bone spavin, which is a bony growth a little lower down and inside this joint. Both are caused by strain or overwork on hard ground, although the conformation of some horses makes them more prone to the complaint. In both cases again, the main treatment is rest; recovery may be aided by hosing daily.

171

Symptoms	Causes	Treatment
Colds Sneezing and nasal discharge which may be thin or thick. Eyes are watery and coat is dull. Horse appears lethargic and loses condition.	Brought in from a ride hot, or wet from rain, and left to stand in a draughty stable, without being dried off. Also by contact with infected horses.	Keep warm in a draught-free stable, well isolated from other horses. Put on a laxative diet and give only very gentle exercise.
Coughs Often accompany colds. May vary from a tickling, irritant cough to a deep, rasping, drawn-out one.	Many causes, from eating dusty hay to contracting broken wind. Teething may cause coughing in young horses.	Consult the vet about the cause of the cough and follow his advice about treatment.
Influenza Fever and temperature accompanied by heavy discharge from the eyes and nose. Animal will be exhausted and distressed.	Contact with other infected animals. Humans can transmit the disease from one horse to another on clothes, shoes, grooming kit, etc.	Isolate the patient immediately and put in an airy, well-ventilated box. Rug and bandage to keep him warm and send for the vet. Prevention is better than cure; all horses should be vaccinated against the disease while young.
Strangles Rise in temperature, accompanied by thin nasal discharge which turns thick and yellow as disease progresses. Rim around eye turns bright red. Possible coughing and swelling of glands in the throat. Usually attacks young horses.	An organism known as the strangles streptococcus. The disease is extremely infectious and, besides direct contact, may be transmitted through bedding, stable equipment, tack etc.	As for influenza.

Thoroughpin This swelling occurs either side of the hock joint and the puffy enlargement can often by pushed through from one side of the hock to the other. Initially the horse may not be lame; but he should be rested.

Infections and vices

Besides lameness, a stabled horse can suffer from a number of other infections, as well as from self-induced vices. Both can be easily prevented. Particularly as far as the latter are concerned, the very fact of being stabled can lead to such problems developing, especially if the horse is not given enough attention or exercise to relieve the boredom.

Horses kept in draughty stables can often develop rheumatism. This will show itself in exactly the same way as it does in man; the horse will be stiff and in obvious pain whenever he shifts position. The affected areas must be rubbed with embrocation and, most important of all, the draughts must be eliminated.

Influenza is one of the commonest and most infectious and contagious of all diseases and,

again, tends to produce similar symptoms in horses as it does in people. These include nasal discharge, general listlessness, lethargy, perhaps coughing and a high temperature. Seek advice immediately from the vet; it will include the complete isolation of the horse, a change in its diet to soft, laxative feeds, and the administering of the relevant drugs.

Strangles is another extremely infectious disease, which attacks the nose and throat, causing swelling of the glands, nasal discharge, dullness and apathy, and a sharp rise in temperature. The membranes of the eye usually turn from their usual healthy pink to a bright red. The disease is most prevalent in young horses. Your vet will advise on treatment; the strictest isolation must again be imposed.

Infectious diseases will run riot through a yard where several horses are stabled unless rigid isolation is practiced. Humans can carry diseases from one horse to another on clothes or by using the same grooming kit on two animals.

Skin diseases, too, are very contagious and

A healthy horse will be alert, attentive, and keenly aware of his surroundings. It will carry its head high, ears pricked, and eyes bright and wide open. His coat will be smooth and glossy. **Above:** If a horse is left to stand in a stable day after day he will become quickly out of condition and bored, resulting not only in various physical manifestations such as swelling of the legs and kidney disorders, but crib biting and other vices as well. Usually caused by a lack of exercise such vices can bring about a loss of condition in the horse.

will soon spread round a stable. Keep a look out for any signs of these – the commonest symptom is a horse rubbing constantly until he makes himself raw – and seek advice from the vet as soon as possible.

Many stable vices occur simply because the horse has become bored with standing in the stable doing nothing. Keep a watchful eye out for any symptoms and try to nip them in the bud; all stable vices are notoriously hard to cure, and thus it is much better to prevent them from even starting.

Chewing rugs As the name suggests, a horse with this habit tears continually at his rugs. Make sure he has a full haynet at all times to divert his attention.

Crib biting Gnawing the edge of the manger or door or gripping hold of it and gulping down air. Try painting the area with creosote, provide full nets of hay and increase work.

Windsucking Here, the horse arches his neck and gulps down air. As with crib biting, windsucking leads to a loss of condition. Special collars are available to discourage the habit;

otherwise the same remedies as for crib biting are recommended.

Weaving Swinging the head and neck rhythmically from side-to-side, usually over the stable door. This can be checked by tying up the horse on a short rope, but the real treatment is to relieve the horse's boredom.

Kicking The horse kicks out at the stable walls or at anyone entering the stable. If caught in the early stages, rap the legs instantly and thereafter handle the horse as much as possible. Strike his hindquarters, using a long pole, if necessary, to get him used to having people near to him. If the habit persists, reinforce the stable walls and cover them with padding to prevent injury.

Biting Horses will often try to take a bite at a passer-by, either because they are naturally bad-tempered, or, more probably, because they are bored. Take steps to relieve this, but, if the problem persists, fit a netted grill to the top half of the stable door. Do not shut the top door as this will serve only to increase the problem.

Tack of the Horse

THE TACK A RIDDEN HORSE WEARS – that is, the saddle and bridle in all their variations, together with their assorted attachments – has existed from the first days of man's association with horses. Although subjected to many changes and refinements over the centuries and in different parts of the world, the reasons for using tack and the principles affecting its design have changed little from generation to generation.

The bridle, and probably the headcollar and halter, were the first items to evolve. This was doubtless because they gave the strongest and most direct control over his horse, whether he was mounted or leading it from the ground. In its crudest form, the bridle consisted of the simplest possible arrangement of straps to hold the 'bit' – a mouthpiece usually made of metal – in the horse's mouth. Straps or 'reins' were attached to the bit; these were long enough for the rider to hold when he was mounted, so that he was instantly in possession of a simple, but effective means of controlling his horse.

Bridles and bits

The bridle used in classic English or European riding varies tremendously in detail – over such points as what type of noseband is used; whether the various component parts are held together by buckles, stud fastenings or stitching; the thickness and colour of the leather; whether the reins are plain, plaited, braided, covered in rubber or made of nylon – and so on. The greatest difference of all, however, lies in the design of the bit, of which there are literally hundreds of types. Almost all of these are variations of two basic bits – the snaffle and the curb.

The snaffle and the curb

The snaffle is the simplest type of bit. Its mouthpiece may be jointed or unjointed, smooth or twisted, straight or curved, according to its individual design and purpose. At each end, it has a circular or D-shaped ring to which the reins are attached. Depending on how the rider uses his or her hands, the bit can be used to exert pressure on the outside of the bars of the mouth, the tongue and the corners of the mouth.

The mouthpiece of a curb bit can also be jointed or unjointed; alternatively, it may have

Care of the saddle, bridle, and other tack is as important as care of the horse. Tack which is not cared for can prove uncomfortable for the horse and dangerous for the rider.

Tack should be stored in a cool and dry place as a warm and dry environment will cause leather to crack and metal to tarnish and rust. Dampness will cause rotting.

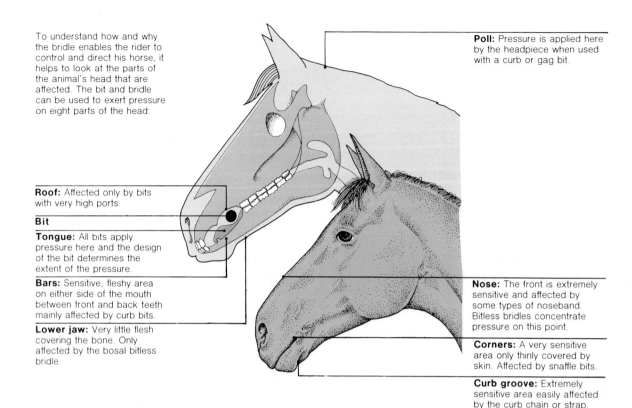

To understand how and why the bridle enables the rider to control and direct his horse, it helps to look at the parts of the animal's head that are affected. The bit and bridle can be used to exert pressure on eight parts of the head:

Poll: Pressure is applied here by the headpiece when used with a curb or gag bit.

Roof: Affected only by bits with very high ports.

Bit

Tongue: All bits apply pressure here and the design of the bit determines the extent of the pressure.

Bars: Sensitive, fleshy area on either side of the mouth between front and back teeth mainly affected by curb bits.

Lower jaw: Very little flesh covering the bone. Only affected by the bosal bitless bridle.

Nose: The front is extremely sensitive and affected by some types of noseband. Bitless bridles concentrate pressure on this point.

Corners: A very sensitive area only thinly covered by skin. Affected by snaffle bits.

Curb groove: Extremely sensitive area easily affected by the curb chain or strap.

a raised section in the center known as a 'port'. It may be 'fixed', in that it is rigidly secured at either end to the cheekpieces, or movable, which means the cheekpieces can move a certain amount independently of the mouthpiece. The slight flexibility this affords tends to lessen the severity of the bit. It also encourages the horse to play with it in his mouth, which helps to create saliva. This, in turn, helps to protect the sensitive tissues of the mouth.

The curb bit has long cheekpieces extending down either side of the mouthpiece, with the rings to take the reins placed at the bottom. In addition, a curb chain or strap, resting in the 'curb groove' under the horse's chin, is fastened to either side of the bit. The lever action produced by the reins exerts pressure on the horse's poll through the head piece (to which it is indirectly attached) and also on the curb groove through the curb chain or strap. The mouthpiece of the bit exerts pressure on the tongue, the bars and – in the case of very high ports – the roof of the mouth.

The double bridle and Pelham bit
Snaffle and curb bits may be combined in one bridle, known as the double bridle. The snaffle used here is called a bridoon; it has a somewhat thinner mouthpiece with smaller rings than most other snaffles of similar design. It is jointed. The curb bit, called a Weymouth, has a slight port and may have a fixed or movable mouthpiece. In the hands of a sensitive, experienced rider, the combined action of both bits gives great opportunity for precision performance and considerable refinement in control.

· The snaffle and curb can also be combined in one single bit known as the Pelham, which again has many variations in design. Most of these look similar to other curb bits, but, in addition, there is a pair of large rings situated either side of the mouthpiece to take an additional pair of reins. These have the effect of giving the bit the action of the snaffle, while the reins attached to the rings at the lower end of the cheekpieces operate the curb action.

Bitless bridles
In addition to the bridles so far mentioned, there are various designs of bitless bridles. As their name suggests, these have no bit and therefore rely on exerting control through areas of sensitivity other than the mouth. The bosal bitless bridle is a traditional bridle used in Western riding, usually in the early stages of training a horse. It is extremely simple in design, the word bosal actually referring to the noseband, which is made of braided rawhide

Top: The snaffle is the simplest bit and can be used to exert force on the outside bars of the mouth, tongue and corners of the mouth. **Left:** The snaffle and curb bits combined create the double bridle. This combination allows for greater control and refinement. **Above:** The hackamore consists mainly of a noseband attached to metal cheekpieces to which the reins are attached.

TYPES OF BIT

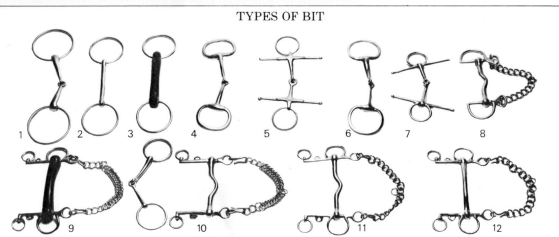

The bit contributes to the overall control of the horse and is used in conjunction with a number of other aids. The pressure exerted by the rider on the horse's mouth sends instructions and the horse's reaction should be one of relaxation and not of fear or pain. There are numerous types of bits ranging from the simple to the complex, however, it is still the skill of the rider which will determine the horse's movements and co-operation. **Above:** (1) German snaffle; (2) straight bar snaffle; (3) rubber snaffle; (4) eggbutt snaffle; (5) Fulmer snaffle; (6) gag-bit; (7) loose-ring snaffle; (8) Kimblewick; (9) flexible rubber mouth Pelham; (10) Weymouth bridoon and curb bits; (11) Pelham bit; (12) Scamperdale.

Left and below; As many variations occur in the design of bridles used in Western equitation as those found in European style riding circles. The bridle shown **Left:** is known as a bosal, one of the oldest designs of all and most commonly used in the training of a horse, control being achieved through pressure on the nose by the thick noseband and behind the chin by the bosal knot.
Below: A bridle featuring one of the many types of curb bit characterized by the long cheek pieces.

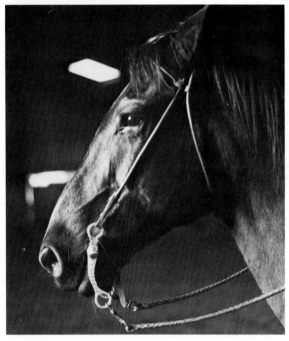

and held in place by an ordinary headpiece. The bosal meets under the jaws (considerably higher than the chin groove), in a thick knot known as the heel knot. Plaited horsehair reins are attached to this. The bosal applies pressure to the horse's nose in front and the lower jaw behind.

Other bitless bridles, known as hackamores (a derivation from the Spanish word for noseband), are somewhat more sophisticated in design than the bosal. The areas the pressure is concentrated upon are the front of the nose and the chin groove. The noseband is attached on either side to metal cheek pieces; the longer these are, the more leverage they afford and the greater the pressure that can be applied. A curb strap is attached to the metal cheekpieces to lie in the curb groove. The commonly-held idea

that a hackamore is necessarily a mild form of bridle as it has no bit, is a fallacy – in the wrong hands, it can be extremely severe. Its severity alters according to the width of the noseband and the type of curb strap used. A thin noseband and single link chain curb strap give the most severity.

Western bridles
Bridles used in Western riding can be bitless, or they may have a snaffle or curb bit of some sort. Western curb bits and spade bits – so-called because of the design of the port – usually have longer, more curved cheekpieces than those used in European riding, in which curb bits are seldom used on their own.

Western bridles fitted with bits rarely have a noseband, but even the few component parts this leaves may vary greatly in design, notably in the material used to make them. This can be plaited or braided rawhide or horse hair; it may be braided, plain or stitched leather; it may be silver-mounted, meaning it is ringed at intervals with silver or it may be braided with contrasting coloured leather. In comparison, the tack of the European or English riding horse looks very dull and conventional.

The reins on Western bridles vary according to whether they follow the Texan style or the Californian style (see page 78). Reins on a Texan-style bridle are always split – that is, not joined together at the end furthest from the bit. This is because the horses are usually trained to 'ground tie'; when the rider dismounts and lets one rein drop to the ground, the horse remains as still as if he was tethered. In the Californian style, it is more common for the reins to be braided together into a single length known as a 'romal'. This the rider can use as a quirt – a whip used for working cattle or swishing against the horse's side.

Putting on a bridle
The principles of putting on a bridle are the same whatever type of bit it has or if it is bitless. First make sure that the throat lash, noseband and curb chain or strap (as applicable) are undone. Then, standing on the horse's near side by the head, hold the bridle's headpiece in your left hand and put the reins over the neck. If the horse is wearing a headcollar, now remove it. Take hold of the headpiece with your right hand and hold it up towards the horse's ears. Hold the bit across the outstretched fingers of your left hand and gently open the horse's mouth by exerting slight pres-

Putting on a bridle Holding the headpiece in the left hand and standing on the horse's nearside, put reins over horse's head and neck. The horse will then be under your control.

Hold top of headpiece in right hand and cradle the bit on thumb and forefinger of the left. Slip left hand under the muzzle and insert a finger between front and back teeth to open the mouth.

Having slipped the bit into the mouth, bring headpiece over the ears, one at a time. Smooth forelock down and check that browband is clear of the ears. Check that no part of the headpiece is twisted.

Fasten the throat lash and noseband. There should be a hand's width between throat lash, jaw; two finger's width between the noseband and nose. The bit should not rest on the teeth.

Left: A horse correctly fitted with bridle. Fitting points include: **Below, left:** You should be able to get a hand's width between the throat and the throat lash. **Center:** You should be able to insert the breadth of two fingers between the noseband and the front of the horse's nose. **Right:** On a double bridle the curb chain is correctly fitted when it comes into contact with the groove when the cheekpieces of the bit are drawn back at a 45° angle to the mouthpiece of the bit. If you are using a metal link curb chain, twist it anti-clockwise until completely flat before hooking it. Hook the end link of any surplus chain onto the hook so it does not hit the bit.

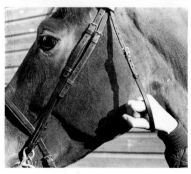

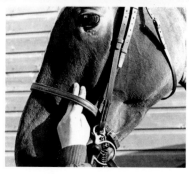

179

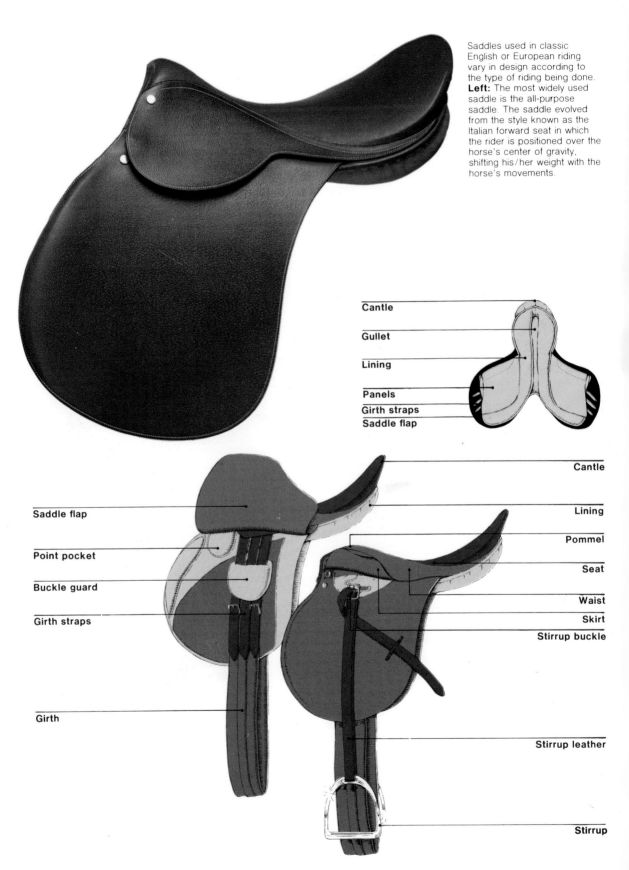

Saddles used in classic English or European riding vary in design according to the type of riding being done. **Left:** The most widely used saddle is the all-purpose saddle. The saddle evolved from the style known as the Italian forward seat in which the rider is positioned over the horse's center of gravity, shifting his/her weight with the horse's movements.

Cantle

Gullet

Lining

Panels
Girth straps
Saddle flap

Cantle

Lining

Pommel

Seat

Waist

Skirt

Stirrup buckle

Saddle flap

Point pocket

Buckle guard

Girth straps

Stirrup leather

Girth

Stirrup

A SELECTION OF SADDLES

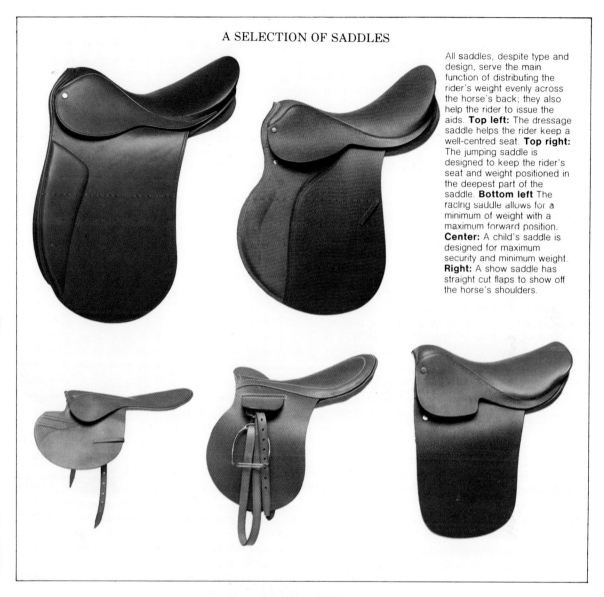

All saddles, despite type and design, serve the main function of distributing the rider's weight evenly across the horse's back; they also help the rider to issue the aids. **Top left:** The dressage saddle helps the rider keep a well-centred seat. **Top right:** The jumping saddle is designed to keep the rider's seat and weight positioned in the deepest part of the saddle. **Bottom left** The racing saddle allows for a minimum of weight with a maximum forward position. **Center:** A child's saddle is designed for maximum security and minimum weight. **Right:** A show saddle has straight cut flaps to show off the horse's shoulders.

sure on the corners with the fingers of this hand. As he opens his mouth, slip in the bit. Take the headpiece over the ears and pull them through the brow band. Buckle the throatlash, noseband and curb chain.

A bitless bridle is fitted in exactly the same way as a bridle with a bit. The only difference is that there is obviously no need to open the horse's mouth to accept the bit.

The saddle

The saddle evolved after the bridle. It came into being in order to make riding a more comfortable experience for both rider and horse. Riding bareback is tiring and somewhat insecure for the rider; it will also eventually injure the horse's back as the rider's weight presses directly on the spine.

All designs of saddle, therefore, have one thing in common – the central gullet directs pressure off the spine and instead distributes the rider's weight evenly on either side of the back over the fleshy muscular area covering the ribs. They also all assist a rider to control his or her mount by giving a firmer position from which to issue the aids.

The key feature of any saddle is a framework known as the tree, around which all saddles are built. The tree is usually made of lightweight wood. When this has been shaped and glued together, it forms the basis upon which webbing and padding will be bound and attached.

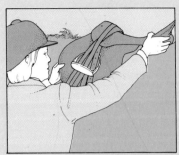

Putting on an all-purpose saddle:
Place the saddle in position, so the pommel is just behind the withers, with irons up and girth across it.

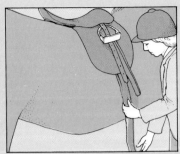

Check that the coat is smooth under the saddle flap. Then move around to the offside of the horse and let down the girth.

Putting on a side-saddle: Standing by the horse's nearside shoulder, lift up the saddle and place it on the horse slightly forward of the withers.

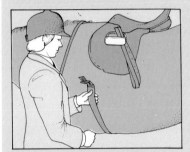

Return to the nearside and pass the girth under the horse's belly. Check carefully to make sure that it does not get twisted.

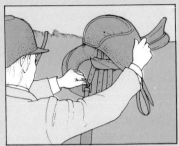

Buckle the girth firmly to hold the saddle securely in position. Adjust the stirrup leathers and tighten the girth again. Then mount.

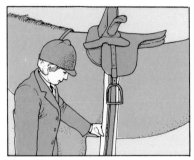

The girth, surcingle and balance strap are now hanging down on the horse's nearside and must be brought over to the offside.

Together, they determine the finished shape and, therefore, the purpose of the saddle.

The most widely used saddle in European riding today is the all-purpose saddle. This evolved from the riding style known as the Italian forward seat, which was developed in that country some 60 to 70 years ago. In this style of riding, the rider is positioned over the horse's center of gravity, shifting his or her position as the center shifts. An obvious example is leaning forward when a horse is jumping. Before this style was developed, a rider sat well back in the saddle, his legs pushed forward; if he had to jump, he would lean further back.

The design of saddles then in use encouraged such a position, so, to further their new ideas, the Italians developed a saddle that encouraged their new style. As this method of riding became widely adopted and practiced, most nations began to produce their own version of this saddle; anyone purchasing an all-purpose saddle today is faced with an enormous range.

Putting on a saddle

When putting on an all-purpose saddle, first make sure that the stirrup irons are run up the leathers so they are resting against the top sides of the saddle. The girth should be folded across the seat, not caught underneath the saddle. Standing by the horse's nearside shoulder, lift the saddle high over his back and place it slightly forward on the withers. Slide the saddle back into place, so the pommel is resting just behind the withers and the hair is lying smooth beneath it. Go around to the offside and take the girth down from the seat of the saddle. Check that the underflaps and the girth buckle guard (if applicable) on this side are lying flat against the lower sweat flap. Return to the nearside, pull the girth through to this side under the horse's belly and buckle it tightly enough to keep the saddle in place. When ready to mount, pull the irons down the leathers and tighten the girth a few more holes.

Side-saddles

Side-saddle riders are faced with a much smaller range of saddles from which to choose – if, indeed, they can find one at all. Nearly all side-saddles are secondhand, since, until the revival of the last decade or so, the art of aside riding – and thus the art of making side-saddles – had almost died out. Most side-saddles, too, were made to fit a specific rider and this is very

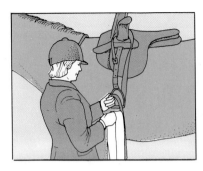

As the girths, surcingle and balance strap are all attached to the nearside of the saddle, undo these and take them down from the seat.

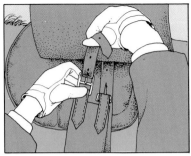

While still on the nearside of the horse, check to make sure that the girth is buckled sufficiently high up on the saddle.

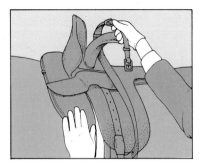

Unhook the surcingle from the pommel. If your horse is jumpy, ask an assistant to hold the saddle in place as it is not yet secured on the horse.

Bring the surcingle and girth through and buckle them securely. Make sure that the hook on the saddle flap is secured on the offside.

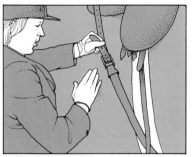

Pull the balance strap under the horse's belly, slotting it through the keeper on the girth. This will help to keep the strap in place.

Mount and ask an assistant to adjust the girth, balance strap, and surcingle, in that order, on the offside of the horse.

FITTING POINTS

Most saddles of European design are padded underneath, between the seat and lining. It is very important that the shape of the padding fits the horse's back and crucial to remember that an ill-fitting saddle or one that is positioned incorrectly will make both horse and rider extremely sore. It is also impossible for the rider to position himself correctly. **Above:** The saddle is placed too far forward. **Right:** The saddle is correctly placed over the spine distributing the weight on the fleshy parts on either side. Remember too that an ill-fitting or wrongly positioned saddle can never be corrected by padding or blankets. Many riders choose to put a numnah under the saddle, to keep the underside clean.

much a point to bear in mind when buying a secondhand one.

Putting on the side-saddle

When putting on a side-saddle, note that the girths, surcingle and balance strap are all attached to the nearside of a side-saddle. They should still be folded over the seat to keep them out of the way. Put the saddle in position on the horse's back from the nearside. Take the girths, balance strap and surcingle down from the seat and make sure that the girth is buckled sufficiently high up on this side as all further adjustments are made on the off-side. Go around to the offside. If you are not sure of your horse, or know it to be jumpy and nervy, get someone to hold the saddle in place, as it is only perched on the horse's back and not secured in any way. Bring the girth under the horse's tummy and buckle it to the girth straps, pulling it as tightly as the horse will allow. Pull the balance strap through under the horse's belly, slotting it through the keeper on the girth if there is one. This helps to keep the strap in place and also stops it sliding off the girth and pinching the horse's skin. Bring the surcingle through and buckle it. Mount and ask someone to adjust the girth, balance strap and surcingle (in that order on the offside). Make sure that the hook on the saddle flap is secured on this side.

Western saddles

There are almost as many designs of Western saddle as there are European ones. The basic design features – the high horn, deep, wide seat and high cantle – were born of practicality and are present to some extent in all Western saddles. However, over the generations, they have been subjected to endless variations and modifications.

The first stock saddle was said to have originated in Mexico, from whence it travelled to Texas, where it was copied. It continued to spread across the country, as ranchmen and cattle began to invade what had previously been buffalo territory. Alterations were made in different places to the rigging (the system of straps and girths that keeps the saddle in place), the horn and the swells (the padded area directly in front of the rider's knees which varies in degree according to taste and the rider's job). In addition, tremendous variations occurred in the actual aesthetic appearance of the saddles, according to the extent and elab-

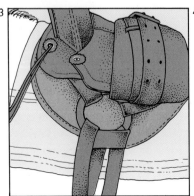

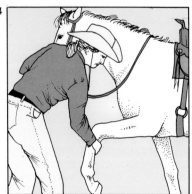

Putting on a Western saddle Western saddles are much heavier than English or European saddles. Because they were designed to carry a person long distances, they were often padded for additional comfort. In putting on a Western saddle, begin by making sure that the hair around and under the saddle is lying flat and smooth. Standing on the nearside, fold a blanket in half or thirds and put it high up on the withers, making sure it is evenly placed across the back. Place the saddle pad on to towards the front and position the saddle, pulling the blanket and pad up into the gullet so that they are not drawn too tightly across the horse's back. Go around to the offside and take the cinch and other straps down from the side of the saddle. Return to the nearside and pull these through under the horse's belly (1) then buckle or tie the cinch (2 and 3). The rear cinch does not have to be secured as tightly as the main cinch. Finally, pick up each of the forelegs in turn and pull them forward to ensure the cinch is not pinching the skin behind the elbow (4).

The Western saddle was designed for practicality. While some are very elaborate with detailed leather-work, most, like the one above, are simple, sturdy and functional. The horn is designed to withstand the stress of roping cattle and most saddles will have a deep seat and pronounced swells that allow the rider to sit relatively comfortably for long hours out on the range.

orateness of the tooling on the leather and the addition of ornate silver buckles and other adornments.

The cowboy's working stock saddle on the home range, differs from that used for Western pleasure riding, or more classic Western riding. Equally, it differs from the saddle used by another ranchhand, whose job involves him spending long hours of each day riding over the range. The cowboy working cows – roping them and jumping out of the saddle hundreds of times a day – uses a saddle with a very strong, reinforced horn that can withstand the strain of a twisting, bucking cow. The saddle also has almost flat swells, so that these do not get in his way as he leaps quickly from his horse's back. The ranchhand riding the range prefers a saddle with very pronounced swells and a deep seat which makes the long hours in the saddle that much more comfortable.

Unlike European saddles, the Western, or stock, saddle, has no padding. This is because the extreme heat of the climate, which would often cause the horse to sweat profusely, would soon affect the padding by shifting it about and making it hard and lumpy. For this reason, Western saddles are always worn with pads and

blankets underneath (these often were used as bedding for the rider when he had to sleep out on the range). Once again, though, the saddle must still fit the horse correctly; an ill-fitting Western saddle can no more be made to fit a horse by putting extra blankets underneath than a European saddle can be.

Putting on a Western saddle

When putting on a Western saddle, the blankets and pads come first. Make sure that the hair around the saddle area is lying flat and smooth. Standing on the nearside, fold the blanket in two or three and put it high up on the withers. Pull it gently back into place, so it lies just behind the withers. Make sure it is evenly placed across the back. Place the saddle pad on top of this towards the front of the blanket. Put the saddle into position and pull the blanket and pad up into the gullet so they are not drawn tightly across the horse's back. If they are, they will exert pressure on the spine. Go round to the offside and take the cinch and other rigging straps down from the side of the saddle. Return to the nearside and pull these straps through under the horse's tummy. Either buckle or tie the cinch. The rear cinch helps to keep the saddle in position, but does not have to be secured as tightly as the main cinch.

Stirrup irons

There are probably as many designs of stirrup iron, both in shape and material as there are

The most important point about any stirrup iron is that it be big enough for a rider's foot to rest comfortably, allowing 2cm (1 in) on the the outside. If not enough space is allowed, the foot may become wedged which is extremely dangerous, particularly in the event of a fall. There are many designs of stirrup irons, depending on the type of riding they are being used for. Obviously, a hunting iron will be designed differently from a child's pony iron. **Above:** Some of the more common irons, including, (1) stainless steel iron; (2) flat racing iron; (3) Peacock child's safety iron; (4) Fillis dressage iron. **Right:** a sample of a Western stirrup leather and iron.

girths and cinches. Those found on European saddles may be made of steel (stainless steel is the best), plated metal or nickel (the last is not recommended as it is rather soft). The design may vary for practical reasons – such as the lightweight stirrup irons used by jockeys or the safety stirrup irons for children – or to satisfy aesthetic or personal preference. Stirrups on most Western saddles are made of wood and bound with leather.

Girths and cinches

Saddles, whatever their type, are held in place on the horse's back by a single girth or a series

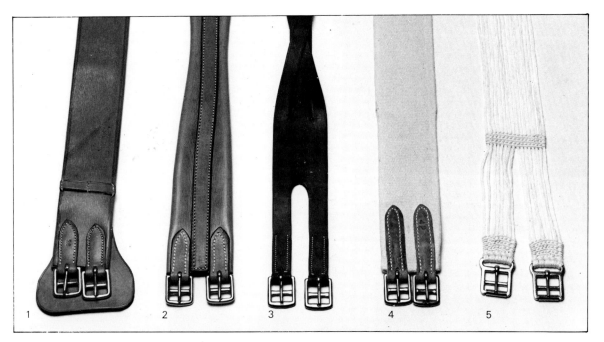

1 2 3 4 5

The saddle is held in place by the girth. Again, there are many styles and types **Above:** Some of the more common girths, including (1) Lonsdale dressage girth; (2) Atherstone leather girth; (3) balding girth; (4) Lampwick nylon girth; (5) nylon string girth. **Right:** Head-collars are used for catching the horse and tethering. **Below:** Some nosebands serve only to enhance the horse's appearance, others have a definite purpose. (1) The plain cavesson; (2) the grackle or figure-of-eight gives the rider greater control; (3) the flash noseband allows a standing martingale and drop noseband to be used simultaneously; (4) drop nosebands are often used on headstrong ponies.

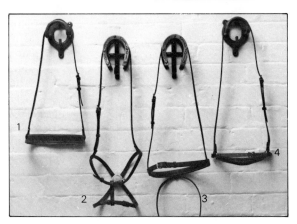

1 2 3 4

of girths, straps and surcingles. The main girth in a Western saddle is called a cinch.

Girths and cinches come in a wide variety of designs and may be made from many different materials.

Ancillary equipment

As mentioned earlier, one of the items that most affects the appearance and design of the bridle is the noseband. The most commonly used noseband is a cavesson; this consists of a simple strap of leather that buckles around the horse's nose (above the bit and inside the cheek pieces). It is kept in place by a thin strap that passes over the top of the horse's head beneath the headpiece of the bridle.

Unless it is used with a standing martingale, the cavesson serves no practical function. However, many riders believe that it enhances the appearance of a horse's head.

Drop nosebands are extremely popular, particularly for use on small ponies, who tend to open their mouths, take hold of the bit and thereafter do what they like regardless of their rider's wishes. The noseband buckles below the bit. When buckled, it should not alter the position of the bit in the horse's mouth by pushing it up into the corners.

The name of the grackle or figure-of-eight noseband comes from the part that lies across the front of the horse's face. This is made of thin leather, arranged, as the name suggests, in a figure-of-eight. The point at the center is padded with a small circle of leather and the straps buckle above and below the bit. It keeps the horse's mouth closed and discourages him from 'yawing' – that is, perpetually stretching his head out and down to open his mouth and reach for the bit. Pressure is also applied quite strongly on the front of the nose by the cross-over point.

A flash noseband is an ordinary cavesson, with two thin straps sewn diagonally across the front central part of the nose strap. These buckle beneath the bit like a drop noseband. The purpose of the noseband is to enable a standing martingale and drop noseband to be used simultaneously.

Martingales

Martingales are among the most commonly used items of ancillary equipment. There are three types in common use. The Irish martingale consists of a short strip of leather with a ring situated at either end for the reins to pass through. The martingale then lies along the reins and helps to keep them close together and positioned evenly on either side of the neck. It is mainly used on racehorses, to help prevent the reins going over the horse's head in the event of a fall by the jockey.

A standing martingale is a long strip of leather, which loops through the girth at one end and the back part of the cavesson at the other. It is held in place by a strap which buckles round the horse's neck. This strap should be kept in position on the main strap of the martingale by a rubber keeper placed across the join. The purpose of the standing martin-

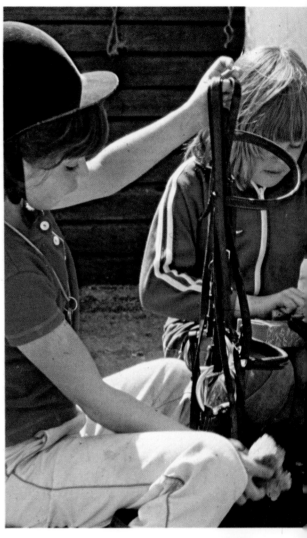

CARRYING A SADDLE

Far left: Rest the front arch in the crook of your left elbow so the central gullet runs along your forearm. Hold the cantle with the other hand to distribute the weight. Pass the bridle headpiece over your left shoulder to free your right hand. **Left:** Carry the saddle facing downwards so the front arch rests on your left hip and support with your left hand. **Right:** Avoid resting your saddle on the ground. If necessary, fold the girth over the pommel and stand the saddle on the front arch. Forward-cut saddles cannot be rested on the front arch and must be leant against a wall. Fold the girth over the back to protect the cantle.

Tack and saddlery are expensive investments and should be cared for accordingly. Proper cleaning and care of your equipment will not only make it last longer, but, in terms of safety, a piece of tack that becomes brittle due to lack of conditioning could lead to an accident. Saddlery should ideally be cleaned each time it is used; if, however, this is not possible, a cursory cleaning should be done following use with a more thorough cleaning done at least once a week. Saddlery not in use should be cleaned once a week as well to ensure that the leather is kept in good condition and kept from cracking and drying out. Keep your cleaning equipment in a box and store in a convenient place.

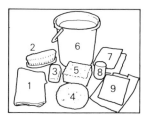

Equipment for cleaning tack (1) a chamois leather; (2) for a saddle with serge lining, a dandy brush; (3) a tin or bar of saddle soap; (4) and (5) two sponges, one flat and one for soaping; (6) a bucket or bowl of tepid water; (7) two cloths, one for polishing; (8) metal polish; and (9) two stable rubbers.

gale is to prevent a horse from lifting his head unnaturally high in the air. However, the martingale should never be so tightly fixed that a horse's head is forced into an unnaturally low position.

The running martingale is similar in design to the standing except that the end attached to the cavesson is divided and, at the end of each strap, is a ring through which the reins are passed. The running martingale serves a similar purpose to the standing martingale, in that it helps to position the horse's head correctly. It acts more directly on the mouth and is slightly less rigid in its positioning of the head. Small leather 'stops' should be fitted on the reins to prevent the martingale rings sliding forward.

Care of saddlery
All items of tack or saddlery are expensive.

Proper treatment and regular cleaning not only makes them last longer; it also ensures that they remain in good condition and are safe to use. Neglected tack soon becomes cracked and brittle but – in the absence of regular inspection – could pass unnoticed until it snaps one day.

The daily treatment of saddlery – how the saddle is carried, stored and put on the ground, the way the bridle is treated when not in use – greatly affects its general condition and the extent of its life.

Cleaning the saddle
Put the saddle on the saddle horse and remove the girth, buckle guards, stirrup leathers and irons. Hang up the girth and leathers or put them over the horse. If the saddle is leather-lined, wash this part with a damp sponge, wrung out thoroughly in the water. Dry it with

the chamois leather. Sponge over linen or scrub if it is very dirty. Brush serge lining and avoid scrubbing it, as it will take several days to dry. Wash the rest of the saddle, beginning under the flaps taking care not to get the leather too wet. This is particularly important when washing the seat, as water may seep through the leather, saturate the stuffing and distort it. Dry all leather with the chamois. Damp the flat very slightly and rub over the saddle soap. Soap all the leather rubbing the soap in a circular movement. If this produces a lot of lather, the sponge is too damp and you will not get a shine on the leather. Check the girth straps as you soap to make sure the holes are not worn or split. Replace the saddle on its bracket (or leave it on the horse) and cover with a clean stable rubber. Before using, rub over the seat and flaps with a damp sponge and dry off with the chamois leather to remove surplus soap. Wash and soap the stirrup leather in the same way and wash the girth according to type. Webbing should be brushed and scrubbed; nylon and string scrubbed; leather is treated as other leather items. Wash the stirrup irons and dry them on the other stable rubber. Clean them

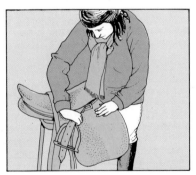

Cleaning the saddle Put the saddle on the saddle horse and remove girth, buckleguards, stirrup leathers and irons. Wash with damp sponge.

Dry all the leather with the chamois. Wash the saddle with soap beginning under the flaps taking care not to over-wet the leather.

Before using the saddle, rub over the seat and flaps with a damp sponge and dry with the chamois leather to remove any remaining soap.

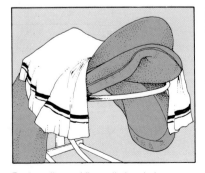

Replace the saddle on its bracket or leave it on the horse if this is where it is usually kept. Cover it with a clean stable rubber.

Wash and soap the stirrup leathers in the same way. Wash all girths according to type: leather as above, webbing brushed and scrubbed, and nylon scrubbed.

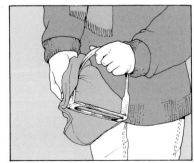

Wash the stirrup irons and dry with the other stable rubber. Polish them with metal polish and shine with a soft cloth.

CLEANING THE BIT

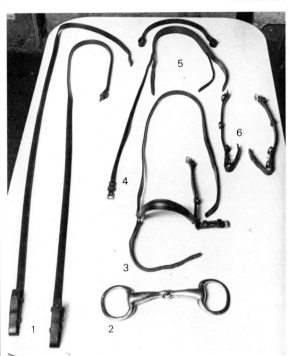

Cleaning the bridle As you will have to dismantle and reassemble the bridle, it is important to be familiar with its various parts. Above:

(1) reins; (2) snaffle bit; (3) noseband; (4) headpiece; (5) browband; (6) cheekpieces.

After dissembling, wash all parts with damp cloth (except metal pieces) and dry with soft cloth.

Wrap the soaped sponge around the straps and rub gently up and down. Rub over with the chamois.

Wash and dry the bit and polish the rings – not the mouthpiece – with metal polish.

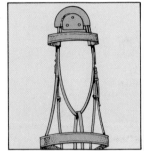

Hang the bridle up by the headpiece, reins caught in throatlash and noseband secured outside the cheekpieces.

with metal polish and shine with the soft cloth.

Ideally, girth and stirrup leathers should be hung on hooks, rather than buckling them back on to the saddle. Stirrup leathers, in particular, wear quickly at the fold.

Cleaning the bridle

Undo all fastenings and lay the pieces out on the table. Note the holes that have been used to ensure you reassemble it correctly. Wash and dry all leather straps the same as for the saddle, making sure you thoroughly wash the underside of the straps. Examine buckle holes to see if any are worn and in need of attention. Soap the leather by wrapping the sponge around the straps and rubbing gently up and down. Rub with the chamois leather. Wash and dry the bit and polish the rings – not the mouthpiece, with metal polish. Reassemble the bridle, buckling the straps on the correct holes and making sure the ends are tucked into the keepers.

A clean bridle should be hung up by the headpiece with the reins caught in the buckled throatlash and the noseband secured outside

the cheek pieces. The noseband is not buckled; instead, the end strap should be passed through the keepers so it remains in place. If the bridle has a curb chain, this should be twisted flat and hooked on either side of the bit, so the chain passes in front of the bit.

If you are giving your tack a quick clean – after daily exercise, say – always clean the underside of the saddle, so the sweat deposited there does not harden and rub the horse's back. Clean the girth and wash and soap the stirrup leathers. If the irons are very muddy, clean them too. Remove and wash the bit, so that any saliva stains do not dry and harden. Wash and soap the reins, particularly if the horse has sweated up on its neck during the ride, and also check over the buckle holes on the rest of the bridle.

Have the saddle and your other tack checked by a saddler once a year. He will check over the tree to ensure it is still in good repair, look at the stitching and assess, too, whether it is necessary to restuff the saddle, all of which will save you money later on.

Horse Maintenance

HORSE MAINTENANCE INCLUDES not only the routines of feeding and cleaning, but also very important areas such as shoeing and illness for which you should establish a good relationship with a qualified farrier and vet.

Horses that are being worked to any extent – whether they are being ridden or used to pull a vehicle – must have their feet shod with metal shoes. Riding an unshod horse soon wears away the hard insensitive horn of the foot and exposes the more sensitive areas. If this happens, these areas become sore and the horse becomes lame within a very short time.

The shoeing of horses is a highly skilled and specialist task, undertaken by a trained craftsman known as a farrier. If the shoes do not fit, or if they pinch the feet in any way, then obviously the horse will not be able to give of its best.

To understand how the farrier goes about his task, it is necessary to have some knowledge of the structure of the horse's foot.

Hot and cold shoeing

There are two types of shoeing – hot and cold. At one time, the former was virtually the only method practiced, but nowadays it has been largely superceded by cold shoeing. This method enables farriers to go to the horse rather than the horse having to be taken to the

The care of the horse's feet is probably the most important part of horsemastership and every rider should know the parts and functions of the horse's hoof.

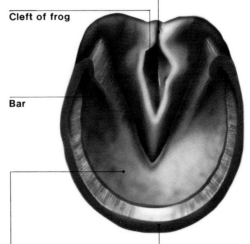

Frog: The frog is V-shaped and leathery, and provides the foot with a natural shock absorber and non-slip device. The farrier never pares back the frog and it needs daily attention to keep it clean and healthy.

Cleft of frog

Bar

Sole: This protects the underside of the foot, however, the outer layer is thin so the inner sensitive area is still quite vulnerable.

Wall: The wall, like the human fingernail, is insensitive and always growing. Because of the latter, the shoes must be removed regularly and the hoof pared into shape.

TYPES OF SHOES

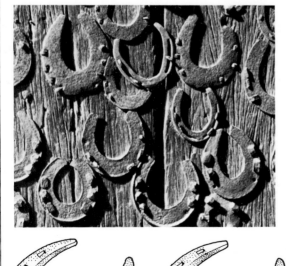

Bottom left: A horseshoe is held in place by nails driven into the tough, horny part of the foot. They are twisted off where they emerge higher up and hammered down. A horse's shoes should never in any way interfere with the horse's natural actions and movements. Clips help to keep the shoe in place. These are small triangular points that fit into the wall of the hoof. Usually there is one clip on the foreshoe and two on the hindshoe. Grip is extremely important and there are several methods for improving it including calks and calking. However, studs are considered the most effective. These are not left in permanently but screwed in place by the farrier. **Right, top to bottom:** Several types of shoes including a hunter shoe, a grass shoe, a corn shoe a leather shoe, and a T-shaped shoe for horses with contracted heels or corns.

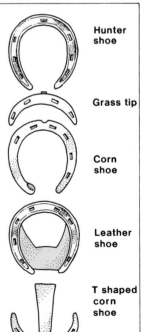

Hunter shoe

Grass tip

Corn shoe

Leather shoe

T shaped corn shoe

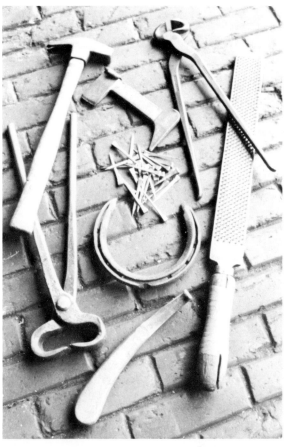

SHOEING – BEFORE AND AFTER

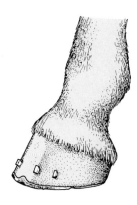

It is absolutely vital that you watch for the signs indicating that your horse needs new shoes. Ideally, this should be done on a regular basis and the shoe and hoof should not be allowed to reach an unhealthy or dangerous state before you get new ones. **Left:** This horse is badly in need of new shoes, the indications being that the shoe itself has worn thin and rough and the clenches have risen and are standing out from the wall. All of these factors are dangerous and unhealthy for the horse.

Right: A newly-shod foot should show certain points indicating that it has been correctly fitted. The shoe should be fitted to the foot and not vice versa; the foot should be rasped and pared evenly and the frog in contact with the ground; a suitable number of nails should be used – never too many nor too few, and the clenches should be neat and evenly spaced. There should be no space between the shoe and the foot and the clip should fit well on each shoe.

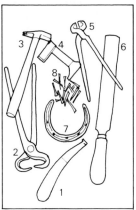

Above: The farrier's skill with his tools will largely determine the fit of the horse's shoe and, consequently, his performance. Some of the tools used by the farrier include: (1) drawing knife used to trim away overgrown horn after old shoe is removed; (2) pincers to remove the old shoe; (3) shoeing hammer to drive in nails; (4) buffer after shoeing; (5) pincers; (6) rasp for filing down hoof to ensure smooth fit; (7) the shoe; (8) nails; usually three per shoe.

smithy and is thus more convenient. Hot shoeing, however, is said to be superior – the maxim being that the shoe is made to fit the foot, not vice versa, as in cold shoeing.

Whatever method is used, the farrier first removes the old shoe, cuts away the excess growth of horn and rasps the surface of the foot to make it even. In hot shoeing, he then places the red hot shoe against the bottom of the foot. It is hard to believe this is not a painful process,

but, in fact, no pain is caused. The mark left by the hot metal tells the farrier whether he needs to alter the shape of the shoe, or needs to rasp the surface of the foot further. In cold shoeing, the farrier can only judge by placing the cold shoe against the foot. It is not as easy to alter a cold shoe by hammering as it is a hot shoe, where the metal is more malleable.

In hot shoeing, the blacksmith cools the shoe once satisfied with the fit. He then hammers it on to the foot using as few nails as possible, but enough to keep it in position; this is usually three on the inside and four on the outside. The points of the nails emerge through the front wall of the hoof and the farrier twists them off with the claw end of the hammer. Finally he hammers the nail heads against the hoof and rasps them smooth so they lie flush against the wall. The point at which the nails emerge in the front is critical; if too low, they may not keep the shoe in place, tearing down through the outer horn to cause cracking, while, if positioned too high, they can bruise the sensitive inner area of the hoof.

How often a horse needs new shoes will

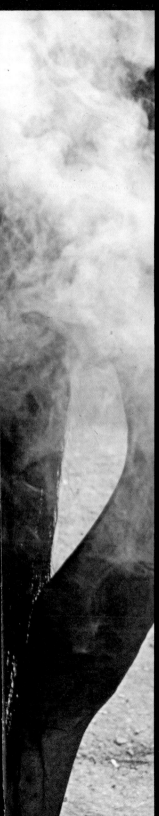

A large percentage of minor, and major, ailments and injuries can afflict your horse due to improper shoeing. It is necessary to realise that the farrier is as important to you and your horse as your vet, and, while it is difficult to find a highly skilled farrier, every effort should be made to do so. Your horse will need new shoes every month, depending on the type and amount of work he is doing. It is a good idea for you to understand the steps taken in shoeing your horse: (1) the horse's old shoes are removed with pincers; (2) the overgrown horn is filed down with a rasp; (3) the new shoes are heated and fitted hot to the horse's foot to locate uneveness of fit; (4) the farrier forges the shoe using his judgement as to fit; (5) the shoe is fitted and nailed to the foot; (6) the new shoe is filed down.

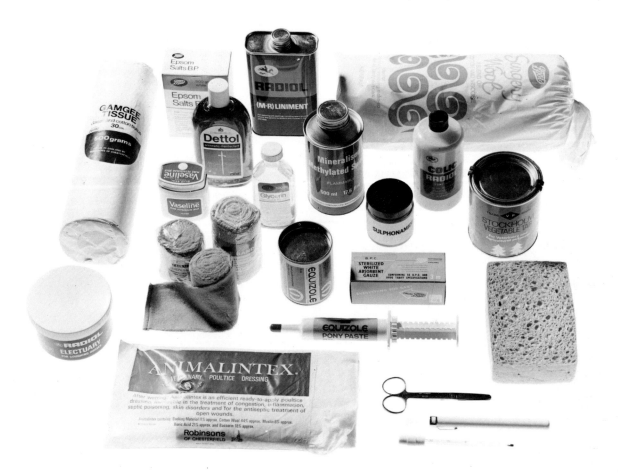

depend to some extent on how hard he is working and on what type of ground. However, most horses should be seen by the farrier once a month, since it may be necessary to cut back the excess growth of horn even if the horse is reshod with old shoes. Even horses out at grass must be looked at by the farrier once a month. They will not move around sufficiently to keep the horn down to a reasonable length and, if it gets too long, it could cause them to trip. The horn, too, may begin to crack and break.

The Horse and the veterinary surgeon
Anyone contemplating buying a horse, should establish contact with a veterinary surgeon, for his advice and services will inevitably be needed at some time in the future. It is just as important to have a vet whom you trust and can rely upon as it is to find an instructor or farrier with these qualities. Having found one, keep his telephone number in a convenient place.

First aid
You should have a set of first aid equipment conveniently at hand. Consult your vet and

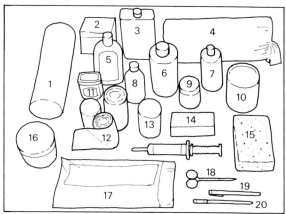

First aid equipment needed: (1) gamgee tissue, (2) epsom salts, (3) liniment, (4) cotton wool, (5) antiseptic, (6) methylated spirit, (7) specific for colic, (8) glycerine, (9) sulphonamide powder, (10) Stockholm tar, (11) petroleum jelly, (12) bandages, (13) worming remedy, (14) gauze, (15) sponge, (16) coughing electuary, (17) poultice, (18) worm paste, (19) round-ended surgical scissors, (20) thermometer.

Every stable should have a first aid emergency kit within easy reach and the kit should contain all the essential items listed **above.** You will be able to treat minor injuries yourself, such as small cuts or saddle sores, but if you are ever in any doubt, the wisest course of action is to call your vet and describe the symptoms to him.

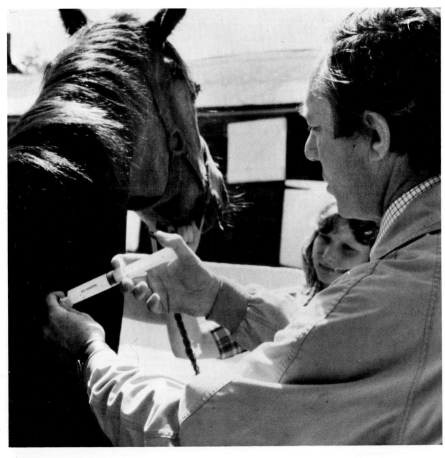

obtain the items he recommends.

There will be many minor injuries and accidents which you can treat yourself with the help of the kit – such as small cuts or various saddle sores – but, if ever you are in any doubt, call the vet. It will help him if you describe the symptoms that have led to your call clearly and precisely. This may avert a visit that would be unnecessary and expensive or help him come to a preliminary diagnosis. If he is going to come to see the horse, have the animal tied up and ready for him in a loose box or field shelter, where there is adequate light for an examination. Do not attempt to give any treatment yourself in the meantime. The golden rule is never to treat a sick or injured animal in any way unless you are absolutely sure what to do; even then, make sure you read the directions on any dressing or medicine pack thoroughly and follow them to the letter.

Dental care

Owners often forget one of the vet's most important tasks – the care of the horse's teeth. Obviously, the horse relies entirely on his teeth

to obtain and make the best use of food; if they are paining him in any way, he will soon stop eating and so lose condition.

In the normal course of events, the horse keeps the surface of his teeth smooth by grinding them together. He chews or masticates his food by grinding the teeth of the upper and lower jaws together in a circular action. In many horses, however, the surfaces of the teeth do not wear down evenly, the result being that razor-sharp pointed edges develop on some of them. These cause the horse considerable pain, as they 'catch' in the soft, sensitive skin on the inner cheeks, and so it is essential to file down the sharp points as they develop. The vet does this with a small, extremely rough rasp, which quickly smooths and flattens the tooth's surface.

Points indicating that dental treatment is necessary are if an animal goes off his food for no other apparent reason, such as identifiable sickness, or if he throws his head up in the air suddenly when out riding without cause. Ask the vet to check the teeth every six months in any case.

In Competition

HOW ONE INITIALLY DECIDES to enter the world of competitive riding depends entirely upon the individual; however, it is a well known fact that, no matter what type of competition or skill required; competitive riding is a demanding sport – mentally as well as physically. Your aim should not be to win but to always work toward perfecting your performance and understanding your faults as well as your capabilities.

Show jumping

Show jumping is a newcomer to the world of competitive horsemanship, having begun in the early part of this century. Now, however, it is one of the best known types of competition and rates as a top spectator sport. Show jumping is truly an international sport; competitors from all over the world compete at the major shows held annually and there are show jumping competitions for all standards of rider.

Gymkhanas

In some countries, competitive mounted games are very much the province of children and their nimble, little ponies. The games form the major part of the many gymkhanas and involve ingeniously devised races, the variations of which seem to be endless. Most gymkhanas will include a few games that have become almost classics – such as bending and the sack race.

In other countries, similar mounted games are equally keenly contested by adults. Most rodeos, for example, include a number of mounted games in addition to the more traditional rodeo events.

Eventing

Eventing has become one of the most popular fields of equestrian competition over the last twenty years, producing hundreds of new competitors each year. It is as international as show jumping and has a much longer history, beginning centuries ago as the ideal way of training horses and men for the cavalry. The three separate phases of eventing – dressage, cross-country jumping and show jumping – demand horses and riders that are extremely versatile.

Competition dressage

Dressage can be defined as the art of training a riding horse so it is well-mannered, responsive,

Right: This immaculately turned-out horse and rider show the standard you should aim at when entering any form of competition. The process should start the day before, with a thorough grooming for your horse. Braids, too, can be prepared, the finishing touches being made the following morning. You should be smart, too.

198

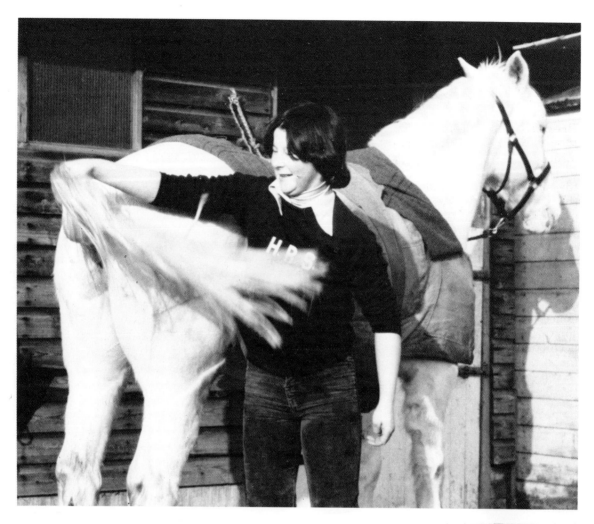

obedient and a joy to ride and watch. It may be conducted competitively to varying standards. All riders now realize the tremendous value of dressage training, which begins with the most elementary school work. At its highest level, the training and movements required from a horse are extremely intricate and must be executed with great precision.

Showing

Showing classes – that is, events in which horses of similar type compete to be judged primarily on appearance – are one of the oldest forms of formally conducted equestrian competition. Horse shows, which are common occurrences the world over and which, in most people's minds are dominated by the more spectacular show jumping events, originally only consisted of showing classes.

Showing is still immensely popular among horsemen and women, even though it does not

Washing: First brush the horse's tail in the usual way to remove any tangles. **Below:** Wet the tail well and apply a hard yellow soap (never a cosmetic soap) and rub the hairs together with your hands. **Right:** Rinse well and run your hands down the length of the tail to remove the excess water. **Above:** To dry, hold the tail by the bottom of the dock and swing it around in a circle.

have the same spectator appeal as other forms of competition. There are many different showing classes, ranging from those for specific breeds to those for countless different types of riding horses and ponies and also styles of riding.

Preparing to compete

If, as a rider, you intend to participate in some form of equestrian competition, you will have to prepare your horse. This involves training the animal in the specific skills necessary for the event, making sure he is fit enough to perform, and also caring for him in such a way that he looks his best on the day.

Anybody who enters his or her horse in a competition will want the animal to look its best. This applies whether the competition is one at a small local gymkhana or a top-level showing class. While the final touches will be done the day before and the morning of the show, a horse will only look its best if it has been fed, ridden, groomed and generally cared for regularly each day for some time. It is impossible to bring a grass-kept horse that has gone without grooming over the preceding weeks into a stable the night before a show and expect to make it look glossy and shining.

Shampooing a horse

You should always give your horse a thorough grooming or strapping the day before the show. If he has any white socks or stockings, these should be shampooed. The tail, too, will look smarter if it is washed.

Hard yellow soap available from saddlers should be used when shampooing any part of a horse; never use soft, cosmetic-type soap. To wash the legs, wet them first with tepid water, then rub them with soap to produce a lather. Scrub very gently using the water brush and then rinse with plenty of clean water, making sure all vestiges of soap have been removed. Rub the legs as dry as possible with a stable rubber, letting them dry completely before bandaging them. If you wash your horse's legs frequently, grease the heels periodically to reduce the risk of the skin cracking through

Tail bandages: Brush out to remove tangles, dampen tail, brush out and unroll a short length of bandage beneath it.

Holding end of bandage against tail, turn once to secure it. Continue evenly down the tail.

The bandage should stop just short of the last bone. The remaining bandage is wound upward and secured.

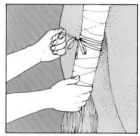

Bend the tail into a comfortable position. To remove, slide downward with both hands.

Foot bandages: Pad beneath the bandage with cotton wool or equivalent.

Roll bandage evenly down from below knee or hock to the coronet.

Continue upward to the start, making sure bandage is remaining even and tight.

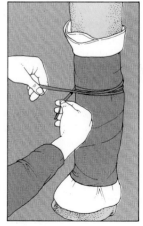

Finish off bandage by securing in the front of the leg. Make sure entire bandage is tight.

BRAIDING THE MANE

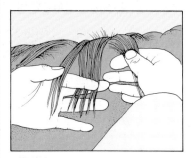

Brush mane to lay hairs, dampen the hair and divide into sections with a water brush.

Begin to braid so that the top of the braid is tight against the roots of the hair.

Secure the end with a needle and thread passed through the braid and wind tightly.

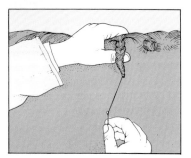

Take loose ends at bottom of braid, wrap tightly with thread and bring under.

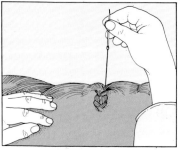

After winding thread around the braid, fold the braid under and stitch it to the braid half way up.

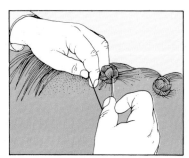

The loop is then rolled up tightly forming a knob close to the poll and is firmly stitched into place.

due to excessive dampness.

To shampoo the tail, first brush it in the usual way to remove any tangles. Then, wet it thoroughly and soap it well. Rub the hairs together with your hands and rinse the tail thoroughly. Run your hands down the length of the tail several times to remove as much water as possible. Then, standing by the side of the hindquarters, hold the tail by the bottom of the dock and swing it round in a circle. This helps to dislodge any remaining water in the same way as a dog does when it shakes itself after a bath or a swim.

Brush the tail out in the normal way, using the body brush and put on a tail bandage which helps to keep the tail clean and ensures the top hairs dry flat. The bandage should not be left on overnight, as it can constrict the circulation in the dock. Thus, you have washed the tail the day before the show. Remove the tail bandage when you bed down the horse and put on another after brushing the tail in the morning.

If a horse's coat is very stained, it is possible to shampoo him all over, but this should only be done if it is absolutely necessary. Only shampoo a horse's coat if the day is warm, dry and preferably sunny. Use the same sort of soap described above with plenty of warm water, and, having soaped and scrubbed the entire coat, rinse it very thoroughly. Remove the surplus water by pulling a sweat scraper across the coat. Then go over the entire body with a dry sponge to 'mop up' as much remaining water as possible. After this, rub it dry, then walk the horse around until the coat has dried completely. Finally, brush the coat in the normal way with the body brush.

Showing routine

If you are keeping your horse at grass – but riding and grooming him daily – at the time of the show or competition, it is a great help to bring him into the stable the night before the show. This ensures that he remains relatively clean after any shampooing or grooming; he is also immediately to hand in the morning.

If you are entering in a show, you will obviously have been riding and probably feeding your horse regularly for some time previously. Do not make the mistake of giving him a huge feed the night before to pep him up. This is far more likely to have an adverse affect on the horse's performance. Give him the usual sized feed the night before and then another sufficiently early on the morning of the show to allow him to eat in peace and still leave you enough time to get him ready.

Having groomed him to shining perfection,

Tail braiding Braid down using side hairs. When two-thirds down, use center hairs.

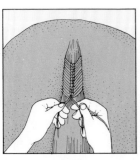

Stitch end of braid with needle and thread, double under and secure half way down.

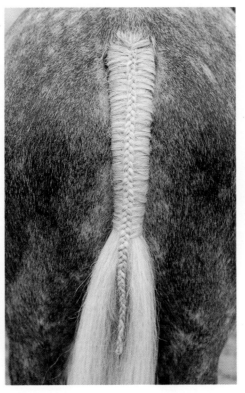

The superficial but important aspects can be done the day before the show and include washing the horse, including the mane and tail, bandaging of legs and braiding the tail and mane. The latter is a matter of personal preference and, if not a necessary aspect of showing, does contribute to the rider's attitude of confidence and pride in his horse and himself.

you can braid the mane if you so wish. This is not a practice confined exclusively to show horses; show jumpers, eventers and ponies entered in small local shows will often be seen with their manes braided. It smartens the appearance and also indicates to the judges and the spectators that you have been prepared to take some time and trouble in getting your horse ready for the show.

If it is an autumn, or even an early spring show on a cold day, your horse will probably need to wear a rug for his journey, if he is being transported in a horse box or trailer. A smart day rug (see page 160) is the most suitable type. In the summer, all that is needed is a cotton fly

Equipment: It is vital to plan all preparations for a show and you should leave enough time to prepare a timetable, the equipment needed, your horse, and yourself. It is a good idea to make out a list beforehand. **Left**: (1) bridle and lead rope; (2) saddle and pad; (3) haynet; (4) bucket for feeding; (5) grooming kit; (6) hoof oil (often overlooked); (7) first aid kit; (8) day rug. **Below**: A horse prepared for showing and travelling.

Above: Lead your horse up the ramp; a layer of straw on the ramp will prevent his slipping. Avoid exciting your horse by shouting or waving your hands. **Right**: Walk in with your horse, looking straight ahead and tie him on a short rope. **Left**: Close the ramp up quickly once inside. Provide your horse with a bowl of feed.

sheet to keep the dust off the groomed coat. It also acts as a protection against irritating flies.

It is also generally best to bandage a horse's legs if he is to be boxed. This protects them from any knocks or bangs against the sides of the box and also helps to keep them clean. A valuable horse may also wear knee caps and hock boots to give added protection. The tail should be bandaged to prevent it getting ruffled against the sides or back of the box; it can be protected further by a tail guard, if necessary.

To remove bandages, untie the securing tapes and unwind the bandage, passing it quickly from hand-to-hand. Remove the protective wool or tissue and rub the legs briskly with your hands to liven the circulation. Do not kneel by the horse's legs as you do this (or as you apply bandages) – you must always be in a position to be able to jump sideways should this ever become a necessity.

Traveling to a show

If the show is near you can ride your horse but the usual practice is to travel in a horse box or trailer. Having got your horse ready, gather together all the equipment you will need.

Whether a trailer or a large horse box is used, there should be a covering of straw to make it as comfortable as possible for the horse. Tie up a net of hay to help relieve boredom.

Boxing a horse

Most horses are used to being boxed and will walk into the confined space without any problems. Lead the horse to the ramp – a thin covering of straw helps to prevent slipping – walking in a straight line so he can see what lies ahead. Walk straight up the ramp yourself and into the box without looking back; more often than not, the horse will follow you. Tie him on a short rope, so there is no chance of him getting a leg caught. It helps if you have a helper who can raise the ramp as soon as the horse is inside the box in case he tries to back out.

If a horse is difficult to box, always coax him in gently; never try to get him into the box by force or by shouting loudly, flapping your arms or hitting him. This will only make him twice as bad the next time. A bowl of feed placed inside the box may act as an enticement and it will help if you feed him in the box, perhaps parked in his field, each day. Always make a fuss of him when he does go into the box and reward him with a titbit.

Driving needs care as well. A horse box

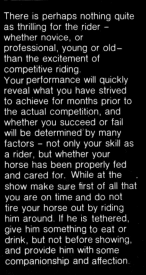

There is perhaps nothing quite as thrilling for the rider – whether novice, or professional, young or old – than the excitement of competitive riding.

Your performance will quickly reveal what you have strived to achieve for months prior to the actual competition, and whether you succeed or fail will be determined by many factors – not only your skill as a rider, but whether your horse has been properly fed and cared for. While at the show make sure first of all that you are on time and do not tire your horse out by riding him around. If he is tethered, give him something to eat or drink, but not before showing, and provide him with some companionship and affection.

Watching your fellow competitors is an excellent way to learn not only what to do but what not to do in competition. Before the actual events take place, it is a good idea to walk the course, noting especially the types of fence being used, their spacing, and degree of difficulty. You will often see riders pacing out the course while walking to get some idea of how they will maneuver their horses while competing. Any turns and bends must be very carefully appraised as well.

should always be driven slowly and steadily; the horse inside is in a very unstable position and he will find it difficult to keep his balance if the box is swung around corners.

Unloading

To unbox a horse let down the ramp, untie the headcollar rope and depending on the design of the box, push the horse's chest very gently to encourage him to step backwards out of the box. In general, it is kinder to tether a horse outside the box (providing it is not in the glaring sunshine) or, better still, under the shade of some trees, than it is to leave him standing in the somewhat cramped conditions of most trailers. Only tether a horse, though, if you are sure he reacts well to such a practice and will not become excited if other horses at the show are ridden past.

At the show

It is advisable to plan entries for a show well in advance, rather than turning up and then making your entries. You may well find that the classes you want to enter are already full and the organizers are refusing to allow any more riders to enter for them.

Horse shows are normally advertized in local papers, the national horse magazines or on posters around the area where the show is to be held. Advertisements will give names of show secretaries from whom you can obtain schedules. From these, you can select the show you want to go to (if there are two or three on one day) and plan which classes you want to enter. Send off the entry form well in advance of the show – either to ensure your entry in a particular class, or to give you time to change your plans if it is already full.

When planning which classes to enter, study the times given in the schedule carefully to make sure you do not enter two that overlap. It can happen that you will be competing in a jump-off, say, at the same time as your next class is called in to the ring. This is disappointing for you and disruptive for the organizers.

On the day of the show, make sure you are on time for your classes; you cannot expect the start to be delayed until you arrive and if you are not there, you may well not be allowed to take part. In jumping competitions, the normal procedure is to go to the collecting ring in advance of the competition and give your number to one of the stewards. He will write it on a board, thereby establishing the order in which the competitors will jump. If you want to jump early on in the event, make sure you get to the collecting ring well before the start of the competition.

Care at the show

During the day, consider the well-being and comfort of your horse before anything else. Do not ride him endlessly round the show ground in between classes, sitting on his back talking to your friends or jumping small practice jumps over and over again. If you are tethering him, make sure he is in the shade and give him a haynet to nibble at. Always offer him a drink of water after a class, taking off his bridle so he can drink more comfortably; do not do this, however, if you are due to ride in another class straight away. Give him a drink again before loading to go home.

When your classes are over, take your horse home immediately. He will be tired and will not want to stand in a cramped box while you watch the other events. If he is very hot and sweaty, walk him round to cool off before loading him. Once home, bed him down in the stable or put him out in the field straight away, rather than fussing over him. All that needs to be done in the way of grooming is to pick out his hooves and take out the plaits. Again, do not give him a large feed as a misguided reward for his hard day's work – give him a normal-size one. When a horse is tired, his digestive system is less efficient than normal and a big feed can easily result in colic. Give him a rest from riding the next day, but check him over thoroughly to make sure he did not sustain any injuries in the way of minor cuts, knocks or bruises, that went unnoticed the day before.

Competition technique

Riders competing against the clock will employ quite a different technique to those used when time is less important. Watch how and where on a course they cut the corners, so you can see in what sort of situation these riders consider it safe to approach a fence at an acute angle. Take note, too, of the places where they take less of a risk and still try to approach the fence in a straight line.

Observe the temperament of different riders – there are those who smile and have a pat for their horses even when they have knocked down a few fences and those who look like thunder when this happens. It is all part of the games-manship of competition riding, but try to emu-late the former. They are understandably the favourites with the crowd and tend to appear among the winners more frequently than those with a more volatile disposition.

If showing horses is your interest, you can learn by observing these classes, too. The tech-niques employed by the riders, however, are more subtle and less obvious. Take note of such things as whether the top-class competitors like to enter the ring at the head of the line of entries or whether they favour a place towards the middle of the group; the technique they employ as they ride directly in front of the judges; the procedure for when they dismount – either for the judges to ride, or so the horse can be viewed unsaddled, and so on.

Walking the course

Begin your observation as the competitors walk the course. A show jumping course is designed to test the skill of the horses and riders; it does this with just two principal types of fences – uprights and spreads. Upright fences, such as those constructed of a number of poles placed directly above each other, a wall or gate – demand great precision and accuracy in jump-ing, while a spread, which is wide as well as high, requires greater impulsion on the approach in order to clear it. Course builders will put uprights and spread fences together, with just one or two strides between them which tests the competitors' skill still further. In addition, there will probably be a water jump on the course, which requires even greater impulsion than a normal spread fence.

While walking the course, the rider measures the strides between the fences. This indicates whether the horse's stride will need to be lengthened or shortened between fences to ensure he meets each one correctly. If an upright fence follows eight or nine strides on after a water jump or a large spread fence, the rider will assess at what point the horse has to be checked in order to get the necessary preci-sion over the upright. He or she will look critically at any turns or bends that must be made on the course in order to judge how widely they must be taken to give a straight line of approach to a jump.

Watch the riders as they ride into the ring – especially whether they keep close to the start of the course or whether they use the whole ring to limber up their horses. Most riders stay quite close to the start, for they must begin the event within a certain time limit after a bell has rung.

Careers in Riding

THOSE WHO WANT to spend their working lives among or closely connected to horses, can find a number of possible careers. Diverse though these are, they all have one thing in common; they demand total devotion to horses and the job chosen. This is simply not the kind of work that can be done between nine to five, five days a week, in a warm, centrally-heated environment.

Instructing

For many, particularly those who do not want to ride competitively themselves, teaching is the ideal career. The qualities needed are the same as those required in any teacher; a profound knowledge and understanding of the subject, coupled with an ability to impart this to others. Many experts in a particular field are totally unable to teach others their trade, so this should be a prime consideration for anyone who wants to become a riding instructor. In addition, he or she must also be a highly competent and efficient rider.

To be a recognized instructor, it is necessary to pass certain official examinations, such as those set in the UK by the British Horse Society. No riding establishment worth its salt will employ an instructor who does not have an appropriate qualification. In the UK there are four possible certificates – the Assistant Instructor, the Intermediate Instructor, the Instructor and the Fellowship. Most people are well satisfied if they become an Instructor.

Riding schools will normally take working pupils, who will receive instruction in return for working around the stable. This prepares them for the first examination – the Assistant Instructors' – in which they will have to satisfy the examiners in four areas – equitation, stable management and horsemastership, minor ailments and instructional ability. Although this qualification will probably enable those who

As a horse lover, you need not feel limited in your career to only riding as there are many paths you might take which offer equal satisfaction and will give you the opportunity to work with and care for horses. Farriers, while obviously in great demand, and a most necessary adjunct in the riding and training of horses, are often difficult to find.

The veterinarian or veterinary surgeon is as vital to the horse as our own doctors and surgeons are to us and require as much skill and dedication as any member of the medical profession. Racing is a sport of high skill and excitement but unfortunately limited to those with the temperament and physical qualifications needed. Jockeys start out very young in their training and often retire early to take up the breeding and training of their own horses. The grooming and caring of horses can be a highly rewarding profession as well, and most horse owners are very dependent on these individuals to raise healthy and strong animals.

hold it to teach at a small establishment, it is advisable to continue training and attempt the more advanced examinations.

Stable Manager

For those who do not want to teach, but who have a flair for administration, the job of a stable manager, particularly at a large riding center, can be very rewarding. The stable manager is responsible for the entire running of such an organization, including the overall welfare of the horses, the training of grooms and working pupils and all the office and business side, such as ordering feed, making bookings and so on. It is a demanding and responsible position for which many riding associations have a special examination.

The groom

Many people want little more out of life than to look after horses – attending to their daily needs and keeping them in prime condition for their riders. If the horses are top-class competition animals, this can be particularly rewarding, as the groom plays a vital part in their success. At one time, the job required no official qualifications and demanded only someone who knew about and loved horses and was totally dedicated to their welfare. These attributes are still necessary, but it is also possible to attain the type of qualification offered by the various national horse societies.

The stud groom or manager

Stud work demands further specialized training and knowledge and is itself a very specialized field of horsemastership. As with the groom, it is possible to attain a diploma in stud work and, if this is your chosen career, it is sensible to study for this qualification. Again, those who have it are more likely to get the most rewarding and interesting jobs with the best prospects. The work involves the complete care of mares and stallions at stud – through all aspects of foaling, including the care of the new-born foal.

The racehorse trainer and jockey

Jockeys fall into two categories – National Hunt jockeys, who ride in steeplechases and hurdle races, and flat-racing jockeys. The two worlds are very different, but the path towards being a jockey is similar in either case. The first step is to become apprenticed to a racing stables, under the overall guidance of a particular trainer. In fact, this apprenticeship does not inevitably lead to the apprentice becoming a

jockey; he or she may find that he would rather remain a groom or 'lad' and work up through the ranks to the position of head lad, when he is responsible for the overall welfare of the horses. Another key position in a racing stables is that of head traveling lad, which, as its name suggests, gives the person concerned responsibility for horses as they travel to and from their races. The other path open to a clever apprentice is to become a trainer, although this will take a considerable length of time plus much talent and hard work.

Although all aspects of work at racing stables have hitherto been dominated by men, nowadays there are also openings for women. Girls can certainly rise through the stable echelons to become head lads or lasses and they are also now permitted to hold a trainer's license. Bear in mind, though, that it is traditionally a man's world and as such, is a very hard and tough life.

Veterinary surgeon and animal nurse

As anyone who has had any dealing with horses knows, the job of the veterinary surgeon is of paramount importance to all horse owners. Before specializing in equine problems exclusively, however, it is necessary to qualify in the normal way as a veterinary surgeon and probably go into general practice for some time.

If qualifying as a veterinary surgeon seems too daunting, you could become a registered animal nursing auxiliary. Here again, the training covers the nursing of animals in general rather than horses in particular. Specialization comes later, either by becoming employed by a vet who specializes in such work himself or by seeking employment at one of the equine research centers.

The farrier

This is another aspect of working with horses which traditionally has been dominated by men, doubtless because the physical work involved is extremely hard and exhausting. It is a field in which there is a crying need for new blood, as farriery has become something of a dying art. Farriers today have more work than they can handle, so there is little chance of ever being unemployed if you choose this as a career.

Learning the trade and the art of farriery is achieved by being apprenticed to a master farrier. The training up to the first examination takes four years, during which time apprentices will have to attend at least one special course on farriery each year. Entry into the profession is regulated by examination.

Glossary

'Against the Clock' A term used in show jumping competitions in which the final round is timed. The winner is the competitor who has the least number of penalty points combined with the fastest time over the course.

Aids Recognized signals used by a rider to pass instructions to his mount. *Artificial aids* include whips, spurs and ancillary items of tack used by a rider to assist him in giving aids. *Natural aids* are the rider's hands, legs, body or voice. *Diagonal aids* are aids in which opposite hands and legs are used simultanously, i.e., the right rein is used with the left leg. *Lateral aids* are hand and leg aids given together on the same side.

Airs Above the Ground High school movements (q.v.) in which, at some stage, all four legs of the horse are off the ground.

Apron Strong, leather or hide apron worn by a farrier (q.v.) for protection when shoeing a horse. *Apron (side-saddle)* Name given to the 'skirt' of the side-saddle habit.

At Grass A horse that has been turned out in a paddock or field.

Balance Strap Leather strap attached to the offside back of a side-saddle which passes under the horse's belly and buckles to a strap on the front of the saddle. It is designed to prevent the saddle from slipping.

Bars (of mouth) Fleshy area between the front and back teeth on either side of a horse's mouth.

Bay A deep, rich, reddish-brown coloured horse, with black mane, tail, and lower legs.

Bit Mouthpiece often made of metal, rubber or vulcanite placed in the horse's mouth and kept in position by the bridle to aid the rider's control. *Curb bits* include any one of a number of bits, the mouthpieces of which vary in design but which include hooks on either side to which a curb chain or strap is attached. This lies in the horse's chin groove and gives the bit its characteristic leverage action. A *gag bit* is a particularly severe form of bit. It may be raised to a greater or lesser degree, thus affecting the severity of the bit. A *snaffle bit* is any one of a number of designs of bit that act on the corners or bars of the mouth. The bit takes only one pair of reins.

Bitless Bridle Bridle without bit. Control is achieved by concentrating pressure on the nose and chin groove. A *bosal* is a very simple bitless bridle, the term actually referring to the rawhide noseband which is its chief component. A *hackamore* is the most widely known type of bitless bridle.

Box, to To lead a horse into a horse box or trailer.

Break In, to Training the young horse to accept and respond to a rider on his back.

Broken Wind Permanent disability to a horse's respiratory system manifesting in a chronic, persistent and rasping cough.

Brushing Striking of the inside hind or foreleg with its opposite. May lead to injury and lameness.

Cantle Extreme back ridge of a saddle.

Cavalletti Adjustable low wooden jump used in the schooling of horse or rider in jumping.

Cavesson Either a simple noseband fitted to a bridle, or a more sophisticated piece of equipment worn by a horse when he is to be lunged (q.v.). In the latter, it is sometimes referred to as a *breaking cavesson*.

Chaff Finely chopped hay mixed with a corn feed to provide bulk and prevent the horse from bolting the feed.

Chestnut An overall yellowish-brown coat, with the mane and tail possibly the same colour.

Cob A type of horse characterized by its smallness and strong, stocky build.

Collected A horse that, while moving forward, indicates it is ready to respond to its rider and so is 'collected' together: neck arched, hocks tucked well beneath it and gait lively.

Colt A male, ungelded horse up to four years old.

Concussion Jarring of a horse's legs, usually caused by fast trotting on the road, or considerable hard work on hard ground. May result in swelling and lameness.

Counter Canter School movement in which the horse canters in a circle with the outside leg leading instead of the inside leg as usual.

Curb Chain Single or double link chain attached to the hooks of a curb bit and lying flat in a horse's chin groove.

Diagonals (left, right) A rider rides on the left or right diagonal at the trot depending on whether he rises as the horse's left or right foreleg moves forward. On a circle, the rider should always rise as the outside foreleg moves forward.

Disunited (canter) Canter in which the horse's legs are out of sequence.

Dorsal Stripe Darkened line (usually black) running along the horse's dorsal ridge.

Double Bridle Traditional bridle with two bits (snaffle and curb) giving the rider greater control than a bridle with one bit.

Draw Rein Severe form of control comprised of a rein attached at one end to the girth, which passes through the bit rings and back to the rider's hands.

Dressage The art of training a horse so that he is totally obedient and responsible to his rider, as well as agile and fluent in his performance.

Drop Noseband Noseband which buckles beneath the bit to prevent the horse from opening its mouth to 'take hold' of the bit, making it easier to ignore the rider's commands.

Dun Generally refers to a 'yellow' coat with black mane, tail, legs and dorsal stripe.

Emergency Grip Position used by side-saddle riders when there is danger of being unseated.

Equitation The art of horse riding and horsemanship.

Eventing Riding in a one or three day event, which combines dressage, cross-country and show jumping.

Extension The lengthening of a horse's stride at any pace. It does not necessarily mean an increase in speed.

Farrier A skilled craftsman who shoes horses.

Fence A *combination fence* is a series of fences (usually three) in a show jumping course, placed to allow only one or two strides between each jump. A *double fence* is two fences in a show jumping course with the same requirement as the combination. A *drop fence* is an obstacle in which the landing side is considerably lower than the take-off side. A *spread fence* is one in which the main feature is the width rather than height, whereas an *upright* is designed to test a horse's ability to jump heights.

Fetlock (Joint) The lowest joint on a horse's legs.

Filly A female horse up to the age of four years old.

Foal A horse of either sex up to the age of one year old. Male foals are usually referred to as colt foals, females as filly coals.

Fodder Any type of food stuff fed to horses.

Forehand Front part of the horse including the head, neck, shoulders, and forelegs.

Frog V-shaped leathery part found on the soles of a horse's feet which act as a shock absorber and as an anti-slip device.

Gait The paces at which a horse moves. Usually, a walk, trot, canter or gallop.

Galls Sores caused by ill-fitting saddlery.

Gamgee Gauze-covered cotton wool used beneath stable or exercise leg bandages for extra warmth or protection.

Gelding A castrated male horse.

Grackle Noseband Thin-strapped noseband with double straps buckling above and below the bit.

Grass Tips Half-moon shaped shoes which cover only the toe area of the hoof. Used for horses turned out to grass to prevent the hoof growing too quickly which creates a falling hazard.

Grey Refers to any colour horse from pure white to dark grey. Further described by such terms as 'dappled' (small iron-grey circles on a lighter background), 'flea-bitten' (specks of grey on a white background), etc.

Groom Person who looks after the daily welfare of a horse.

Grooming Kit The various brushes and other tools used in cleaning a horse's coat.

Ground Line Pole or similar placed in front of a fence to help horse and rider judge the take-off point.

Habit Traditional riding kit worn by side-saddle riders.

Hack A type of horse characterized by its pleasing appearance, fine bone structure, good manners and complete obedience to its rider's commands. Also a term used to describe going for a ride.

Half Pass Dressage movement performed on two tracks (q.v.) in which the horse moves forwards and sideways simultaneously.

Half Volte A school movement in which a horse is asked to leave the track and perform a half circle of a given diameter after which he rejoins the track to continue in the opposite direction.

Hand The recognized measurement used for determining the height of a horse or pony. A hand equals 10cm (4 ins).

Haynet Large net or bag made of rope designed to hold a horse's hay.

Head Lad Used in racing stables to describe the head groom – the one who has overall responsibility for the welfare and general condition of the horse.

High School The classical art of riding, in which the traditional advanced school or dressage figures are practiced.

Hock The joint in the center part of a horse's hindlegs. Responsible for most of the horse's forward force.

Hoof Pick A small metal implement with a pointed hook on one end used to remove dirt, stones, etc. from a horse's hooves.

Horn The hard, insensitive, outer covering of the hoof.

Horse Box Self-propelled vehicle used for the transportation of horses.

Horsemanship The art of equitation or horse riding.

Horsemastership The art of caring for and attending to all aspects of a horse's welfare, under all possible circumstances.

Hunter Any type of horse considered suitable to be ridden to the hounds.

Hunting Head The top of the two pommels found on a side-saddle. The hunting head is in a fixed position and supports the rider's right leg.

Impulsion Strong but controlled forward movement in a horse.

Indirect Rein The opposite rein to the direction in which a horse is turning. When giving an indirect rein aid, the instruction to turn comes by pressing the opposite rein against the horse's neck.

Inside Leg The leg or legs of rider or horse on the inside of any circle or track being described.

Irons Stirrup irons are metal items of tack attached to the saddle by the stirrup leathers to hold the rider's feet.

Jog Western style riding term for trot. Also used in European style riding to describe a slow, somewhat shortened pace of trot.

Jumping Lane A narrow track, usually fenced on either side in which a series of jumps are placed.

Keeper Small leather loops found on the straps of a bridle, designed to contain the end of the strap after it has been buckled, giving a neat appearance.

Leading Leg The front leg at a canter or gallop that appears to be leading the leg sequence.

Leading Rein Long rein attached to the bit by which the horse may be led. Usually used in the early stages of being taught to ride.

Leaping Head The lower of the two pommels on a side-saddle with a small amount of adjustability.

Leg-up A method of mounting in which an assistant stands behind the rider and supports the lower part of his left leg as he springs up off the ground.

Livery (stables) Riding establishment where an owner may keep his horse for a fee.

Long Reins Long webbing reins attached to the bit of a horse's bridle and used in the animal's training.

Lunge, to The act of training a horse by directing it around in a circle while on a long 'lunge' rein. This rein is attached to a cavesson (q.v.). Schooled horses may be lunged as a form of exercise or during the course of teaching a novice rider.

Lunge Rein A long, webbed rein used in the above action.

Manège A marked out area or school used for the teaching, training, and schooling of horse and rider.

Mare A female horse over four years old.

Martingale Ancillary item of tack, the purpose of which is to give a rider a greater degree of control.

Muck Sweat Condition of a horse when, through hard work or over-excitement, it has sweated to such an extent that its neck is covered with lather.

Mucking Out Daily stable chore involving the removal of dirty, soiled bedding and sweeping of the stable floor before replacing the bed.

Nearside The left hand side of a horse.

Neck Reining The art of turning a horse by using the indirect (q.v.) or opposite rein to the direction of the turn.

Neckstrap A simple leather strap buckled around the horse's neck used to give added security to a novice rider. Also refers to the strap of a martingale that buckles around the horse's neck.

Numnah A pad worn under the saddle, usually cut in the shape of the saddle. It may be made of felt, rubber or sheepskin.

Offside The right hand side of a horse.

Overbend A horse that has arched its neck acutely, thereby bringing its head too far into its chest. Usually caused by a rider exerting too much pressure on the reins while urging the horse forward.

Paddock Fenced-in area of grassland in which horses are turned out. Generally used to denote a fairly small area.

Palomino Colour of horse. The coat may be various shades of gold and the mane and tail white.

Pelham Various types of curb bit with a single mouthpiece to which two reins may be attached. Aims to combine the two bits of a double bridle in a single mouthpiece.

Piebald Refers to a coat irregularly marked with large patches of black and white. Pinto is an American term for piebald and skewbald horses (q.v.).

Pirouette A dressage movement in which the horse describes a circle in which the forelegs describe a small circle while the hindlegs remain in the same spot, one of them acting as a pivot.

Points (of a horse) Names given to the different parts of a horse. Also used to describe the mane, tail and lower legs.

Pommel The center front of an astride saddle. In some designs, the pommel is more pronounced.

Pony A small horse that stands 14.2 hands high or less.

Port A raised section in the center mouthpiece of some curb bits. It may be raised to a greater or lesser degree, thus affecting the severity of the bit.

Pull, to (mane and tail) The process of thinning the mane and tail.

Quarter, to Superficial grooming of stabled horses before taking them out for exercise.

Rein Back To instruct the horse to move backwards. In order to execute the movement correctly, the horse must move back with the diagonal fore- and hindlegs moving in unison.

Reining Patterns Type of dressage test in Western riding in which advanced movements are executed.

Renvers A school movement also known as quarters-out, in which the horse moves along the side of the school, his hindlegs on the track and his forelegs on an inside track.

Rising Trot The action of a rider rising from the saddle in rhythm with a horse's trot.

Roan Colour of horse. A blue roan refers to a coat in which black and white hairs are mixed giving an overall blue effect; a strawberry roan refers to a coat in which chestnut and white hairs are mixed to give an overall reddish effect.

Roller A strap which passes around the horse's back and belly used to keep rugs in place.

Rug Up, to To put on a horse's rug or rugs. A horse wearing rugs is described as being 'rugged up'.

Saddle Horn The prominent pommel featured on Western saddles. The lariat is looped or twisted around it when a steer has been roped to help restrain the animal.

Saddle Horse A horse suitable for riding, as opposed to one that works in harness.

Saddle Soap Specially prepared soap to be rubbed into the leather of all saddlery to help preserve it.

Saddlery A comprehensive term for all equipment worn by a horse.

School Marked-out area used for training and exercising horses and riders. To school is the art of obedience training and education of the horse.

Serpentine A school movement in which the horse, at any pace, moves down the center of the school in a series of equal-sized loops.

Shoe, to The act of fitting and securing metal shoes to the horse's feet, usually done by a farrier (q.v.).

Shoulder-In A two-track movement (q.v.) in which the horse is evenly bent along the length of its spine away from the direction of its movement.

Shy, to Wherein a horse jumps to one side having been frightened by a real or imaginary phenomenon.

Side Reins Reins used while training to help position the horse's head. They are attached at one end to the bit and at the other to the girth or roller buckled around the horse's saddle or belly.

Skepping Out Stable management term used to describe the removal of droppings from the stable bed by putting them into a skep or skip.

Skewbald Refers to the coat of a horse irregularly marked with large patches of brown and white.

Snaffle (bit) Any one of a number of designs of bit that act on the corners or bars of the mouth. The bit takes only one pair of reins.

Spurs Small metal devices (usually blunt) worn on the rider's boat to help reinforce the leg aids.

Stable Management The art of looking after one or more stable horses including all aspects of their welfare.

Stall Old-fashioned stabling of horses with several stalls usually incorporated in one building. Mainly found nowadays in large establishments, such as studs.

Steeplechase A horse race in which the horses gallop around a marked-out course which contains several solid brush fences. A steeplechase course refers to any course which includes such fences.

Stock A specially designed cravat, worn as part of a formal riding outfit, usually hunting dress.

Strapping The thorough grooming of a stabled horse.

Surcingle A webbing strap which passes around a horse's back and belly and is used to keep a rug in place. Show jumpers and jockeys often buckle a surcin-

gle around their saddle as an added precaution against the girth breaking.

Tack Comprehensive term for saddlery (q.v.). A tack room is where tack is stored.

Tail Guard A piece of equipment made of leather, jute or wool, designed to completely cover the dock (q.v.) and protect this area of the tail. Frequently used when traveling.

Thoroughbred One of the most well-known breeds, the thoroughbred, known also as the English racehorse, was bred for speed in the 17th century.

Trailer The transportation vehicle of one or two horses which is drawn behind another vehicle.

Transition The act of changing pace. A walk to a trot and a trot to a canter are known as *upward transitions*. A canter to a trot and a trot to a walk are *downward transitions*.

Travers Similar to a renvers (q.v.) except the forelegs stay on the outside track of the school while the hindlegs move on an inner track.

Turn On The Forehand A school movement performed from a halt in which the hindquarters describe a circle around the forehand, with one foreleg acting as a pivot.

Turn Out, to To put a horse out to grass or turn it loose in a paddock.

Two Track School movements in which the hindlegs follow a separate track from that made by the forelegs.

Vice Any one of a number of bad

habits which may be learned by a horse. Unless curtailed when young, they are very hard to cure.

Volte A circle of 3m (10ft) executed at a given point in the school.

Water Jump An obstacle, usually comprising a low hedge, behind which is a wide expanse of water. Used in show jumping courses.

Wisp A coiled or woven 'rope' of straw used in strapping (q.v.) a horse to massage the skin and muscles and improve circulation.

Withers Point at the bottom of the neck of a horse from which a horse's height is measured.

Wither Pad A small pad, made of either felt or sheepskin placed under the front of the saddle to give added protection. In a well-fitting saddle, this should not be necessary.

Yawing A horse that continually opens its mouth and stretches its head outwards and down to the ground in an attempt to evade the bit.

Yearling A colt or filly between one and two years old.

Index

Acknowledgements
Photographs by
Leo Burnett (Marlborough), 92;
Gerry Cranham 4, 126r;
English Tourist Board 45, 47;
Farming Press (TV Vet Horse Book) 144tr, 145tr;
Mike Fear 184, 186b;
J P Ferrero 121, 133t, 145   -left;
G. Francis 96, 109, 110, 111;
Michael Freeman 192b;
Bill Holden 180, 181, 186, 187,
Kit Houghton 57, 73, 114b, 124, 125, 128t,br, 178b, 199,
202, 203;
Ian Howes 321,r, 136b, 140, 141, 183;
Ed Lacey 76t, 76bl, 77, 148t, 206tl;
Peter Newark's Western Americana 79, 95t, 97tr;
Picture Point 210b;
Peter Roberts 2, 26, 40, 42, 46t, 46b, 66r, 69, 76bl, 78t, 86;

87, 88, 89, 96, 97tl, 97bl, 114t, 116, 123, 126, 128bl, 132b,
133bl, 134, 136tl, 144tl, 147, 155m, 160, 161tl, 161tr, 166,
172, 173, 188tl, 194, 197, 206, 207, 208;
Western Horseman 94;
Simon de Courcy Wheeler 81, 9, 10t,1,r, 11, 15, 16, 21t, 22,
23, 29, 31, 33, 35, 38, 51, 52, 54t, b, 58, 59, 63, 67, 70, 71,
74, 75, 99, 100, 148b, 149, 150, 156t, 157, 158, 159, 162, 165,
169, 174, 177, 179, 188b, 189tr, 190, 191, 195b, 200, 204t,b,
205, 211br;
Trevor Wood 43, 49, 80, 81, 84, 95b, 132t, 95b, 132t, 138,
139, 155t, 168;
Terry Woodford 137;
Jon Wyand 8r, 18, 21b, 25, 62, 66, 98, 102, 105, 106, 107,
108, 115tb, 142, 161, 164, 183, 193, 195tr, 211t;
All illustrations by Chris Forsey and Marilyn Bruce except
for the following by Q.E.D. 9tr, 12, 18b, 34t, 40t, 41r, 43,
50, 51, 66, 118, 119, 120, 121, 122, 130, 132, 134, 140, 142,
144br, 149, 158, 161, 171, 179, 180b, 192t;